Managing Manic Depressive Disorders

Edited by Ved Varma

Jessica Kingsley Publishers
London and Bristol, Pennsylvania

First published in the United Kingdom in 1997 by
Jessica Kingsley Publishers Ltd
116 Pentonville Road,
London N1 9JB, England
and
325 Chestnut Street,
Philadelphia, PA 19106, USA.

www.jkp.com

Second impression 1999

Copyright © 1997 Jessica Kingsley Publishers
Foreword copyright © 1997 Myra Fulford
Appreciation copyright © 1997 Dennis Friedman

Library of Congress Cataloging in Publication Data
A CIP catalogue record for this book is available from the Library of Congress

British Library Cataloguing in Publication Data
A CIP catalogue record for this book is available from the British Library

ISBN 1 85302 347 7

Printed and Bound in Great Britain by
Athenaeum Press, Gateshead, Tyne and Wear

Contents

List of Figures

List of Tables

Dedication

This book is dedicated, by the editor, with affection and love, to all people affected by manic depression.

Acknowledgement

I would very much like to acknowledge the help, inspiration and support of John Martin who was interested, practical, kind and wise throughout the preparation of this book.

Ved Varma

Foreword

I want to pose a challenging question at the beginning of this book. Do you honestly believe that the condition of manic depression can be effectively managed and people continue to live useful and creative lives? If you are a mental health professional working in the NHS your perception will be of people who are angry and in crisis. If you are a member of the general public the words 'severe mental illness' will be tainted by the sensational and almost wholly negative picture you will have received of mental illness through the tabloid press. I suspect the answer is more than likely a negative.

Mental illness affects one in four of the UK population and manic depression (Bipolar Affective Disorder) affects one in 100. Despite this high incidence there remains considerable ignorance about mental health problems and this ignorance causes fear, anxiety, stigma and discrimination. From our perspective, in The Manic Depression Fellowship, any book that addresses the needs of people who have manic depression and which is written from an encouragingly large number of viewpoints and both educates and informs is to be applauded. But it is still disappointing to find so many contributors writing about 'manic depressives' – a label which defines people only by their illness and which most certainly does not lead to holistic treatment of the individual. And why, when the Disability Discrimination Act 1995 has just become law is there not a chapter about the employer's role? That possibly says a lot more about society and the lack of enlightened employers than the Editor's perceptions.

Books on manic depression are few and far between and Ved Varma deserves our congratulations for editing a book which gives as much weight to psychotherapeutic and self management approaches as to drug treatments. All the contributions are commendably accessible to lay and professional readers alike and as such will play an important part in educating and reassuring people of the real possibility of managing the condition.

And let's hope the book will serve as a catalyst for mental health professionals to devote more time, energy and interest to researching the psychotherapeutic, cognitive behavioural and self management approaches to manic depressive disorders.

Myra Fulford
Director of The Manic Depression Fellowship, UK
8–10 High Street
Kingston-Upon-Thames
Surrey KT1 1EY
Tel. 0181 974 6550

Professor Hugh Freeman
An Appreciation

Dennis Friedman

Hugh Freeman's ten eventful years as Editor of the *British Journal of Psychiatry* did much to further interest in the discipline to the world wide readership. During this time, the total amount of material that was published in the journal grew considerably. Additional sections – the Brief Reports, Supplements, and *Review of Books*, as well as the series of *College Seminars* and other books – were introduced. Through his eclecticism, the variety of subjects covered also increased, with a particular emphasis on the psychotherapies. These innovations, together with extra space in the supplements, allowed more data about new treatments to be published. All added to the body of clinical and scientific information which is essential to a journal of international repute. These efforts, together with a new structure of financial management, went a long way towards establishing the independent position of the journal on a firm basis.

It is no coincidence that an appreciation of the contributions made by Hugh Freeman to psychiatry appears as the preface to this new work on depression. Although those who know him would agree that he is good natured, calm and life loving, a momentary sadness as milestones are passed and tasks given up is nevertheless entirely appropriate. It emphasises the attachment felt to that which has been left behind – in this case, a responsibility of ten years' duration.

Academic life began for Hugh Freeman with a history scholarship to St John's College, Oxford. He had been on the arts rather than the science side of school, and had come to medicine largely because of family influence. Specialising in psychiatry meant something of a sideways move from an earlier interest in social history to the psychosocial experience of the individual, which provides essential information for the later management of psychological and emotional problems. A more recent concern with the psychiatric aspects of politics may well have grown out of this earlier interest.

Leaving Oxford with an honours degree in psychology, philosophy and physiology, Hugh's career took him via the Manchester Royal Infirmary, the Maudsley Hospital and a further period at Oxford to a post as Consultant at Salford. His long period there culminated in an honorary professorship at the University of Salford's Department of Sociology and Anthropology. He was also made an Honorary Visiting Fellow of Green College, Oxford and is an honorary or corresponding member of seven national psychiatric organisations in other countries, including the USA.

The thread running through these clinical and academic experiences has been the acquisition and dissemination of knowledge. The many papers he has presented at international congresses and the frequent invitations to address learned bodies testify to this. His particular contributions to the advancement of psychiatry has been reflected in the considerable body of research in which he has been involved, particularly into the community and epidemiology of schizophrenia.

His leisure activities are, as one would expect, an extension of these academic concerns. A search for meaning in art and literature has resulted in much of his spare time being spent in both a visual and written interest with aspects of history. In the art galleries and museums, as well as through his reading, he has sought to evaluate what lies behind the two-dimensional facade of the word or the image. His erudite reviews in many newspapers and journals, including *Nature* and the *Times Higher Education Supplement*, are not only thoughtful evaluations of the books in question, but literary models in themselves. His preoccupation with hidden meaning and search for the intrinsic good has led to a deep interest in the often destructive fragmentation of the psyche seen in psychotic illness. In this way, a junction is made between the creativity of the artist and that distorted thinking which often frustrates the innate talents of the mentally ill.

This love of history coupled with scientific curiosity, has taken Hugh's concern not only into the primitive unconscious of the individual, but even further back into the biochemical and genetic factors responsible for psychotic illness. In this, the aim has been to create order out of chaos, to attempt to piece together life as it should have been for the mentally ill, rather than as it is. It is perhaps surprising that of the 85 papers published by Hugh Freeman since 1958, only five – all relatively recent – are on the subject of depression; possibly, 'looking back' has a more intellectual, rather than an emotional meaning. While his academic concerns are mainly with the here and now, he has none the less returned to an interest in the past by co-editing two volumes of *150 Years of British Psychiatry* and is working on a lengthy study of mental health policy in post-war Britain. Community care for the mentally ill has been another of his major interests, growing out of clinical experience and a long-term responsibility for an industrial community in the north of England.

More voices such as Hugh Freeman's would ensure that communication and awareness, reason and debate would take precedence over suppression and denial. In this way, the psychological needs – both of the individual and of society – would be better served.

Introduction

Ved Varma

The management of persons with manic depressive disorders has always been a source of worry, concern and anguish to those who have to deal with them because, among other things, in this illness the subject has excessive changes of mood from elation to depression. Therefore, manic depressives can be very awkward and unproductive to deal with when manic, and unresponsive and unhelpful while depressed. Briefly, manic depressive disorders are a major mental/affective illness with mental pain, unhappiness and puzzlement all round. This is why we need to know more about manic depressives, about how they think, feel and/or behave as they do.

This interesting book on the important subject is an excellent account in this discipline. The contributors include consultant psychiatrists, psychologists, psychotherapists and social workers – all of whom are recognised authorities in their respective fields. Accordingly, their views command every respect. This is why I wholeheartedly recommend this helpful, practical and pleasant book to readers concerned with manic depressive disorders in any way.

Further reading

Jamison, K.R. (1993) *Touched with Fire: Manic Depressive Illness and the Artistic Temperament.* New York: The Free Press.

McKeon, P. (1991) *Coping with Depression and Elation.* London: Sheldon Press.

Paykel, E.S. (1982) *Handbook of Affective Disorders.* Edinburgh: Churchill Livingstone.

Wigoder, D. (1987) *Images of Destruction.* London: Routledge.

CHAPTER 1

Manic Depressive Illness
Services

David Kingdon

Research into services for people who have manic depressive illness is relatively underdeveloped despite its practical importance. This may be because the benefits of hospital services which provide asylum, sanctuary and respite have been seen as self-evident. However, the development of alternative and complementary care has been much more controversial. This is leading to a re-evaluation of evidence about hospitalisation and new research into other elements of service provision. Much of this research has been into services for people with mental illness generally, as the services for people with manic depressive illness being provided are similar to those for other mental illnesses, for example, schizophrenia. There are advocates for specialised services for manic depressive illness resistant to conventional treatments – 27 out of 36 UK Professors of Psychiatry surveyed recently (Beasley, Brockington and Crisp 1996) believed such services should exist but only 13 of the areas had such services. The most important priority has been for services that are accessible and local.

Relevant epidemiology

The National Psychiatric Morbidity Survey (Office of Population Censuses and Surveys (OPCS) 1994) found about one in seven adults in private households, aged 16–64, are suffering from significant anxiety or depression in any week. Moreover, 0.4 per cent suffer from a severe mood disorder or schizophrenia in any year. The categories used in the results of the survey published so far do not fully distinguish manic depressive illness from schizophrenia and other psychoses on the one hand and less severe depression on the other. Therefore the following is rather over-inclusive, but focuses on current contacts with services and specific symptoms, such as suicidal ideas, which are most relevant.

Half of those aged 16–64 with anxiety, depression and other neurotic disorders had a long-standing physical complaint (compared with 30 per cent without neurotic disorders). Twenty-nine per cent (compared with 14 per cent) had severe lack of social support. One in eight with these disorders is currently having treatment – in two-thirds this is medication, with one-third having counselling or psychotherapy; they were twice as likely to consult a GP in the two weeks before interview. For psychotic disorders, men equalled women in incidence with about half in the age group 16–34 (38 per cent were 25–34). They were twice as likely to be unemployed, and half were on medication or receiving counselling or psychotherapy. In the 12 months prior to interview, 82 per cent received some sort of service: two-thirds from a GP for 'emotional problems', half from outpatient appointment, a quarter had an inpatient stay. Suicidal ideas were occurring in 1 per cent in the week prior to interview; two-thirds of these were women, one-half aged 16–34. One-fifth were on antidepressants and 30 per cent had seen a GP in the past week. Half had been outpatients, 30 per cent inpatients, 10 per cent had had home visits in the previous year. One-half were living by themselves or were lone parents (OPCS 1995a; 1995b).

Needs of patients

Services should be configured to meet people's needs, rather than the reverse which has often happened in the past, that is, peoples' needs are met only in so far as they fit the services delivered. The needs of people with mental health problems generally have not changed over time, but the way local authorities and the NHS try to meet them has. Individuals need:

- homes to live in
- help with money and jobs
- someone to talk to
- information about their problems and the choices available to them
- treatments that work
- services which are:
  - available when they need them
  - acceptable to them
  - responsive to their needs, including the need for physical care.

Those with manic depressive illness have this range of needs but individual health and social care assessment is necessary to establish which should be prioritised. There are also certain aspects of services which are likely to be of particular importance and these will now be discussed.

Primary health care

Primary health care teams (general practitioners, practice nurses, receptionists, and so on) will usually be the first, and often only, point of contact for those with less severe and persistent problems. If dealt with effectively, mental health teams will never need to be involved. However, expertise in detection and management of mental health problems, specifically depression, in primary care has been demonstrated repeatedly to vary considerably and the potential for improvement in care is at least as great as in improving the care provided by specialist services. About half of all people developing depressive disorders seek help, especially those with biological symptoms, those lacking social support and those limited functionally by their illness, for example, those prevented from working (Meller *et al.* 1989). But where the presenting symptoms of depression are through physical symptoms, for example fatigue, or where patients are reticent to admit that their mood is disordered, detection is especially poor. Even when detected, if the symptoms seem 'understandable' because of social circumstances, treatment may not be initiated. A consensus statement has been produced by the Royal Colleges of General Practitioners and Psychiatrists to improve this situation (Paykel and Priest 1992).

Community mental health teams

Community mental health teams cover specified population groups so that responsibility for any individual's care is clearly defined. They include social workers, mental health nurses, psychologists, occupational therapists and psychiatrists. They have some skills specific to their particular profession and others in common, but they are expected to use them flexibly to work together to meet the full range of needs of those referred to them. Trained and experienced mental health staff are essential to any service caring for people with manic depressive illness and while this is obvious in theory, in practice shortages or poor targeting have meant serious deficiencies in the UK and elsewhere. Personnel planning has failed to deliver sufficient psychiatrists to fill even funded vacancies and has artificially held down numbers. Psychologists and occupational therapists are similarly scarce, with nursing staff numbers also barely sufficient. This inevitably restricts services available and easily means that services become crisis-led rather than being able to reach out to those needing them to provide interventions at an early stage rather than when symptoms are entrenched and critical.

Interprofessional collaboration has been a key issue for teams and almost universally problematic (Kingdon 1992). Either teams have become very inward-looking and exclusive or riven by professional disputes. The teams which seem to have been most successful operate within networks including the wide variety of agencies, for example housing, probation, police and employment services, respect each individual's strengths and diversity, and are well managed and led.

The links between primary and community mental health teams are vitally important in meeting the physical, psychological and social needs of those with severe mental health problems through maintaining continuity of care; specific members of the latter have often been attached to practices. Where this acts as a bridge between teams it can be effective, but often the mental health worker has loosened ties with the community mental health team and a neglect of those with more difficult problems has occurred. Where psychiatrists have developed collaborative attachments to primary health care teams, this has not, however, been noted as a problem.

The links between local authority social services and housing departments and community mental health teams are also essential to meet social needs which may be of much greater concern to the individual and significantly influencing more apparent mental health symptoms. Similarly, the links between all the purchasing agencies – district health authorities, GP fundholders and local authorities – must be close to provide the co-ordination of care essential for those with severe mental health problems. This involves dialogue to ensure that purchasing intentions complement each other and target and encompass the needs of those with severe mental illness. As resources allow, purchasing will need to expand to meet the mental health needs of others but prioritisation is essential to the efficient delivery of the range of treatments and services according to need.

Early detection

Early detection of manic depressive illness reduces the damage that can be done to a person's reputation, financial situation, employment, relationships and self-esteem. One episode of hypomania can be damaging but that damage may be remediable; repeat episodes can multiply the damage and produce secondary effects which make depression more likely and certainly reduce future quality of life. However, by its very nature, with diagnosis usually dependent on repeated episodes, early intervention is difficult. Recognition of the possibility of such illness and ready availability of expert care if it recurs, may, however, be possible.

Early intervention on first and subsequent illnesses has been described by Perry, Tarrier and Morriss (1995). Such evidence of effectiveness is currently anecdotal but nevertheless makes clinical sense. Recognition of a 'relapse signature' – a personalised sequence of symptoms which lead up to a hypomanic or depressive episode – such as has been described in schizophrenia, can enable the individual to seek help early and make adjustments to medication or current life circumstances, for example particular stresses at work or home.

Risk assessment

At the same time and subsequently, there is a need for risk assessment and management – especially of harm to self, including suicide, or others – and also the risks accompanying hypomania through poor judgement and disinhibition, for example breach of road traffic regulations, financial misjudgement or through sexual vulnerability. In the UK, the Drivers Licensing Authority restricts anyone suffering from an episode of hypomania from driving for five years. This can be a major disincentive to patients and relatives from notifying the authority but invalidation of their licence and insurance results from their continuing to drive. Regulations for those driving heavy goods or passenger service vehicles are even more stringent. Risk of aggression to others is unusual but the *Confidential Inquiry into Homicides and Suicides by Mentally Ill People* (Boyd 1994) emphasised its importance. In men, risk is more commonly associated with schizophrenia but in women affective disorder is more common. Danger where it exists appears to be to those who are close to the individual, especially family members. Irritability can develop in depression or hypomania and frustration leads to verbal and occasionally physical hostility. Disinhibition about financial matters can also be very serious.

For hypomania, Bennett (1982) advises medical staff and relatives to persuade the patient to hand over car keys, credit cards and cheque books at the first sign of illness and put their affairs in the hands of a solicitor, friend or relative. If appropriate, application can be made to the Court of Protection to take over the person's affairs. There may also be occasions when allowing the family or staff member to review and, if necessary, censor mail is judicious. Unfortunately the disinhibited behaviour while hypomanic can severely affect lifestyle, employment, personal relationships and self-esteem, with lasting effects on the individual and those around him or her, and be a precipitant of depression subsequently with prognostic implications.

Availability of treatments

A variety of treatments now exist, including *medication* and *psychological* treatments. Services to deliver physical treatments need to take into account the needs patients have for information about their treatments and compliance issues. Lithium clinics run specifically for people with manic depressive illness may provide high quality monitoring of medication and health care needs and can be associated with support groups. However, there is some debate about whether they are appropriate to more local provision of services and whether social and psychological care needs can be neglected. They need to be well supervised by senior staff, as delegation of responsibility to junior staff for long-term patients can lead to discontinuity of care, poor compliance and missed opportunities for early recognition of deterioration. Availability of facilities for the administration of electroconvulsive therapy needs to be assured in dignified and comfortable settings with modern equipment and suitably trained and qualified staff (Freeman 1995).

Psychological treatments, for example cognitive behavioural, psychodynamic and family therapies, have become increasingly available as a large and growing body of research has demonstrated the effectiveness of specific techniques in depression and anxiety. However, there remains much greater demand for these than is currently being met. Successful use of these techniques has been described for patients with resistant symptoms in combination with pharmacotherapy, behaviour therapy, family therapy and inpatient care (Scott 1992), increasing self-esteem and reducing hopelessness.

More widely available is simple counselling. This may also be of benefit but the evidence is less conclusive and, while the demand for it is also considerable, appropriate training and supervision is essential. Brief, structured interventions making full use of self-help techniques (for example Barker 1993) generally appear to be most cost-effective (Tyrer et al. 1988). Unfortunately it has been all too easy for practitioners autonomously to provide services at public and private expense which are of dubious efficacy – to the detriment of more seriously ill people, including those with manic depressive illness who could benefit from their time and experience (Audit Commission 1995).

Social care is also of importance as home, financial, employment and family circumstances frequently precipitate relapse and interfere with recovery. Fadden, Bebbington and Kuipers (1987) found that spouses of depressed patients were frequently very tolerant but found coping with worrying, irritability and nagging by patients most difficult. Other effects on patients' families included reduction in income, restrictions on social and leisure pursuits and strain on marriages. However, Hooley and Teasdale (1989) found that the most significant prognostic indicator in unipolar depressives was the answer by patients to the question: 'How critical is your wife of you?'. The greater the perceived criticism, the worse the outcome. Marital and family therapies are therefore potentially of considerable importance, although research into these areas has been relatively underdeveloped.

Co-ordination of services

There are now more agencies providing care in increasingly dispersed settings. People when they have manic depressive illness may not be able to use conventional services, for example outpatient clinics, or accept needs for care, for example supported accommodation, day care or medications. These complexities require a co-ordinated, flexible and collaborative response which defines responsibilities and ultimately ensures that services are provided when and where needed in an acceptable form. The Care Programme Approach (Kingdon 1994a,b) has been introduced in districts since 1991 to make this aim a reality. It sets standards for care; everyone accepted by specialist mental health services must have one person, a *keyworker*, responsible for seeing that their health and social needs are fully assessed, that a care plan is negotiated with the individual themselves and their carer (if one is involved) and that this is then acted on and reviewed by those involved in care as needed. Occasionally there may be particular concern that, at that time, somebody is at significant risk of suicide or self-neglect, or (rarely) of violence towards someone else. To make sure that their needs are given highest priority, they may be included on the local supervision register (Department of Health 1995).

Such risk assessment and management remains, at best, an inexact science (Department of Health 1994b) but the following can help:

- making sure relevant information is available

- conducting a full assessment of risk, for example discussion with the person themselves and consideration of known risk factors

- defining situations and circumstances known to present increased risk.

The Mental Health Act (1983) allows for somebody to be assessed and treated for mental disorder in hospital, not just when that person is thought to be at risk to themselves or others, but also in the interests of their health. This is particularly important in manic depressive illness as it can allow intervention before risk has developed. Unfortunately, however, professionals approved under the Act have frequently failed to use it in this way when it would have been appropriate to do so (Department of Health 1993). Supervised discharge, recently introduced, may improve the care of some people who are at risk in the community but will only apply to those meeting criteria for inclusion on the supervision register and currently detained under section 3 of the Mental Health Act. It does not allow for compulsory treatment.

The range of treatment settings has changed since the days when the only alternatives were the traditional hospital or at home with visits to an outpatient clinic (see, for example, Groves 1990; Kingdon *et al.* 1991). It is now becoming much greater and therefore providing more choice and flexibility to meet needs, as shown in Table 1.1.

Table 1.1 Range of services

	Acute/emergency care	Rehabilitation/continuing care
Home-based	Intensive home support	Domiciliary services
	Emergency duty teams	Key workers
	Sector teams	Care management and Care Programme Approach
Day care	Day hospitals	Drop-in centres
		Support groups
		Employment schemes
		Day care
Residential support	Crisis accommodation	Ordinary housing
		Unstaffed group homes
	Acute units	Adult placement schemes
		Residential care homes
	Local secure units	Mental nursing homes
		24 hour NHS accommodation
		Medium secure units
		High security units

Acute care

Most patients continue to live in their *own homes* while they are helped with their mental health problems. They may visit their family doctor for treatment or a member of the community mental health team, or be visited by them as individual assessment at home has been shown to be cost-effective (Burns *et al.* 1993). During periods of crisis, support may be given to them at home which is generally what people prefer. Intensive support in the home has been provided for people with severe mental illness, including manic depressive illness, by teams who may visit repeatedly during the day or remain with them for periods while carers do other things. This has been demonstrated to be as effective as hospital admission, generally preferred by patients and carers and to be, if anything, less expensive (Burton *et al.* 1980). However, it is also demanding on staff and the sustainability of such schemes has been questioned in the UK. Support to carers is an essential part of services and voluntary groups, such as the Manic Depression Fellowship and Depression Alliance, need to be supported locally and nationally. These organisations run support groups for patients and their families and provide them with a wealth of useful information.

If patients are not making progress or need support in the day when family members are away, a *day hospital* (Creed *et al.* 1990) may then provide alternatives to hospitalisation. These are suitable for even quite ill patients, for example those with depression or hypomania, and are appropriate settings for group therapies and more intensive support for outpatients. Most patients attend for short periods of up to three months. This can provide respite for carers during the day so that they can, for example, continue at work.

Home care may be unsuitable for people who live in adverse social circumstances and those at significant risk to themselves or others. For the former, *crisis accommodation* where people can stay overnight with varying levels of support, can be sited in various settings such as mental health centres, hostels or ordinary housing. For the latter and others needing inpatient care, *acute treatment units* provide a protective environment which is safe and structured and assist in stabilisation, treatment and re-establishment in the community. They can also be places of sanctuary for vulnerable patients and provide respite for relatives.

Watson and Bouras (1988) describe factors determining the effectiveness of inpatient stay. Personal factors are relevant such as age, sex, ethnicity and specific mental disorder; when wards combine wide age groups, lack privacy and cannot meet individual cultural needs, their effectiveness will be limited. The ward environment would be expected to affect mood, although direct evidence for this is limited. The physical structure can range from the bleakest of old institutions through crowded district general hospital wards to modern purpose-built units with homely environments. Locations of acute units are now most frequently on district hospital sites but there are some alternatives as, in cities particularly, these may have poor access, be excessively large and in design more suited to general medicine or surgery. They can be developed offering a more user-friendly design: small local acute units exist, for example, in Newcastle, East Birmingham and Stoke-on-Trent.

The social environment of the acute ward also affects the individual through the quantity and quality of personnel. Decision-making about their care and communication systems with them, for example through the multidisciplinary team review and ward meetings, will be of importance and what research there is suggests that alternative, more effective ways of working than the traditional medical-led group interview of patients exist (Watson and Bouras 1988). The beliefs and value system, policies and procedures of a ward are relevant alongside the interaction patterns with staff, patients and visitors to the ward. There is therefore a complex of issues, some of which are of specific relevance to manic depressive illness, which are of daily practical importance but of which only rudimentary research exists. Nonetheless Department of Health instructions to purchasing authorities emphasise that the development of a 'spectrum of care' must include the provision of sufficient local acute psychiatric beds.

The old mental hospitals met needs for shelter and sustenance but meant people usually had to leave their homes and localities. Local services tend to overcome those problems but have also highlighted the risk of people with mental health problems becoming homeless or ending up in prison. Inquiries into incidents involving harm to self or others have received considerable publicity and services have been criticised as poorly organised and unresponsive. Some excellent services exist but too often they exist in isolation, with surrounding services poorly co-ordinated and frequently demoralised. Pressures on admission beds have often meant that services become distorted towards crisis management rather than developing strategies to allow early intervention, crisis resolution and prompt discharge by efficient meeting of housing needs with continuing and consistent support. The reasons for the reported pressures on beds, particularly in the inner cities in the UK, are many and varied, including insufficient beds in some settings (Mental Health Task Force-LP 1994) but more frequently poor discharge planning and development of local services (Flannigan *et al.* 1994).

Longer-term care

Some patients require longer-term support and rehabilitation. About 10–15 per cent of 'new long stay' patients, the second largest category after schizophrenia, have manic depressive illness (Robin *et al.* 1983). A further 10–30 per cent, not requiring long-term residential care, have evidence of moderate or severe social impairment. This latter is usually related to loss of confidence and motivation, as persistent psychotic symptoms and gross behavioural disturbance are unusual. Enduring symptoms may be as much from the collapse of family and other supports or continuing but unrecognised pressures, as from the illness itself. High levels of expressed emotion have been shown to correlate with relapse in manic depressive illness as well as in schizophrenia (Hooley and Teasdale 1989). Underlying relationship problems may not be obvious but subtle rejection by partners, fellow employees and family members seems frequently to lead to conflicts within that setting and in the individual themselves. Pressures at work may be obvious to all but the patient themselves. Support away from the home or job environment in these circumstances can be diagnostic and therapeutic in itself and also allow for a reconsideration of those relationships, change of job or even early retirement.

It is also important to assess premorbid personality traits, for example dependency and obsessionality, as these may be underlying factors in persistent depressive illnesses and need to be taken into account in the provision of services to the individual. Isolation may also be of importance. This may have occurred for reasons beyond the person's control, but there is also evidence that depressed patients may show deficits in their ability to mobilise social support prior to the onset of illness (Bhugra 1989).

Therefore for people with longer-term problems, rehabilitation services may have much to offer. The services provided will be based on the individual's needs and specific diagnosis is of little relevance, for example poor motivation and concentration will be managed in a similar way whether someone has manic depressive illness or schizophrenia. *Social skills training* and *befriending schemes* may be relevant. Day centres can provide community-based rehabilitation and continuing support. *'Drop-in' centres* can allow social contact to be gradually increased and engagement with services commenced. *Community mental health centres* can provide local team bases including interview facilities, and bases for clubs, adult education, advocacy and other schemes. *Employment schemes* to assist people in returning to work exist in many areas. Links with local placement, assessment and care teams, especially their Disablement Employment Advisers, based at job centres run by the Department of Employment can make the transition back to work more successful. They can provide confidential advice on training schemes and concerns about loss of social security benefits.

Where accommodation is needed, unstaffed *group homes* or *flatlets* with communal living are an option for some patients who have good relationships with each other. A small number of patients will need the support of group homes with staff present in the homes for extended periods of the day or giving 24 hour cover, for example in *residential care homes*. In the latter case, sleeping-in staff provide the least restrictive, while appropriately supportive, option for a significant number of patients. Some schemes have developed on a 'core and cluster' model with staff from the more highly staffed hostels also supporting those which are more independent. *Mental nursing homes* may provide asylum or sanctuary care for extended periods. Of particular importance, *24 hour nursed NHS residences*, sometimes called hospital hostels, are an essential component of all services for rehabilitation purposes and continuing care. They tend to be more cost-effective than using acute wards sporadically and inappropriately for the care of people who need continuing intensive support. *Local secure units* complement acute units and provide short-term care for patients either during acutely disturbed episodes, or as part of a rehabilitation plan in levels of progressively reducing security. *Medium secure units* provide care and treatment in conditions of security for patients who are not such a risk as to require a place in a high security unit. Failure to assess and provide the number of places required has led to unsuitable placements in the special hospitals, in lesser secure provision or in prison. *High security units*, the special hospitals, provide care for the very few people who are mentally disordered and dangerous to others.

However, there are still districts without access to the full range of treatments and services and even more lack sufficient places or trained staff. While this suggests that insufficient resources are available, the evidence from many sources, including the Audit Commission (1995), is that the resources available in a district seem to bear little relationship to how well the services meet the needs of people with severe mental health problems. The Clinical Standards Advisory Group (1995) has produced standards for use by purchasers and providers of care and it has concluded that morale and leadership seemed to be the most important factors in determining quality of care. Services for people who may develop mental health problems should be at least as well provided as those provided for physical problems; to achieve this, their importance needs to be appreciated and that importance acted upon, led by managers of high quality, supported by staff in all branches of the NHS and local authorities who have been trained and are valued for their roles in, as the first target in the English 'Health of the Nation' strategy states, 'improving the health and social functioning of mentally ill people' (Department of Health 1994a).

References

Audit Commission (1995) *Finding a Place*. London: HMSO.

Barker, P.J. (1993) *A Self-Help Guide to Managing Depression*. London: Chapman & Hall.

Beasley, J., Brockington, I.F. and Crisp, A. (1996) 'Survey of highly specialised psychiatric services.' *Psychiatric Bulletin 20*, 129–130.

Bennet, D.H. (1982) 'Management and rehabilitation of affective psychoses.' In J.K. Wing and L. Wing (eds) *Handbook of Psychiatry. Volume 3: Psychosis of Uncertain Aetiology*. Cambridge: Cambridge University Press, pp.173–176.

Bhugra, T.S. (1989) 'Social support and social networks.' *Current Opinion in Psychiatry 2*, 278–282.

Boyd, W. (1994) *Confidential Inquiry into Homicides and Suicides by Mentally Ill People. Preliminary Report on Homicide*. London: Department of Health.

Burns, T. *et al.* (1993) 'A controlled trial of home-based acute psychiatric services. I: clinical and social outcome.' *British Journal of Psychiatry 163*, 49–54.

Burton, A.. *et al.* (1980) 'Alternative to mental hospital III: economic cost benefit analysis.' *Archives of General Psychiatry 37*, 400–405.

Clinical Standards Advisory Group (1995) *Schizophrenia. Volume 1 & Volume 2. Protocol for Assessing Services for People with Severe Mental Illness*. London: HMSO.

Creed, F. *et al.* (1990) 'Randomised controlled trial of day patient versus inpatient psychiatric treatment.' *British Medical Journal 300*, 1033–1037.

Department of Health (1993) *Legal Powers on the Care of Mentally Ill People in the Community*. London: Department of Health.

Department of Health (1994a) *Health of the Nation. Mental Illness Key Area Handbook*. London: HMSO, 2nd edition.

Department of Health (1994b) *Guidance on the Discharge from Hospital of Mentally Disordered People and Their Continuing Care in the Community*. Department of Health: Fleetwood.

Department of Health (1995) *Building Bridges. A Guide to Arrangements for Inter-Agency Working for the Care and Protection of Severely Mentally Ill People*. London: Department of Health.

Fadden, G., Bebbington, P. and Kuipers, L. (1987) 'Caring and its burdens. A study of spouses of depressed patients.' *British Journal of Psychiatry 151*, 660–667.

Flannigan, C.B. *et al.* (1994) 'Inner London collaborative audit of admissions in two health districts. III. Reasons for admission to psychiatric wards.' *British Journal of Psychiatry 165*, 750–759.

Freeman, C.P. (1995) *The ECT Handbook: The Second Report of the Royal College of Psychiatrists Special Committee on ECT.* Council Report CR39. London: Royal College of Psychiatrists.

Groves, T. (1990) 'After the asylums: the local picture.' *British Medical Journal 300*, 1128–1130.

Hooley, J.M. and Teasdale, J.D. (1989) 'Predictors of relapse in unipolar depressives: expressed emotion, marital discord and perceived criticism.' *Journal of Abnormal Psychology 98*, 229–235.

Kingdon, D.G. (1992) 'Interprofessional collaboration in mental health.' *Journal of Interprofessional Collaboration 6*, 2, 141–148.

Kingdon, D.G. (1994a) 'The care programme approach.' *Psychiatric Bulletin 18*, 2, 68–70.

Kingdon, D.G. (1994b) 'Making care programming work.' *Advances in Psychiatric Treatment 2*, 41–46.

Kingdon, D.G. *et al.* (1991) 'Replacing the mental hospital: community provision for a district's chronically psychiatrically disabled in domestic environments.' *British Journal of Psychiatry 158*, 113–116.

Meller, I. (1989) 'The use of psychiatric facilities by depressives: results of the Upper Bavaria Study.' *Acta Psychiatrica Scandanavica 79*, 27–31.

Mental Health Task Force (1994) *Priorities for Action.* London: Mental Health Task Force.

Office of Population Censuses and Surveys (1994) *National Psychiatric Morbidity Survey. Report 1.* London: HMSO.

Office of Population Censuses and Surveys (1995a) *National Psychiatric Morbidity Survey. Report 2.* London: HMSO.

Office of Population Censuses and Surveys (1995b) *National Psychiatric Morbidity Survey. Report 3.* London: HMSO.

Paykel, E.S. and Priest, R.G. (1992) 'Recognition and management of depression in general practice: consensus statement.' *British Medical Journal 305*, 1198–1202.

Perry, A., Tarrier, N. and Morriss, R. (1995) 'Identification of prodromal signs and symptoms and early intervention in manic depressive psychosis patients: a case example.' *Behavioural & Cognitive Psychotherapy 23*, 4, 399–409.

Robin, G. *et al.* (1983) 'The Scottish survey of "new chronic" in-patients.' *British Journal of Psychiatry 143*, 564–571.

Scott, J. (1992) 'Social and community aspects.' In E.J. Paykel (ed) *Handbook of Affective Disorders.* London: Churchill Livingstone, 2nd edition.

Tyrer, P. *et al.* (1988) 'The Nottingham study of neurotic disorder: comparison of drug and psychological treatments.' *Lancet 2*, 235–240.

Watson, J.P. and Bouras, N. (1988) 'Psychiatric ward environments and their effects on patients.' In K. Granville-Grossman (ed) *Recent Advances in Clinical Psychiatry 6.* London: Churchill Livingstone.

Further reading

Tyrer, P., Ferguson, B. and Wadsworth, J. (1990) 'Liaison psychiatry in general practice: the comprehensive collaborative model.' *Acta Psychiatrica Scandanavica 81*, 359–363.

CHAPTER 2

What Psychodynamic Approaches Can Do To Help

Charles Lund

The threats to manic depressive order

This book rightly and understandably has as its focus manic depressive disorder since it is the disordered state of affairs that concerns manic depressives, their relations and friends and which brings them to the attention of various mental health professionals.

However, it is worth first reflecting on the state of manic depressive order since an important contribution of psychodynamics is that of helping in the understanding of the condition and its context. While some crudely expressed biological models of manic depressive illness assume a 'normal' personality upon which is intermittently inflicted an illness state, most psychological theories of manic depressive illness take into account long-standing attitudes in the manic depressive which can predispose them to illness (Gelder, Gath and Mayou 1989; Scott 1995). These attitudes and behaviours may undergo considerable change during the course of an illness and may or may not revert back to the previously held position when recovery comes.

Reduced to its essentials, the psychodynamic view of the mental state of a manic depressive in a non-illness state can be summarised as:

1. Within the internal mental life of the manic depressive can be identified three elements:

    (a) the normal, well adjusted, rational, adaptive self

    (b) a grandiose, expansive, visionary, aggressive, even ruthless self

    (c) a vulnerable, defensive, passive, depressed self.

2. Manic depressives have to manage more unconsciously than
    consciously:

    (a) aggressive feelings and actions

    (b) dependent feelings and vulnerabilities.

Not only do manic depressives vary in their ability to identify the different
elements in their make-up, their insight can vary markedly at different points
in their life. Moreover, by the interpersonal mechanism of projection, one self
element of the manic depressive's three selves may be lodged in another person,
particularly in a spouse or partner (Horwitz 1983).

Viewed in these terms it is worth reconsidering the marriage of the Duke of
Wellington and Kitty Pakenham (Longford 1969; Longford 1972). The Duke's
feats as soldier and statesman and his prodigious levels of energy and self-belief
are legendary. Many have queried why such a man remained married to an
apparently inadequate depressed woman like Kitty Pakenham until death parted
them, particularly when the opportunities for an alternative consort abounded.

One possible psychodynamic explanation is that at some level of his complex
being, the Duke recognised that Kitty was performing an indispensable function
for him, namely relieving him of his depressive inadequate self so that the
grandiose self in conjunction with his adaptive self could perform the deeds
for which he is properly renowned. On this basis one may muse that first
Napoleon and later Wellington's political opponents helped him manage his
aggressive drives while Kitty helped him manage his vulnerable dependency
needs to such an extent that a supremely successful life of manic depressive
order was lived unshaken by any manic depressive disorder.

With this example in mind we can sketch the conditions under which a
person with a potentially manic depressive mental life can avoid illness:

1. A clear split is maintained between the grandiose and the vulnerable
    selves. This is usually achieved by ascribing the unwanted
    characteristics to another, usually a partner who, more unconsciously
    than consciously, is prepared to accept the projection. Sometimes,
    however, the split can be managed within the individual in that over
    periods of time there can be periods of grandiosity, activity and
    enterprise alternating with periods of inactivity, withdrawal and
    dependency associated with illnesses that may sometimes be physical,
    sometimes emotional.

    It is particularly when the period of illness is mental that there is
    the greatest threat to the self-esteem that is maintained by the split.
    That is to say, whatever may have initially precipitated the
    breakdown, be it psychological or physical, the impact of the fact of
    the illness breaking down the split between the grandiose and

dependent selves itself becomes an important trauma maintaining the illness state.

It follows from this that one way of helping the patient to recover is to help reinstate the split by assuring them that the crisis is a one-off brought about by extreme circumstances. If the precipitating circumstances are indeed considerable and it is the first episode that ploy may well work. It is unlikely to work if the episodes recur and the circumstances are less severe. Any attempt by the carer to repeat the ploy is liable to run the risk of damaging their credibility.

2. The manic depressive has a range of activities which can absorb their aggressive needs. In conditions of health these may include business activities, ruthless career development and competitive, physically demanding sport.

    Difficulties arise and may threaten illness if one or more of these outlets is denied. For example, physical illness may severely curtail sporting activity or redundancy or retirement may deny the person enough outlets for their aggression which compounds the loss of prestige.

3. The manic depressive person is able to gain some reality-based support for their internal grandiose self. This may come about via two sources:

    (a) their own talent and energetic application may bring its own social rewards

    (b) by proximity to the famous and socially prestigious they may be satisfied with reflected glory

    (c) some combination of (a) and (b) whereby their own achievements bring them to the attention of the more celebrated and their accomplishments gain praise from eminent practitioners in their field.

    Again it follows that a breakdown into disorder threatens if either the person's talent or energy fails. The artistic, literary and theatrical world is full of stories where such a work crisis has precipitated a breakdown, though it is often later portrayed that the breakdown precipitated the work crisis. Similarly, the loss of reflected glory through bereavement, divorce or withdrawal of patronage can destabilise the previous order.

4. The manic depressive person's dependency needs are met either in ways of which they are unaware or in ways that do not threaten their

self-esteem. The means by which manic depressive dependency needs can be met are manifold and range from the Wellington/Pakenham solution through to the person meeting their own needs by caring for others, often in the health or social service professions. Breakdowns often occur in relation to the ending of such unconscious arrangements through bereavement, divorce, retirement or redundancy when no alternative arrangement is in place to support that aspect of the personality.

The tabloid press has for long reported the messy divorces of comedians, artists and other celebrities whose performances are noted for their manic quality. So often the marital pattern is that of a partner who has supported the artiste in the early years and has usually had the major part in holding the household together and meeting the dependency needs not only of the children but also of the despondent struggling performer. This partner not infrequently succumbs to a dependency problem, often problem drinking, a condition sometimes shared in some measure by the performer. The arrival on the scene of a fellow artiste of some celebrity as an alternative partner shifts the balance such that dependency is ostensibly repudiated in favour of like finding like. While substance abuse may escalate during the divorce proceedings, it not infrequently abates in the performer later. The question that begs to be asked is whether the manic depressive has divorced their spouse, who is left in a despondent state, or has attempted to disown and leave behind some aspect of themselves.

Loss and manic depressive disorder

For anyone, having any diagnosis applied to themselves, be it physical or psychological, is a disturbing yet mystifying experience. So often the words are familiar, yet previously little or no thought has gone into what the experience behind the phrase might entail. At best, or more often at worst, all that is attached to the words are headline associations which in matters psychological are often of the most lurid and outlandish kind.

The first contribution that the psychodynamic approach can make therefore to someone suffering from a manic depressive illness, or to someone concerned for them, is to contribute towards articulating something of the sufferer's experience as it has been and will continue to unfold over time. For the psychodynamic approach is essentially based on a corpus of knowledge derived from the descriptions of a wide variety of persons, be they normal, neurotic or psychotic. It summarises their experiences when depressed or distressed and explains their inward mental states of mind when in the throes of mental distress and also when they are in a calmer frame of mind.

At this point it is worth pausing briefly to consider the etymology of the phrase 'manic depressive'. Both in psychiatric and lay usage it implies connected but polar opposites. That is to say the frenzied, or euphoric state of mania is, by implication, contrasted with the retarded disconsolate state of depression. Superficially there does indeed appear to be a marked difference and, given that several aspects of the treatment and management of these conditions are at some considerable variance from each other, it is hardly surprising that the idea of such polarity should be widely held.

Yet the phrase 'manic depressive' can also be approached in another way. Also in psychiatric classifications and descriptions are phrases such as 'agitated depression' or 'retarded depression'. This draws attention to the idea of 'manic depression' as essentially a depressive state but distinguished from the others by the intercurrence of manic states. That is to say that 'manic' is used as an adjective to describe a particular kind of depressive.

It is from this usage of the phrase manic depressive that it is most easy to gain access to that aspect of psychodynamic description and thinking that is psychoanalytically based and which bears on manic depressive disorder. What has to be emphasised here is that what follows is not *the* single definitive all-encompassing psychoanalytic statement on *the* cause of all manic depressive states. What should soon become apparent is that within the time course of any manic or depressive illness of any individual, let alone during the course of their life, there are a number of inter-related causes and effects, patterns and meanings which defy superficial all-embracing attempts at a single, simple causal explanation. The role of genetics is known to be important but in what way genes produce their influence is as yet ill understood and is in any event influenced by psychosocial influences as well as internal psychological events.

In approaching the psychodynamic understanding of manic depressive states it is important to remember that although the mental states and behaviour of the manic depressive patient can be extreme, the underlying personal attitudes, feelings and mental mechanisms vividly displayed by such distressed patients are, in more muted or contained form, shared by us all. The mentally ill have been banished less for appearing alien, more for having too much in common with the rest of mankind. In the descriptions and case vignettes that follow there will be overlap between the experiences of those who have lived through normal, neurotic or psychotic levels of depression yet also points of difference between them.

It is helpful to consider three inter-locking areas of human experience to gain an appreciation of the complex dilemmas facing the manic depressive patient. A little of these ideas has already been introduced in relation to manic depressive order. The areas to be reviewed are in the realms of feelings, relationships and attitudes to the self (Jacobson 1971; Lund 1991).

Regarding feelings, at first sight it would appear that the only feelings involved are depression and, in the case of mania, euphoria. Yet closer acquaintance shows that even within depression there is a complex amalgam of feelings, of which depression may not be the most predominant. Other feelings that are commonly present, in varying degree at different times in the illness and life of the manic depressive, are anger, guilt, sadness, shame and countless other more personal and idiosyncratic shades of affect. If one attends only to the cardinal emotions of anger, guilt and sadness one senses that the manic depressive person (in common with, but more vividly than the more usual person) has cycles of sustaining a particular tension state of feeling then discharging it.

At other times certain areas of feeling appear to be totally absent. This can occur when, in the context of a psychotic depressed state, the patient hears of the death of someone known to them. Others about them may be shocked to realise that the manic depressive in that state of mind shows no sadness or other more usual feelings of loss. At that phase in their illness such is the predominance of destructive feelings and bleak internal images that the death of another is of no more consequence than the death of a fly amid the horrors of the Holocaust. Only later, as that phase works itself out or is treated, does the capacity to remember relating to the dead person return and with it a capacity to feel sad for the death of the person and at the loss of that relationship.

It is in relation to loss and bereavement that the dynamics of manic depressive states, indeed of any depressive states, can best be understood. In the opening section it will have been noted that it is some form of loss of a relationship that so often threatens manic depressive order. In this context it is helpful to note that relationships may be entered into either on the basis of the difference between the people concerned in terms of their attributes or else on the basis of their similarities. In the first case the other has nurturant qualities that can be available and supplied to oneself. In the second case, on the basis of similarity a person is attracted to another in that a desired aspect of oneself is found mirrored in the qualities of another.

Whichever form a relationship takes, or whatever degree of admixture of these possibilities there may be in the relationship, when that relationship ends, or is threatened with termination, the familiar litany of bereavement responses is progressively played out – shock, denial with or without manic activity, anger, guilt and, with increasing health, reparation leading to resolution.

In severe depressive states much of the dynamics is around the phases of the emotional or affective states of anger, guilt and desperate reparative atonement, even involving ideas of self-sacrifice up to and including self-destruction. In manic states one can often understand a particular manic episode as a more or less desperate attempt to stay in the denial phase of grief, thereby warding off the pain of loss by a false brittle joviality and/or frenetic activity unconsciously designed to crowd out the image of the loss.

This dynamic was evident as hypomanic promiscuous activity displayed by a gay musically talented clerical worker from a deprived background who had been living with his professional musician lover for some time before the latter began to betray evidence of infidelity to a degree that threatened the relationship. The response of this gay manic depressive was to seek to retain the relationship by acceding to dangerous threesome sexual liaisons. He himself then actively encouraged ever more frenetic sexual activity in a sustained mood of high spirits which belied his distress at the threatened loss of the relationship which had given him both support and prestige. He needed considerable psychotherapeutic help first to recognise the connection between his dangerous manic sexual acting out and his fear of the loss of the relationship and then to work through his feelings about the end of the relationship.

As indicated earlier, in the area of the self, depressive patients generally, and manic depressive patients particularly, can be thought of as operating with three aspects of self: a normal realistic sense of self, a diminished, impoverished, denigrated sense of self and a grandiose, self-important sense of self. Feelings generally, but those feelings associated with loss particularly, are closely associated with the vicissitudes of the states of self. Which one of the three selves described that comes more to the fore in organising the person's mental life will determine the clinical features of their episode of illness.

Like the rest of humanity manic depressives have relationships, some of which cater for their needs for nurturance and affiliation and some of which sustain their self-regard by association with their perceived highly valued qualities, real or imagined. These latter forms of relationship mitigate the effects of the low self-esteem generated by the denigrated self because the grandiose self is sustained by close affinity to a person, cause or activity that is more or less prestigious. The loss of such a close association, which may have been striven towards for years and attained at great cost, can be devastating. Its effects may be temporarily warded off by manic activity. Alternatively the person is plunged into despair under the influence of the denigrated and denigrating self.

For example, a deaconess with a background of both maternal and paternal emotional neglect coupled with high moral expectations formed a long-standing intense, largely fantasised attachment to a fellow clergyman of some local stature. Proximity to this priest was gained by assiduous religious devotion. Her mental state was all but entirely dependent on her perception of whether she felt he cared for her in any way. If he appeared disinterested she was filled with rage, self-loathing, despair and a level of depression that included suicidal ideas and required antidepressant medication. If he appeared to offer her about the same recognition as other church members she lifted out of clinical depression but felt jealous of her peers. If he went out of his way to support or praise her, she became euphoric and would successfully take on strenuous hobbies and re-double her religious duties, combining these with a literary output that put her in ever closer contact with the priest. While capable of sustaining this level of activity for months, eventually fatigue would set in, contact with the priest would diminish and she would become despondent and depressed before the cycle began again.

Given the intensity of her feelings for the priest an unusual but mutually supportive matrix involving the manic depressive deaconess, the priest and the deaconess's husband gradually evolved. The husband sustained an astounding tolerance for the intense, albeit platonic, relationship between his wife and the priest, although it required much emotional work involving the bearing of much personal pain on his part to help maintain his wife's meta-stable mental equilibrium. Later still in the life of this menage, communication developed between the husband and the priest which enabled them both to cope better and help the deaconess achieve a considerable measure of productive stability.

In reading these necessarily brief descriptions, while the reader may be more or less content to accept that the author is not offering an across-the-board explanation of manic depressive psychosis, he or she may yet protest that the points made could well apply equally to persons of their acquaintance who had never suffered an episode of mania nor of significant depression.

This criticism would be entirely valid partly on the grounds that there are a wide range of manic depressive clinical states, some of which are mild and remit spontaneously or improve with unlabelled help from a general practitioner and which never became common knowledge. More importantly, the comment would highlight that while this book focuses on helping manic depressive disorder, it is easy to overlook the reality of the previously discussed manic depressive order and the variants of mental life between. That is to say that, with luck, it is possible to live a life with all the attributes and internal characteristics of a manic depressive but without ever demonstrating any florid clinical manifestation of such a potential vulnerability.

From what has gone before it may be surmised that if a predisposed person goes through life with freely available close intimate support in time of bereavement, self-esteem-sustaining partnerships that do not suddenly collapse and friends who can cope with the unusual range of their emotions, then there is no reason why even the idea that they are manic depressive should cross their mind. It is only when personal disasters befall or when a person carries the knowledge of a family propensity to manic depressive disorder that the underlying mental attitudes are suspected.

A 50-year-old music teacher had just had his divorce confirmed but was not yet fully committed to another relationship when he came under increased pressure in terms of job demands and potential job insecurity. He also received the news that his recent ex-wife had developed cancer. In his background there was a strong family history of manic depressive psychosis which he had long feared.

Beset with these problems he became increasingly agitated and irritable, his sleep pattern became disturbed and his concentration became poor. The combined effect of these changes was to lead to a greater emotional distance between him and his new-found partner and increasing alienation between him and his headmaster and other colleagues. This increasing emotional and professional distance in its turn precipitated a burst of inappropriate manic activity which produced more disruption than productive work, at least from the point of view of colleagues. From the patient's point of view, his 'intellectually limited' colleagues could not appreciate the breadth and scale of his vision for the re-styling of the curriculum nor match his boundless energy and enthusiasm. He felt that their attitude and actions towards him were motivated by envy and malice. Faced with a situation which neither he nor anyone else could manage any longer and from which everyone he knew felt forced to withdraw, he reluctantly accepted admission to hospital.

Help

From the brief, heavily disguised, case vignettes already described it will have become obvious that whether the potential helper be relative or friend, whether the condition be manic depressive order or manic depressive disorder, the would-be helper is often already emotionally involved in complex ways in the condition itself. Moreover, it will have become evident that whatever the friend or relative does will be perceived in different ways at different times by the manic depressive person. Furthermore, whether or not to stay involved, whether or not to get more involved, whether or not to act in a different way throw up many perplexing, difficult moral and emotional issues which go to the heart of marital, familial, working and friendship relationships.

As John Lennon put it when nearing the zenith of his fame yet when he was in his most despairing state, in needing help he needed 'somebody, but not just anybody'.

The response that may be offered must be personal and taken as a considered response, having regard to the potential short-, medium- and long-term consequences for the manic depressive and the putative helper.

To some extent the position of the professional helper is a little easier if their role is essentially to offer a short-term aid to recovery to impart some skill, even a complex skill such as cognitive therapy. The position is potentially more complex if the professional, for understandable and legitimate reasons, undertakes to provide part of the long-term supportive psychotherapy for the manic depressive. It is in this situation that a knowledge of the dynamics of manic depressive states becomes essential for the well-being of all concerned since the helper too, for good or ill, may be recruited to the internal world of the patient.

In terms of a psychodynamic approach to helping manic depressive disorder the next issue for the psychodynamically informed psychiatrist, mental health worker, pastor, friend or relative is: 'Help towards what?'. That is to say, does the helper have an implicit or explicit sense of normality foreign to the sufferer towards which he or she is trying to guide the manic depressive sufferer? Or is their aim both more modest and personalised in that they are attempting to guide the person back to their previous manic depressive order, rather sadder but perhaps wiser?

Other authors writing chapters in this book will indicate the particular approaches of other disciplines at the different phases in the care, support, treatment and management of people with manic depressive disorder. In this chapter I have summarised certain issues which need attending to at all phases of the manic depressive life, though the nature of that attention will vary not only as between the non-clinical normal state and the clinical state, but also between the poles of the manic depressive illness and the degrees of its severity.

Regarding feelings therefore, at times these are so extreme as to require physical containment in the sense of the person being in hospital, pharmaceutical containment with either tranquillisers, mood stabilisers or antidepressants, and also personal emotional containment by the ward staff. This personal containment involves trained humane staff being present when few others can cope with being with the manic depressive *in extremis*. Later, as the person is able to settle enough to listen, staff members can give information about what the manic depressive is going through, which helps to reduce the extent of the otherwise formless chaos of emotions and experience.

The formation of a therapeutic relationship is crucial both as a link to others, as a point of attachment and as a source of much needed information upon which the enterprise of rehabilitation will be built.

Part of that rebuilding includes the re-formation of the sense of self. For many the 'nervous breakdown' can be used creatively as the basis of a 'nervous breakout'. As the other authors in this volume will show, if the person can emerge from the experience with a more realistic sense of themselves coupled with a stronger adaptive self, they will be less encumbered with an unflattering view of themselves linked to an unhealthy interplay between their denigrated and grandiose selves. This will render them less vulnerable. Linked to this is if they can distinguish the difference between sustainable realistic relationships that can support them from unhelpful relationships that pull them down or glossy relationships which sustain only their grandiose selves, then again they may be better protected.

Rarely is sensible pre-emptive advice sought or heard by someone who is experiencing the excitement of another way of being. Before, that is, they are shaken by some form of breakdown. However, if a therapeutic alliance can be established, patient work over months and years, having regard to dynamically based principles, can make a significant contribution to mental health.

By itself, psychodynamic psychotherapy is rarely, if ever, the single mode of treatment for a manic depressive. However, practitioners of other therapies with a psychodynamic knowledge will bring to the manic depressive a broader understanding of their condition and its context and they will thereby be in a better position to adjust their goals, style or technique accordingly.

Conversely, psychodynamic understanding and specific psychodynamic psychotherapy may be part of a management strategy. By way of examples we can reconsider the case vignettes previously described.

In the case of the gay musical clerical worker, a psychodynamic under-standing first helped the therapist to make sense of why that man had become ill in that way at that point in his life. During sessions with the man, the therapist was progressively able to share his understanding with his patient, who was gradually able to work with the explanation and begin to modify his behaviour.

The second overlapping phase of psychodynamic work was that of focused therapy concerning the loss of his relationship in which the therapist was present as a supportive figure. His role was not confined to this, in that he also encouraged his patient to talk through and come to terms with the loss of the various aspects of his former relationship without recourse to dangerous manic activity.

Concerning the second case, that of the deaconess, the psychodynamic understanding of her therapist was shared, in some measure, both with the deaconess and her husband. In some ways, the deaconess was less psychologi-cally minded than the gay musician and it therefore took months rather than weeks for her to understand that the ups and downs in her relationship with her priest, while they had their realistic aspects, often were largely an expression of her mental state. In the increasing light of this understanding she was able to manage the relationship without embarrassing and potentially destructive incidents.

Conjoint sessions involving the deaconess, her husband and the therapist helped consolidate the marriage as the primary relationship. It also provided the opportunity for the therapist to give the husband as much psychodynamic understanding of the situation as she could, within the constraints of the core relationship she had with the deaconess and given the sensitive nature of the relationships concerned.

In the third case, that of the music teacher, having regard to the floridly psychotic nature of his presentation and the strong family history, the mainstay of his treatment was lithium and antipsychotics. However, he was referred for psychotherapeutic help in respect of a number of inter-related life issues. These included his understandably confused feelings for his ex-wife in which his feelings about the divorce, initiated by his wife, conflicted with his feelings of compassion for his ex-wife and his concerns for the best arrangements for their children. These major disruptions to his life, combined with work issues, provoked a mid-life crisis of Job-like proportions. Therapy therefore not only involved grief work in respect of the marriage and anticipatory grief work in respect of his wife's terminal illness, but also work-related counselling and a life review in preparation for a radically different future.

References

Gelder, M., Gath, D. and Mayou, R. (1989) *Oxford Textbook of Psychiatry*. Oxford: Oxford University Press.

Horwitz, L. (1983) 'Projective identification in dyads and groups.' *International Journal of Group Psychotherapy 33*, 259–279.

Jacobson, E. (1971) *Depression. Comparative Studies of Normal, Neurotic and Psychotic Conditions*. New York: International Universities Press Incorporated.

Longford, E. (1969) *Wellington: The Years of the Sword*. London: Weidenfeld and Nicolson Limited.

Longford, E. (1972) *Wellington: Pillar of State*. London: Weidenfeld and Nicolson Limited.

Lund, C. (1991) 'Psychotic depression: psychoanalytic psychopathology in relation to treatment and management.' *British Journal of Psychiatry 158*, 523–528.

Scott, J. (1995) 'Psychological treatments for depression: an update.' *British Journal of Psychiatry 167*, 289–293.

Further reading

Bookshop shelves are lined with books about depression, variants of psychodynamic psychotherapy and enthusiastic accounts of therapy for depressives. The difficulty about recommending many of these texts is twofold. First, too often 'depression' is used as a term as if it were describing a single condition which varies only in its degree of severity across its entire range. By analogy, it is as if bronchopneumonia was the same condition as the common cold, only more severe. In fact the pathologies of the two conditions are quite different.

The second difficulty about recommending many books follows from this, namely that psychotherapeutic remedies for the depressive equivalent of the common cold, such as a normal bereavement reaction, may have little relevance to, and indeed may without modification be harmful to, the depressive equivalent of bronchopneumonia that is fulminating manic depressive disorder.

One book that is very alert to these issues and careful in its descriptions of the levels of depression is *Individual Psychotherapy and the Science of Psychodynamics* by David H. Malan (1979). Not only is the book positively enjoyable to read, the reader will finish it with a sound grasp of the psychodynamics of a wide range of conditions, including normality. Of particular interest in the manic depressive context are Chapters 12 and 14 which delineate the different levels of depression and describe clearly when psychotherapy is indicated with or without psychiatric back-up, and when it is contraindicated.

Regarding wider reading, the biographies and autobiographies of many of the shapers of our destiny, our artists and comedians can be read as accounts of manic depressive order, as in the previously cited biographies of Wellington by Longford, or of manic depressive disorder (Milligan, 1986).

Approached in this way, these accounts of lives lead one to wonder whether the forms, structure and basis of the Arts, indeed of civilisation, are but the coral formed by the current and past lives of manic depressives in conjunction with those whose fortunes are enmeshed in their's.

Malan, D.H. (1979) *Individual Psychotherapy and the Science of Psychodynamics.* London: Butterworth.

Milligan, S. (1986) *Where Have All The Bullets Gone?* London: Penguin Books.

CHAPTER 3

What a Cognitive Behavioural Approach Can Do To Help

Alison Jenaway and Denis O'Leary

Introduction

It is surprising how little has been written about using cognitive behaviour therapy (CBT) with patients who suffer from manic depressive illness. Indeed, most books about manic depressive illness ignore the role of psychotherapy as a specific treatment for the illness, focusing instead on how it may be used to improve compliance with medication. This lack of attention to psychotherapeutic treatments for patients with manic depressive illness is probably due to three main factors, as summarised by Scott (Scott 1995): first, early psychoanalysts, including Freud, tended to view bipolar patients as resistant to psychoanalysis; second, there was a generally held belief that patients with manic depression were completely well between episodes; and third, most mental health professionals believe that manic depressive illness has a stronger genetic and biochemical basis than pure depressive illness and these aspects of the illness have tended to receive most research attention. The belief in the biological approach to treatment has been even stronger since the introduction of successful drug treatment for depression and mania, and of lithium as a prophylactic to prevent future episodes of illness.

Unfortunately, it has become clear from several studies that treatment with medication is often inadequate. Although lithium does appear to be more effective than placebo in preventing further episodes of illness in controlled trials (Prien, Caffey and Klett 1973; Stallone *et al.* 1973), the evidence from research carried out in clinical settings is less optimistic. Lithium was used increasingly for prophylaxis in manic depressive illness from the early 1970s, yet the number of patients re-admitted to psychiatric hospitals with mania does not seem to have declined after this, as one might expect if lithium was totally effective in preventing further episodes (Dickson and Kendell 1986; Symonds and Williams 1981). Similarly, follow-up studies in which treatment is carried out according to usual clinical practice, have found that some patients continue to have further episodes while on lithium, and that even between episodes some patients still have considerable problems in social and work adjustment (Gitlin *et al.* 1995; Harrow *et al.* 1990).

It seems clear that early views about manic depressive illness were very polarised. In the early part of this century, psychotherapy was attempted in the absence of medication and deemed to be impossible (Abraham 1953; Fromm-Reichmann 1949). More recently, medication has been seen as the only answer with no need to attend to the psychological aspects of the illness. Hopefully, the time has come to bring the two treatment options together as allies against an illness which causes so much distress. Since cognitive behavioural approaches have been used with some success in unipolar depression and, more recently, in schizophrenia (Kingdon, Turkington and John 1994), it seems appropriate to consider how they might be used in manic depressive illness. We will first define the terms we intend to use throughout the rest of this chapter, then describe briefly the main elements of CBT for depression, and go on to discuss which aspects of manic depressive illness might best be targeted using cognitive behavioural techniques.

Definition of terms

There is an important distinction between *unipolar depression*, in which patients suffer from episodes of depression only, and manic depressive disorder, also known as *bipolar affective disorder*, in which patients may have episodes of mania or depression. These two groups of patients show differences in genetic predisposition and in the course of the illness over time. There are also some differences in response to treatment, so it is useful to make the diagnosis whenever possible. Throughout this chapter we will use the terms 'unipolar' or 'bipolar' to make it clear to which group of patients we are referring. We will refer to an *episode* of illness to describe the period of time during which the patient has symptoms of either depression or mania, *remission* for the point at which the patient no longer has significant symptoms, and *relapse* for the onset of a further episode.

CBT for unipolar depression

Several theories about depression have been developed which include a link between cognitions (thoughts), behaviour and mood. Early behavioural theories about the cause of depression concentrated on ideas about reinforcement. A reinforcer is defined as anything which increases the frequency of a given behaviour. The most powerful reinforcers for most people are pleasure, satisfaction after achievement and praise from important others. Thus loss of reinforcement might be due to lack of ability to feel pleasure, inability to achieve or the loss of an important person in one's life. Depression was seen as a condition resulting from a lack of positive reinforcement, leading to the person giving up and withdrawing from society. This makes sense but involves a very mechanical view of human beings. Scope for therapy is limited to encouraging people to seek out reinforcers, training them if they have specific skill deficits or encouraging them to find others who can give them praise. These behavioural techniques remain an important part of CBT, but a more complicated model is required if we are to take into account a person's thoughts and the way they make sense of the world. The actual amount of reinforcement may be less important than how the person perceives it and what value they place on it.

The most influential model resulting in treatment methods has been Beck's cognitive theory of depression (Beck 1976). This arose out of clinical observation of depressed patients. Beck was struck by the pervasiveness of the negative thoughts that these patients have. He described a negative cognitive triad in which patients have a negative view of themselves, the world and their future. These negative thoughts are called 'automatic' as they seem to occur spontaneously rather than as the result of deliberate thought. In addition, Beck identified a series of systematic, logical errors which tend to occur in depressive thinking, for example:

1. *Arbitrary inference*, such as assuming that because a person hasn't contacted you, then they must not like you any more.

2. *Over-generalisation*, for example, believing that you have failed at everything just because you have made one mistake.

3. *All-or-nothing thinking*, such as, 'if I am not perfect then I am useless'

4. *Selective abstraction*, attending to negative aspects of a situation and ignoring the positives.

The cognitive model asserts that these errors increase the frequency of automatic negative thoughts. The negative thoughts lead to changes in behaviour such as social withdrawal, which results in further lowering of mood and more negative thoughts. Thus a vicious circle is set up which maintains the depressive syndrome. This model can be useful whatever the theoretical cause of the depression in the first place, as treatment can be effective when aimed at any point in the vicious circle (see Figure 3.1). Drugs act specifically on brain chemicals which alter mood; behaviour therapy aims to get people active and doing things they might enjoy; cognitive therapy aims to correct the negative bias in thinking and help patients to assess their situation more realistically.

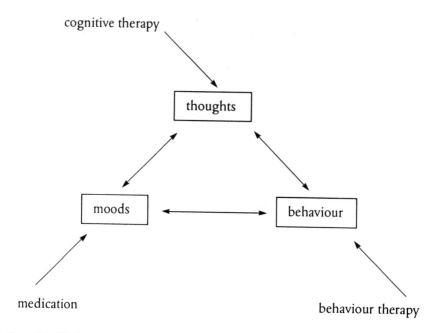

Figure 3.1 The interaction of thoughts, behaviour and mood

In general, a cognitive behaviour therapist would start by explaining the model to the patient. If they are unable to understand it, or feel that it does not apply to their depression in any way, they are unlikely to engage in the treatment. It is also necessary for patients to be able to form a collaborative relationship with the therapist for any useful work to be done. Once the patient understands the model, the therapist would encourage them to start testing it out to see if it is true for them. They would probably start with behavioural techniques, particularly for a patient who feels they are unable to do anything at all to help themselves. The first step might be just to keep a diary of what they are doing during the day and to give each activity a score for how much sense of achievement it gave (mastery) and for how pleasurable it was. Gradually the patient would be encouraged to build up their activity, bit by bit, so that they start to feel more capable and are able to return to some of their previous interests. These changes in behaviour can be used as experiments to identify the automatic negative thoughts which stop the patient achieving what they want to. For example, thinking, 'this is not going to make me feel any better' right from the start rather than keeping an open mind. Later, patients are encouraged to recognise these thoughts and identify their own logical errors, learning to challenge them and check out the evidence for them. This might involve behavioural experiments, for example, telephoning a person who hasn't been in contact for a while and seeing how they react.

The techniques described so far are aimed at treating the depressive symptoms. However, cognitive therapists also believe that they can reduce a patient's vulnerability to future episodes. This is based on the idea that some people have beliefs, even when well, which make them vulnerable to developing depression. These beliefs are thought to arise out of early life experiences as the developing child struggles to make sense of the world. Eventually, each person constructs a system of beliefs about the world and about themselves which is used to make sense of current experience. Some beliefs are clearly very useful, for example, if you believe that, 'in order to be successful, I should work hard' you are likely to go far. However, someone who believes that, 'in order to be successful, I must never make a mistake' might well be vulnerable to depression. For such a person, any mistake could trigger a marked mood change as it automatically means 'I am a failure'. These beliefs are thought to be so ingrained that a person may not even be aware that he or she is acting as if the belief were true. Cognitive therapy techniques can help the person learn to become more aware of their own beliefs, and examine them more closely. They may be out of date, or too rigid, and therefore unhelpful. Modifying the unhelpful beliefs, and being more aware of when they are causing mood changes, may make a future episode of depression less likely.

CBT can be given individually or in a group setting. Most research has been based on 10 to 15 hourly sessions of therapy. There are several self-help books encouraging people to try the technique for themselves (Barker 1992; Blackburn 1987) but this can be difficult without the support of a therapist who can help to motivate the patient and suggest ways of overcoming difficulties.

How CBT might be effective in bipolar affective disorder

There are a number of ways in which CBT might be helpful for patients with bipolar affective disorder. Unfortunately, as mentioned earlier, research is sadly lacking in bipolar patients and we can therefore only speculate from the work done with patients suffering from unipolar depression and other disorders in which CBT appears to be effective. We will discuss three main targets for CBT techniques. First, CBT could be used to treat the symptoms of depression or mania, in an attempt to shorten or lessen the severity of each episode. Second, it may be possible to use CBT to prevent the development of further episodes. Third, it could be used to modify other aspects of the patient's life which are causing problems. This would be worthwhile even if it did not specifically target the illness because the aim would be to improve the quality of life between episodes.

As any therapy would involve a substantial investment of time and effort from both the patient and the therapist, it would be essential to test out these ideas using controlled research trials in patients with bipolar affective disorder.

Treatment of the symptoms during episodes

DEPRESSIVE EPISODES

Studies of patients with unipolar depression suggest that cognitive therapy is as effective as medication for depressive illness (Dobson 1989). Even patients who have endogenous symptoms (those which indicate a biochemical basis to the depression, such as poor sleep, appetite disturbance, lack of energy and concentration difficulties) seem to respond as well to CBT as those with a less biological type of depression, although there is evidence that severe depression responds better to medication (Elkin *et al.* 1989). Unfortunately, perhaps due to the bias mentioned already, most studies of cognitive therapy exclude patients with bipolar illness so we do not yet know whether depression in bipolar patients responds as well to CBT as unipolar depression. It is possible that the treatment would be as effective in bipolar depression as it is not directed at the original cause of the depression but at the resulting symptoms and behaviour. There is no convincing evidence that the symptoms of depression in bipolar patients are systematically different to those seen in unipolar depression, or that there are significant differences in their response to antidepressant treatment (Perris 1992). However, the cognitive model of unipolar depression has been tested and refined using basic research over many years, and it is important not to assume that the same model necessarily fits bipolar depression, even though the symptoms are similar.

CBT is unlikely to become the main treatment for bipolar depression but it might find a place where patients have failed to respond fully to antidepressant treatment.

MANIC EPISODES

Many authors have written about the difficulty of treating patients with mania using psychotherapy, and this is probably one of the main reasons that bipolar patients have generally been excluded from trials of cognitive therapy. Kahn described the attitudes of early psychoanalytic writers who found manic patients difficult to deal with because of their lack of concentration and grandiose ideas (Kahn 1990). However, Janowsky, Leff and Epstein (1970) warned against just relying on medication for acute treatment and described the sort of interactions in which manic patients may engage. The experience of elation and irritability may lead to certain 'games' that can be played out between manic patients and those attempting to treat them. In particular, the patient may adversely affect the self-esteem of others by picking up on any vulnerability, for example commenting on the doctor's age or appearance. They may also expose conflicts within the staff team by constantly testing boundaries and questioning staff decisions. Clearly, when patients are severely manic they would be unable to attend a formal psychotherapy session. Similarly, patients without insight into the fact that they are ill would resist attempts at therapy. This seems to place manic patients in the category of those who are not able to establish a positive collaborative relationship with the therapist, probably the most important indication of suitability for CBT.

In a sense, however, what clinicians do with such patients has some similarities to informal CBT. We reduce stimulation and try to get them to reduce their overactive *behaviour*, either by negotiating more realistic activities or by setting firm limits of what is acceptable. We challenge their grandiose *thoughts* by asking them how realistic they are and getting them to think about the possible consequences of their actions. These means are used at present to cope with a manic patient until the medication has started working. It may not be possible for a new therapist to engage a patient at this stage of the illness, but trusted staff who are already known to the patient could perhaps use CBT techniques in a more structured way.

Hypomania is a milder form of manic episode and it might be possible to engage hypomanic patients in a more formal CBT session. It would be important to be sure that the patient had good insight into the fact that he or she was ill and was prepared to work with the therapist. At present there is no specific CBT for manic symptoms and this would have to be developed with experience. The focus would presumably be on explaining the model and then trying to understand how cognitions and behaviour were reinforcing the elated mood, resulting in a kind of positive vicious cycle. It might be necessary to help the patient see that this was having adverse consequences in their interactions with others, or was likely to cause long-term problems for them, perhaps by reviewing the effects of previous episodes of hypomania. The goals of treatment would have to be mutually agreed in order to engage the patient in the therapy. Unfortunately, unlike the depressed patient, for whom a CBT session may improve their mood, the hypomanic patient might leave a successful session feeling less elated. This would be unlikely to promote compliance with the therapy! It remains to be seen whether the use of CBT techniques is effective in treating hypomania.

Prevention of future episodes

Patients with unipolar depression and those with bipolar illness remain vulnerable to further episodes. Thus although the chance of recovery from a given episode is good, attention has turned to the prevention of relapse. Recently there has been some suggestion from follow-up studies of unipolar patients that CBT can prevent relapse. In several controlled trials, patients who had gone into remission following CBT were less likely to suffer a relapse of their depression than those treated with antidepressants (Blackburn, Eunson and Bishop 1986; Evans *et al.* 1992; Simons *et al.* 1986). In one of these studies the effect of having had CBT was as good at preventing relapse as continuing on long-term antidepressants (Evans *et al.* 1992). It is not yet clear why this is so. It may be because CBT provides patients with a sort of 'do it yourself' treatment kit which they can use to treat their symptoms as soon as they start to feel an episode of depression coming on. A more exciting alternative explanation might be that CBT changes certain underlying beliefs, thus making the patient less vulnerable to depression. This would be a major breakthrough in the treatment of depression as no medication appears to alter the course of unipolar depression after it has stopped being taken by the patient.

Again, we do not know whether this effect of relapse prevention would be seen in bipolar patients as the research has not yet been carried out. If the trigger for an episode of bipolar depression is some kind of biological change in brain chemistry and the onset is sudden, patients will be less able to use cognitive techniques to prevent the development of a full-blown episode. For the same reason, underlying beliefs may be less important in bipolar patients. However, there is increasing evidence that stressful life events can precipitate episodes of illness in bipolar patients (Ellicott *et al.* 1990; Hunt, Bruce-Jones and Silverstone 1992). This suggests that the cause of relapse is not simply a spontaneous biochemical change and that cognitive behaviour therapy might make patients less vulnerable to the stress of life events.

Another important area to focus on might be working with the patient and their relatives, to identify early warning signs of a relapse. Some patients may become more irritable as the initial symptom of a manic episode, others may have early morning waking as the first sign of depression. If these signs are taken seriously and acted upon, it may be possible to avoid a full-blown episode of illness.

Treatment of other problems

THE EFFECTS OF LIFE STRESSES AND THE STRESS OF LIVING WITH A CHRONIC ILLNESS

People with manic depressive illness are just as likely as anyone else to have had difficult childhood experiences. They may have developed maladaptive beliefs from these experiences or unhelpful ways of coping with stressful situations which would operate, even when euthymic. In addition, a patient with manic depressive illness, like a patient with any chronic condition, has to cope with stresses which result from the illness itself. As mentioned above, stressful life events appear to precipitate some relapses. Thus a vicious cycle may occur of worsening illness and worsening psychosocial environment, possibly leading eventually to chronic illness. The sort of stresses which may result from the illness include:

1. Disruption of certain developmental tasks, if the illness begins during adolescence or early adulthood, such as leaving home, education and forming relationships.

2. Effects on the family, spouse, children and difficulties in these relationships after repeated episodes.

3. Realistic losses which occur during episodes of illness, for example employment lost through depression or debts incurred when manic.

4. Symbolic losses due to the illness itself, or the treatment. These may include feelings of being defective and having to rely on medication, loss of self-esteem and loss of dreams for the future.

Many of these issues could be addressed in CBT and the patient helped to come to terms with things they cannot change and work gradually on things which could be improved. The specific cognitive behavioural techniques which are likely to be used for these problems will depend on a careful analysis of the problem itself, a process known as a formulation. This generally involves taking a detailed description of the problem, including how frequent it is, things which seem to aggravate or relieve it and the consequences of it. In addition to the patient's full psychiatric history, this can be used to work out the likely factors which predisposed the patient to develop the problem, what precipitated it originally and why it is being perpetuated. The therapist can communicate the formulation to the patient and suggest ways in which therapy could help. The work is likely to be aimed at changing factors which are perpetuating the problem. This might involve assertiveness training, improved communication skills or behaviour family therapy. Detailed descriptions of these techniques are beyond the scope of this chapter but can be found elsewhere (Stern and Drummond 1991).

CBT FOR THE PROBLEMS OF NON-COMPLIANCE

Compliance with medication is often taken for granted by treating clinicians but patients' views and behaviour vary a great deal. It is likely that between 20 and 50 per cent of patients on lithium decide not to take their medication at some time (Cochran 1984). They may either stop it completely or just reduce the dose. In some patients compliance is probably highest immediately after an episode of illness and then declines as the person remains well and no longer sees the need for continuing medication. In others, compliance is poor initially because the patient denies that they are ill, but improves after several episodes when they start to gain insight into the nature of their condition.

Although unpleasant side effects appear to be one reason for non-compliance in many patients (Bech, Vendsborg and Rafaelsen 1976), this is clearly not the only reason. Attitudes towards illness and medication play a large part in compliance behaviour. This is highlighted by the findings from one study in which patients reported that the primary reason for their non-compliance with lithium was that they were bothered by the idea that their moods were being controlled by the medication (Jamison, Gerner and Goodwin 1979). Of course, for the clinician, this is the main aim of the treatment! In an attempt to model the complex reasons behind non-compliance, Cochran and Gitlin (1988) questioned 48 patients attending a lithium clinic and found that a patient's normative beliefs (beliefs that relevant others such as family, friends, personal psychiatrists and lithium experts want the patient to take lithium) appeared to be important in influencing compliance.

The question remains whether these influential attitudes and beliefs can be explored in therapy so that patients are able to make an informed decision about their own treatment and discuss this openly with their treating clinician. Coercion should be avoided. Persuading patients to take medication that appears to be ineffective for them or causes unacceptable side effects would be pointless. A rational exploration of the benefits and risks of the patient continuing with prophylaxis should be the aim. Many psychiatrists would see this as part of normal clinical practice. However, some patients may appear to have a distorted view of their illness or treatment. This may call for specific cognitive techniques. For example, a patient who believes that taking any long-term medication is a weakness, and who believes that they must appear strong at all times, will be unlikely to continue with lithium however effective it is for preventing further episodes of illness. These beliefs could be explored in therapy and perhaps modified so that they are less rigid. Does the patient consider diabetic patients weak because they need insulin? What is their fear about admitting any weakness? Is this a realistic fear or one based on past experiences which are no longer relevant? Doctors may not realise the importance of exploring patients' views about compliance. In the study by Jamison et al. mentioned above, psychotherapy (usually psychodynamic psychotherapy in this study) was rated as very important in maintaining lithium compliance by 50 per cent of patients, but by only 27 per cent of clinicians.

Only a few studies have looked at ways of improving lithium compliance. All of these have emphasised the importance of educating patients about lithium. One controlled study tested the effects of an educational package on 60 patients attending a lithium clinic. The package consisted of a 12 minute video and written handout about lithium, combined with a home visit during which patients could ask questions about lithium. The group receiving the educational package had significantly greater knowledge of lithium than the control group at follow-up. They also had more positive attitudes towards it and showed better compliance as measured by lithium levels. If such a brief intervention can affect attitudes and compliance, it seems likely that psychotherapy would have some effect. In addition, there are reports in the literature that individual (Benson 1975) and group (Shakir, Volkman and Bacon 1979) psychotherapy appears to improve compliance. The most encouraging findings are those from the only controlled study of CBT in bipolar patients. Cochran (1984) examined the effect of six sessions of CBT, adapted from Beck's approach for the treatment of depression (Beck 1976), on 28 new attenders at a lithium clinic. Over the next 6 months, the 14 patients allocated to the therapy were significantly less likely to be rated as having major problems with compliance, to terminate lithium against medical advice or to suffer an episode of illness precipitated by non-compliance than the control patients.

REHABILITATION OF THE CHRONICALLY ILL PATIENT

Bipolar illness has traditionally been distinguished from schizophrenia by the fact that patients recover between episodes. Certainly the prognosis is better than that of patients with schizophrenia, but in studies carried out before lithium was widely prescribed, around 25 to 30 per cent of patients developed a chronic illness with difficulty in working or functioning socially (see Coryell and Winokur 1992 for a review of these studies). It is possible that such a chronic course is less likely since the introduction of lithium and other mood stabilisers, but the risk of chronic illness is unlikely to have been eradicated completely. Other patients may enter a phase of 'rapid cycling' at some point in their illness, where episodes recur four or more times a year for a period of time. In addition, any patient who has spent a substantial time in hospital may find it difficult to adjust to life in the community and may require active rehabilitation. The need for rehabilitation has been increased by the programme of closing large psychiatric hospitals and resettling patients in the community. Much work has been done on reversing the effects of institutionalisation. Institutionalised patients have been used to a rigid hospital routine where most tasks of daily living are carried out by the staff and they are not required to structure their day or plan their life. Cognitive behavioural techniques may be useful in breaking down these complex skills into smaller tasks which can be learned one at a time. It may also be important in helping patients to adjust to living in the community and the new stresses this creates.

PATIENTS WHO ALSO HAVE OTHER CONDITIONS

Some patients with bipolar affective disorder also have other psychiatric conditions. This phenomenon, known as co-morbidity, can make it more difficult to diagnose and treat the bipolar illness. One common co-morbid condition is that of alcohol or drug abuse. This may be an attempt to self-medicate during an episode of illness, or to escape the stress of other life difficulties. Studies have shown that around 35 per cent of patients with bipolar illness abuse alcohol to some extent (see Goodwin and Jamison 1990). Cognitive behavioural techniques could be used to treat the substance abuse, helping the patient to identify triggers to their drinking or drug-taking. Strategies can then be developed so that triggers are avoided or dealt with in a different way. Having any depressive illness appears to increase the likelihood of also suffering from an anxiety disorder about tenfold (Boyd et al. 1984). CBT could be helpful for bipolar patients who have comorbid conditions such as generalised anxiety, phobias or panic disorder. A psychological approach is probably preferable to introducing further drug treatment. A more detailed description of the sort of techniques used in other conditions can be found elsewhere (Stern and Drummond 1991).

Conclusion

CBT has not been explored enough as a treatment for patients with manic depressive illness. We have considered how it might be useful for such patients and reviewed some of the limited evidence that it might be effective. Any good therapy should be flexible enough to adapt to the needs of the individual patient and there is no doubt that, if CBT were applied to those with manic depressive illness, new techniques would have to be developed. New insights might emerge about the complex relationships between mood, thoughts and behaviour, and the therapy might gain as much from the experience as the patients!

References

Abraham, K. (1953) 'Notes on the psychoanalytical investigation and treatment of manic-depressive insanity and allied conditions.' In *Selected Papers of Karl Abraham*. New York: Basic Books.

Barker, P.J. (1992) *Severe Depression, a Practitioner's Guide*. London/Glasgow: Chapman and Hall.

Bech, P., Vendsborg, P. and Rafaelsen, D. (1976) 'Lithium maintenance treatment of manic-melancholic patients: its role in the daily routine.' *Acta Psychiatrica Scandanavica 53*, 70–81.

Beck, A.T. (1976) *Cognitive Therapy and the Emotional Disorders*. New York: International University Press.

Benson, R. (1975) 'The forgotten treatment modality in bipolar illness: psychotherapy.' *Diseases of the Nervous System 36*, 634–638.

Blackburn, I.M. (1987) *Coping with Depression*. Edinburgh: Chambers.

Blackburn, I.M., Eunson, K.M. and Bishop, S. (1986) 'A two-year naturalistic follow-up of depressed patients treated with cognitive therapy, pharmacotherapy and a combination of both.' *Journal of Affective Disorders 10*, 67–75.

Boyd, J. *et al.* (1984) 'Exclusion criteria of DSM III: a study of co-occurrence of hierarchy-free syndromes.' *Archives of General Psychiatry 41*, 983–989.

Cochran, S. (1984) 'Preventing medical noncompliance in the outpatient treatment of bipolar affective disorders.' *Journal of Consulting and Clinical Psychology 52*, 873–878.

Cochran, S. and Gitlin, M. (1988) 'Attitudinal correlates of lithium compliance in bipolar affective disorders.' *The Journal of Nervous and Mental Disease 176*, 457–464.

Coryell, W. and Winokur, G. (1992) 'Course and outcome.' In E. Paykel (ed) *Handbook of Affective Disorders*. Edinburgh/London: Churchill Livingstone.

Dickson, W.E. and Kendell, R.E. (1986) 'Does maintenance lithium therapy prevent recurrences of mania under ordinary clinical conditions?' *Psychological Medicine 16*, 521–530.

Dobson, K.S. (1989) 'A meta-analysis of the efficacy of cognitive therapy for depression.' *Journal of Consulting and Clinical Psychology 57*, 414–419.

Elkin, I. *et al.* (1989) 'National Institute of Mental Health Treatment of Depression Collaborative Research Program. General effectiveness of treatments [see comments].' *Archives of General Psychiatry 46*, 971–82.

Ellicott, A. *et al.* (1990) 'Life events and the course of bipolar disorder.' *American Journal of Psychiatry 147*, 1194–1198.

Evans, M.D. *et al.* (1992) 'Differential relapse following cognitive therapy and pharmacotherapy for depression.' *Archives of General Psychiatry 49*, 802–808.

Fromm-Reichmann, F. (1949) 'Intensive psychotherapy of manic-depressives.' *Confina Neurologica 9*, 158–165.

Gitlin, M.J. *et al.* (1995) 'Relapse and impairment in bipolar disorder.' *American Journal of Psychiatry 152*, 1635–1640.

Goodwin, F. and Jamison, K. (1990) 'Alcohol and drug abuse in manic-depressive illness.' In F. Goodwin and K. Jamison (eds) *Manic-Depressive Illness.* New York/Oxford: Oxford University Press.

Harrow, M. *et al.* (1990) 'Outcome in manic disorders.' *Archives of General Psychiatry 47*, 665–671.

Hunt, N., Bruce-Jones, W. and Silverstone, T. (1992) 'Life events and relapse in bipolar affective disorder.' *Journal of Affective Disorders 25*, 1, 13–20.

Jamison, K., Gerner, R. and Goodwin, F. (1979) 'Patient and physician attitudes toward lithium.' *Archives of General Psychiatry 36*, 866–869.

Janowsky, D., Leff, M. and Epstein, R. (1970) 'Playing the manic game: the interpersonal manoevres of the acutely manic patient.' *Archives of General Psychiatry 22*, 252–261.

Kahn, D. (1990) 'The psychotherapy of mania.' *Psychiatric Clinics of North America 13*, 229–240.

Kingdon, D., Turkington, D. and John, C. (1994) 'Cognitive behaviour therapy of schizophrenia.' *British Journal of Psychiatry 164*, 581–587.

Perris, C. (1992) 'Bipolar-unipolar distinction.' In E. Paykel (ed) *Handbook of Affective Disorders.* Edinburgh/London: Churchill Livingstone.

Prien, R., Caffey, E. and Klett, C. (1973) 'Prophylactic efficacy of lithium in manic-depressive illness.' *Archives of General Psychiatry 28*, 337–341.

Scott, J. (1995) 'Psychotherapy for bipolar disorder.' *British Journal of Psychiatry 167*, 581–588.

Shakir, S., Volkman, F. and Bacon, S. (1979) 'Group psychotherapy as an adjunct to lithium maintenance.' *American Journal of Psychiatry 136*, 455–456.

Simons, A.D. *et al.* (1986) 'Cognitive therapy and pharmacotherapy for depression. Sustained improvement over one year.' *Archives of General Psychiatry 43*, 43–8.

Stallone, F. *et al.* (1973) 'The use of lithium in affective disorders, 3: a double-blind study of prophylaxis in bipolar disorder.' *Archives of General Psychiatry 48*, 1082–1088.

Stern, R. and Drummond, L. (1991) *The Practice of Behavioural and Cognitive Psychotherapy.* Cambridge: Cambridge University Press.

Symonds, R. and Williams, P. (1981) 'Lithium and the changing incidence of mania.' *Psychological Medicine 11*, 193–196.

CHAPTER 4

What Psychologists Can Do To Help

Anne Palmer and Paul Gilbert

The awareness that people can suffer from elevations and depression of mood was noted over two thousand years ago by the Greek physicians (Jackson 1986). In 1854, Falret used the term *'folie circulaire'* to describe bipolar illness (Sedler 1983) and Kraepelin classified manic depression as one of the major forms of serious mental illness (Kraepelin 1921). However, it was the work of Leonhard (1959), Perris (1966) and the advent of lithium which was responsible for the unipolar–bipolar distinction evolving into its current significance. Over the last 20 years, a differentiation of the bipolar disorders has been suggested. These distinguish between Bipolar I, Bipolar II and Bipolar III (Cohen and Dunner 1989; Depue and Monroe 1978). However, the criteria for these distinctions have varied in recent years and remain the subject of research (Goodwin and Jamison 1990).

It is now well recognised that bipolar illness is a serious, long-term, relapsing condition which, if untreated, can have serious social and personal conse-quences. Suicide rates are higher than for other psychiatric risk groups and at least 25–50 per cent of patients make one suicide attempt (Goodwin and Jamison 1990). Even when using mood-stabilising medication, patients can experience serious mood shifts and subclinical symptoms of affective disorder between the episodes of mania and depression which interfere with work and social relationships (Carlson *et al.* 1974; Goodnick *et al.* 1987; Scott 1995). Moreover, mood shifts can be associated with life events (Ambelas 1987). Even when patients recover, they can be faced with shame and guilt for being ill, have fears of relapse, of being a burden to family and of taking risks. They may experience loss of trust in self, changes in long-term aspirations, and may avoid various social and employment opportunities (Coyne and Calarco 1995; Goodwin and Jamison 1990).

Recently, the American Psychiatric Association (1994) provided a major review of the epidemiology, course and treatment recommendations of this disorder. It is increasingly recognised that in treating conditions such as bipolar illness one cannot be a 'one-club golfer'. People suffering this condition require a variety of inputs, both bio-medical and psychosocial, and help and support may be needed even when a patient has recovered (Coyne and Calarco 1995). This chapter explores only the psychological input but it should be emphasised that a psychological approach should be part of a comprehensive approach to care, treatment and management and follow a biopsychosocial approach (Gilbert 1995; Vasile *et al.* 1987).

Theory development

Psychologists have a major role to play in theory development. Theories regarding emotional disorders are important because they can generate new therapies. This is particularly true, for example, in the case of cognitive therapy (Beck *et al.* 1979), behaviour therapy (Rehm 1988; Wolpe 1979), family therapy (Beach, Sandeen, and O'Leary 1990) and interpersonal therapy (Klerman and Weissman 1994). Once the clinical cognitive model illuminated the importance of thinking patterns in the maintenance of emotional disorders it became possible to target cognitions with specific techniques to alter them. More recently, developments within cognitive science and clinical psychology suggest that the focus of therapy should not be on challenging the intellectual interpretation of events by the patient (the propositional meaning), but on adapting and altering the generic model(s) held by the patient which give rise to implicational interpretations of those events (what is 'felt') (Teasdale and Barnard 1993).

Cognitive theory

The cognitive theory of depression suggests that depressed moods are accentuated by patterns of thinking that amplify mood shifts. For example, as people become depressed they become more negative in how they see themselves, their world and future (this is known as the 'negative cognitive triad'). Hence they tend to jump to negative conclusions, over-generalise, see things in all-or-nothing terms, and personalise and self-blame to an excessive degree (known as 'cognitive distortions'). By teaching patients how to challenge and dispute these thinking styles, the patient is helped to gain a better perspective on their problems, learn how to generate alternatives to negative ideas and be more sensitive to the evidence for and against their negative ideas (Beck *et al.* 1979; Gilbert 1992; Greenberg and Padesky 1995; Williams 1992).

The cognitive model of hypomania suggests that hypomania is a mirror image of depression and is characterised by a positive cognitive triad of self, world and future, and positive cognitive distortions (Newman and Beck 1993). The self is seen as extremely loveable and powerful with unlimited potential and attractiveness. The world is filled with wonderful possibilities and experiences are viewed as overly positive. The future is seen as one of unlimited opportunity and promise. Hyper-positive thinking (stream of consciousness) is typified by cognitive distortions, as it is in depression, but in the opposite direction. For example: jumping to positive conclusions (I'm a winner; I can do anything); an underestimation of risk (there's no danger here, I can surmount all obstacles); minimisation of problems (nothing can go wrong) and overvaluing of immediate gratification (they should do what I want now). Thus cognitive distortions reflected in thoughts provide biased confirmation of the positive cognitive triad of self, world and future. Positive experiences are selectively attended to, and in this way underlying beliefs that guide behaviour, thinking and feeling are maintained and strengthened. Examples of such underlying beliefs include: 'Being manic helps me to overcome my shyness'; 'I'm not accountable to others'; 'I can change the world and make it a better place'; 'I'm chosen', and so on. Cognitive therapy offers a point of entry into the process of the illness and may offer many benefits in teaching self-management strategies. We will explore a cognitive group therapy approach in more detail shortly.

Evolution theory

An evolutionary approach to mental illness begins by suggesting that humans have evolved special processing systems to deal with social challenges (for example, care of offspring, mating, acquiring status and building alliances) (Cosmides and Tooby 1992; Gilbert 1989; Gilbert 1995). Hence an evolutionary theory of bipolar illness suggests that its root lies in the malfunctioning of normal systems of mood control and social behaviour. Gardner (1982, 1988) suggested that bipolar illness represents a disorder of the normal mechanisms that control social rank (winning and losing status). If this is the case, the special processing systems that may be involved in bipolar illness are related to those for rank acquisitions and decline. The manic patient experiences hyper-levels of energy (as if he or she has just won a major contest) and appears to behave as if he/she is a leader of extremely high status. When the person swings into depression the defeated, subordinate profile of behaviour is expressed, noted by extreme ideas of inferiority, failure and withdrawn subordinate behaviour (see also Gilbert 1992; 1993; Price 1972). In bipolar illness, these innate mechanisms for winning and losing are grossly amplified and distorted.

In this approach cognitions offer windows on underlying brain systems that have become activated. Illuminating what these underlying systems may be is the task of future work. However, there is now evidence of major biological and behavioural differences between dominant and subordinate animals (see for example, Ray and Sapolsky 1992; Sapolsky 1990a, b, 1994) and that rank interacts with personality. While some dominant primates are relaxed, affiliative and confident others are tense and aggressive. Sapolsky (1990a, b) notes that there are differences between secure and insecure dominance and thus the 'state of dominance' is not uniform.

A caution

A problem with some approaches is the tendency to see mania and depression as bipolar opposites (as the name implies), although in fact it is recognised that patients can be both depressed and hypomanic at the same time – this is known as dysphoric mania (Post *et al.* 1989). In cognitive therapy this implies that positive and negative schema are not mutually exclusive. From the evolutionary view the low rank, defeat state and the high rank winning state are seen to be controlled via separate modular processing systems (Gilbert 1989; Gilbert 1992), thus allowing for their co-existent activation in certain states of mind.

Psychological therapy

Partly because of the power issues and dominance issues, hypomanic patients have often been regarded as poor candidates for psychotherapy. In other words it is not the thoughts *per se* that are the therapeutic challenge, but the fact that in the hypomanic state patients are so sure they are right and are resistant to taking advice from others, especially if this is seen to dampen their chances of reaching overvalued goals. They become, as it were, their own authority and not motivated to seek or use help from others. Nonetheless, as Goodwin and Jamison (1990) note, although when hypomanic, patients see themselves far more positively than others see them, as they recover they are able to recognise that their behaviours were dysfunctional and ideas distorted.

The therapist treating bipolar people in a hypomanic state can expect to engage in power plays and must try to avoid getting into unprofitable conflicts while at the same time helping to set boundaries. Recognising the typical social behaviour of the hypomanic patient is especially important when patients are hospitalised. Generally, however, it is our experience that nurses and other professionals are more positively disposed to mania because it is seen as 'genuine illness', in contrast to personality disorders which can activate problematic counter-transferences.

Individual therapy

There has been much written on individual therapy from different perspectives (American Psychiatric Association 1994; Goodwin and Jamison 1990). Elsewhere Gilbert (1996) has outlined developments in the interpersonal cognitive approach to the treatment of depression and has discussed therapy with a man suffering a bipolar disorder. As with most individual therapies it is important to obtain a good history, articulate core self–other schema and basic attitudes, and recognise typical social behaviours (especially ways of perceiving and dealing with interpersonal conflicts) and triggering events. Individual therapies involve providing support and education on the nature of the disorder (including other family members); insight into vulnerable self–other perceptions (schema); strategies for challenging distortions in thinking; strategies for coping with interpersonal conflicts; early recognition of mood shifts requiring preventive actions; and the need to take a biopsychosocial view of the illness, including use of medication.

The therapeutic relationship is a key component of this work because the bond between patient and therapist is often crucial to the ability of the patient to work collaboratively. Sensitivity to the ambivalence that some patients have about medication is important and the therapist may need to explore gently the advantages and disadvantages of medications to help compliance and coping with side effects of medication. This does require sensitivity and at times discussion with psychiatrists if there are fears of under- or over-medication. The psychologist may have difficulties working on this issue if they themselves have worries about medication.

Because the onset of the disorder can be associated with a collapse of ideals and hopes for the future, especially during the recovery phases, therapists should be sensitive to the issues of grief (over losses) in the disorder (Gilbert 1995; Graves 1993). A similar concern has been noted for schizophrenia (Appelo *et al.* 1994; Atkinson 1994). It is possible that a lack of attention to the grief aspects increases risk of subsequent depression and/or denial of problems.

At the present time there are few adequate treatment trials that attest to the success or otherwise of individual therapies for bipolar depression. However, this does not mean that it is not susceptible to psychological treatment, rather that treatments may have to be specifically tailored for this condition. One area where this is being developed is in group approaches.

Group therapies

There is now increasing interest in the role of group therapy approaches for this condition (Goodwin and Jamison 1990; Graves 1993). The American Psychiatric Association (1994) suggests the development of:

1. Specific psychosocial interventions, including family work.

2. The use of specific therapies for depressive episodes such as cognitive therapy or interpersonal therapy.

3. Specific therapies for manic episodes which usually involve preparing action plans for patients before they become hypomanic.

4. Specific therapies for complications and co-morbid difficulties.

5. Support groups, especially to help patients set boundaries for each other, to gain more information on the nature of the disorder, and to offer support when a member becomes unwell.

Within groups cognitive techniques for hypomania follow the basic format of cognitive therapy but with some changes. In setting up such a group patients can be invited to attend structured group work for a set period. Below we outline such a group, how it operates and the result of outcome research. This approach has been utilised by Palmer, Williams and Adams (1995).

GENERAL

In conducting any group therapy therapists should be familiar with basic group processes and the typical stages through which a group will pass (Yalom 1986). These will include early forms of bonding, and issues around leadership, trust, mutuality, altruism, formation of small alliances, dependency, hope and endings. In regard to bipolar depression these phases are often marked, as patients may move between confronting authority, trying to take leadership roles and dominating others, to being depressed and withdrawn. Other issues surround feelings arising when fellow patients experience a relapse (Graves 1993).

As for other forms of cognitive therapy, patients are educated into the form therapy will take and the therapeutic rationale. Of special importance are the skills of mood and thought monitoring and insight into how thoughts are related to moods. Patients are encouraged to use 'homeworks' to practise thought monitoring and challenging dysfunctional beliefs. In addition, information is given on the nature of bipolar disorder.

The full outline of the programme used by Palmer, Williams and Adams (1995) is given in Appendix 1 to this chapter.

STRUCTURE AND CONTENT OF SESSIONS

Each session has the same overall structure. Once the group is formed, the first item on the agenda is the completion of measures used to check the integrity of the treatment programme, then homework is reviewed. The therapist uses illustrative and current examples from the patients to reinforce learning. Homework is set and time allocated to the discussion of any predicted problems in completion. Homework always includes self-monitoring of mood states and completing and updating action plans. A table of the main techniques used is given in Appendix 2. Since these are less well known, some of the specific methods for cognitive therapy of hypomania will now be discussed in more detail.

The detection of early warning signs of hypomanic episodes allows the patient to take preventive action to interrupt escalation and so reduce the impact of the relapse. In a recent study, Smith and Tarrier (1992) found that patients could recall the early warning stages of an episode and described what they termed as their own 'relapse signature'. Palmer, Williams and Adams (1995) found that, besides being able to identify retrospectively their own first signs of troubles, patients can also detect them during their occurrence.

A list of common warning signs, taken from the literature and/or a card sort (Table 4.1) helps patients to discover their own early warning signs. For a card sort, symptoms are written on cards, and the patient sees which ones they recognise, identifies those which have occurred earlier in an episode, and finally adds any which are not included but are unique to themselves. Examples of idiosyncratic early warning signs include the inability to inhibit use of expletives, and feelings of unworldliness – which for the patient may presage delusions. Some patients describe changes in their dreams which for them mark a switch in mood state. This is consistent with Beauchemin and Hays' finding that hypomanic episodes are often preceded by dreams of death and injury. Once mood was elevated, dreams were bizarre (Beauchemin and Hays 1995).

Table 4.1 Card sort of specific early warning signs

Feelings	*Behaviour*	*Thoughts*
Example 1		
Tense, on edge	Beginning conversations with strangers	I'm a chosen person
Alienated		On top of things
Purposeful	Reorganising things in the home	Can do everything
Irritable		Must do a lot
	Walking at night	
Example 2		
Energised	Staying up all night	I love life
Loving	Racing other cars	Everyone wants to be near me
Light-headed	Spending money	Why is she frightened? I'm driving perfectly
Happy	Argumentative	
Fearless		Why are they miserable when I'm so happy?
		The world is wonderful

To help patients learn to anticipate difficulties before activity and mood escalate out of control, feelings, behavioural symptoms and thoughts associated with their hypomanic episodes are recalled.

Patients describe the early stages of hypomania as 'feeling great', as being 'a time when they get things done' and often 'feel powerful and superior to everyone else'. Indeed, changes in social comparison (feeling superior to others) may also be an early warning sign as predicted by evolution theory.

Using a visual analogue scale to chart changes in mood state provides a constant overt reminder to be alert to variations in mood state, which in turn is a reminder to look at Action Plans to check for any first signs of difficulties. Some patients find it helpful if they keep a Daily Warning Signs Chart which includes warning signs and 'what to do' tick-lists. If appropriate, patients agree ahead of time with significant others to accept their help to spot changes.

LIFE EVENTS AND STRESSFUL SITUATIONS

Healey and Williams (1989) propose a model of mood change which postulates a relationship between life events which cause breaks in daily routine and hypomania. They suggest that disruptions in circadian rhythms cause elevation in psychomotor activity which is misattributed in a self-enhancing manner and so intensifies and maintains hypomania: 'I'm so active because I'm so powerful'. Given the probable role external events play in manic episodes (Ambelas 1987), it is important for patients to learn to recognise those life events and situations which, for them, 'ring alarm bells'. These include both general situations where life events cause breaks in daily routine, to which most bipolar patients are probably vulnerable, plus those which are specific to the individual.

Patients can work together to identify 'break in routine' (danger) situations which represent an increased risk of re-occurrence; for example taking a job which involves shift work, or late night parties. Other personal risk situations may involve having too much to do and excessive stimulation, and these need to be identified. For one patient these included joining extreme and active political campaigns, and entering risky situations when travelling alone. For another, it involved attending meetings where she agreed to work on too many jobs. While some patients are well aware of what situations must be treated with caution or avoided, the awareness of others may need to be prompted with checklists or through discussion with fellow sufferers.

It is important to caution patients to avoid such events whenever possible, but where unavoidable, such as beginning a university course, to be vigilant for early warning signs, particularly states of sleeplessness and hyperactivity. If such signs are noticed, they must seek help immediately (Bauer *et al.* 1991).

TAKING EARLY ACTION

If an episode does occur, and once it has been recognised, patients need to take action to protect themselves. Again ahead of time, the therapist and group helps the patient to arrive at their own decisions about what they are willing to try to do to stop things escalating out of control. Cory Newman's techniques (Newman and Beck 1993), adapted by Palmer, Williams and Adams (1995), give some indication of strategies patients have been prepared to consider.

Bauer *et al.* (1991) propose activation level as the core characteristic of the manic syndrome. Emphasis is therefore placed on agreeing to pace activities when behavioural activation is excessive. One very important way of preventing the patient from driving him or herself into a manic phase through over-activity and sleep deprivation is activity scheduling, where emphasis is placed on decreasing activities. Patients are encouraged to ask a trusted friend or relative to look over their plans for each day and help them to eliminate one or more activities; especially over-stimulating and exciting ones.

Rules patients might make *for themselves* are ones such as 'take 48 hours before acting or taking irreversible decisions' and the 'two-person feedback rule' (Newman and Beck 1993). Good ideas, which are bold and fun but risky, are noted down and the patient either waits two days before taking action, reminds him/herself to keep big decisions for a neutral mood state, or discusses it with at least two close friends, relatives or the therapist. Reminders, such as, 'the two day wait is an insurance policy, a protection, and if it is a good idea now it will still be in two days' time', and, 'never act on a great idea without first discussing it with at least two people', written to themselves before an episode occurs, are more likely to be followed than any suggestion from others at the time. Use of their own reminders also means that they still have control.

OTHER TECHNIQUES

When hypomanic, patients tend to underestimate the impact of their disorder and its associated behaviours on their relationships. It often does little good for the family or the therapist to point out the dangers. These efforts can be seen as holding back the patient and may be turned into sources of conflict that increase arousal, determination to resist others and might drive the person further into their mood shift. Instead, fellow sufferers are more able to challenge the value attached to hypomanic episodes and may be more able to challenge superiority thinking. Bipolar patients help one another, with prompts from the therapist, to generate examples of the effects of their hypomanic behaviours in the following areas of social adjustment: family, work, leisure and interpersonal. It helps patients to decide on what they want to avoid happening again. Some decide to write down the disadvantages of high moods or give themselves reminders. This is one reason why a homogeneous group for this disorder can be beneficial.

Learning to consider the costs and benefits of hypomanic behaviours is further aided by using the two-column technique. This can be used to analyse acts of maladaptive generosity under the headings of 'benefits to self' versus 'benefits to others', and risky behaviours can be analysed for 'productive potential' versus 'destructive risks' (Newman and Beck 1993). One of the patients used the technique very effectively to look at the positive and negative effects of increased activity. This allowed him to arrive at his own conclusions about the effects of his behaviour on his child. Previously he had seen the hyperactivity as purely a positive feature of his life.

Finally, to help with refusal to take directions from others, self statements are written out on flash cards. The purpose of this is to interrupt accelerations in thinking and behaviours, and to hold back over-spontaneous behaviours: 'take it one step at a time', 'easy does it'. 'I can be in more control of the situation if I think things through slowly and carefully'. In addition, some patients make tape recordings of their own values and things they promised themselves that they would try to avoid happening again (Newman, personal communication).

ACTION PLANS

The early warning signs identified and the strategies chosen by the patient feed into an Action Plan, which is their personal record of plans for managing their illness. This includes behavioural plans, ideas for cognitive techniques and reminders of beliefs which may have been activated, and ends with details of help-seeking behaviours if the patient's own efforts do not enable them to get the situation under control.

DOES THE THERAPY WORK?

There are few well-controlled outcome studies of the efficacy of psychological interventions, and those which do exist suffer from methodological difficulties (Goodwin and Jamison 1990; Scott 1995). Thus a key component of responsible, accountable practice is the monitoring of therapeutic progress and evaluating the effectiveness of what is being attempted. Some appropriate standardised self-report measurement scales and other methods for this group of patients follow.

THE EXTENT TO WHICH USE IS MADE OF A TREATMENT PACKAGE

In order to assess the extent to which bipolar patients have awareness of symptoms and make use of skills and strategies for manic and depressed states, a version of the Personal Questionnaire Rapid Scaling Technique, developed by Mulhall can be used (Mulhall 1976; Shapiro 1961). The method enables the internal consistency of answers to be assessed and can be completed once the various skills and strategies have been introduced.

MONITORING CHANGES REGULARLY AND SYSTEMATICALLY

To assess the severity of manic and depressive symptoms simultaneously, the Internal State Scale II developed by Bauer *et al.* (1991) can be used. Because it gives scores which indicate depression, mania/hypomania or remission, it can be used to assess the integrity of the treatment package. Bauer *et al.* state that construct validity is supported by significant relationships between Activation scores and clinicians' ratings of mania; and between Depression Index scores and clinicians' ratings of depression.

MEASURING PRE-, POST- AND FOLLOW-UP CHANGES IN SYMPTOMATOLOGY

To assess symptomatology, the Symptom Checklist-90 Revised can be used (Derogatis and Cleary 1977). This is a 90-item scale designed to measure levels of distress. It has nine sub-scales which assess different psychiatric symptom constructs and estimate overall symptomatology. Evidence for internal consistency is given by ranges of alpha coefficients (0.80–0.90) and test/re-test coefficients (0.78–0.90).

MEASURING PRE-, POST- AND FOLLOW-UP CHANGES IN SOCIAL ADJUSTMENT

To assess social adjustment, the Social Adjustment Scale which has been re-worded for a British population can be used (Cooper *et al.* 1982; Weissman and Bothwell 1976). This assesses social functioning in six role areas: work as worker, housewife or student; social and leisure activities; relationships with extended family; relationship with spouse, functioning as a parent; and functioning in the family unit. Reliability is established by the alpha internal consistency ($r = 0.74$) and test/re-test stability ($r = 0.80$). Weissman *et al.* (1978) also state that raters' agreement across all items averaged 83 per cent. Concurrent validity is supported by significant differences in the impaired and non-impaired groups and the scale's sensitivity to change.

MONITORING THEIR OWN MOOD STATE ON A REGULAR BASIS

To alert bipolar patients to changing patterns in their mood states, a visual analogue scale anchored between -10 (most depressed state) and +10 (most manic state), with 0 as a neutral state, can be used (Mood Charts). The patient marks the point which represents overall mood for the day. To control for diurnal variations, ratings are recorded twice a day at the same times throughout the treatment programme.

Bipolar patients in the study of Palmer, Williams and Adams (1995) reported that they felt that they had acquired, and were using, a new repertoire of skills for dealing with their changing mood states. This is consistent with Teasdale and Barnard's Implicational Cognitive Subsystems Model (Teasdale and Barnard 1993). Effective therapies are those which help patients repeatedly to use active problem-solving techniques and coping strategies which become encoded within, and help the patient to build up, adaptive self-schematic models.

ADVANTAGES OF GROUPS

As the above indicates, it appears that patients who are homogeneous with respect to bipolar diagnosis, but not particularly so in other ways (such as age, gender, socioeconomic, marital or parental status) can benefit from structured group work. Therapists can tailor their skills and theoretical concepts specifically to problems of bipolar disorder. A second advantage of groups is that they enable patients to discover that some of their behaviours and experiences are not unique to themselves and to be with others who share the same problems and concerns. For many it may represent their first experience of being with similar others. They all have in common the experience of being (at times) unable to control emotions and behaviour, and all know the difficulty of confronting the emotional pain associated with the consequences of their manic behaviours. Feedback from patients reveals that they often feel able to talk about their experiences, particularly hallucinations and delusions, with fellow sufferers because they see themselves as less likely to be rejected or shamed. Mutual support and encouragement is important and this often continues outside the therapy. Graves (1993) writes that the group may need to set boundaries to protect against excessive phone calls or visits if a person becomes hypomanic. However, Palmer, Williams and Adams (1995) did not find this a problem in their work.

Sharing knowledge about the disorder helps those who deny or underestimate the problem to gain insight. As noted above, there is a strong tendency for patients to value their hypomanic phases. They report a sense of power, elevated levels of energy and optimism, which cause them to minimise the danger of progression to a manic state. Attempts by carers to help are seen as threats to autonomy and are resisted. When a group member points out the negative consequences of hypomanic behaviour, however, it is more likely to be accepted.

Issues to be sensitive to include mixtures of hopelessness in being unable to manage their illness, the reluctance to give up hypomanic episodes and unrealistic expectations of the treatment package. All these can pervade the group in the early weeks. If a patient comes to a group feeling discouraged or unrealistically optimistic, contagion can be a problem and result in other patients feeling the same way. In the group run by Palmer and Williams it was found that having two therapists was a distinct advantage. One of the reasons for this is that each therapist will have someone to keep him/her functioning at an energetic or calming level as appropriate. Working with bipolar patients can be difficult and emotionally taxing, and therapists need to be sensitive to their own limitations and needs when working in this area.

Another major issue is to try to ensure good working relationships with psychiatrists who may be called upon urgently to provide admission or change medication. Serious problems can occur if psychiatrists devalue psychological inputs, have problems in collaborative working or undermine therapeutic efforts with statements such as 'your illness is purely biological'. It is of the utmost importance, therefore, that all those involved in the care of the bipolar patient should understand the role of each carer involved, the nature and aims of the treatment given, and the importance of a biopsychosocial approach to care delivery. Nothing is more undermining of patient confidence than to receive contradictory messages from care professionals.

Conclusion

We began this chapter by noting that bipolar illness is a serious, relapsing condition, carrying a high risk of suicide and family disturbance. Within the context of a biopsychosocial approach to theory and care delivery, psychologists have a major role to play. There is increasing evidence for genetic vulnerability to this disorder. However, enabling patients to gain more insight into the nature of the disorder, develop self-control processes, learn to deal with interpersonal conflicts in new ways, and derive benefits from the support of fellow sufferers can all help to instill hope and control over the illness. Psychological treatments are still in their infancy but sufficient information is now available to begin to offer comprehensive services for this patient group.

As for all such developments more research is needed, both on the internal psychology which contributes to mood swings and the interventions that are most likely to be effective.

References

Ambelas, A. (1987) 'Life events and mania: a special relationship?' *British Journal of Psychiatry 150*, 235–240.

American Psychiatric Association (1994) 'Practice guidelines for the treatment of patients with bipolar disorder.' *Archives of General Psychiatry (Supplement) 151*, 1–36.

Appelo, M.T. *et al.* (1994) 'Grief: its significance for rehabilitation in schizophrenia.' *Clinical Psychology and Psychotherapy 1*, 53–59.

Atkinson, S.D. (1994) 'Grieving and loss in parents with a schizophrenic child.' *American Journal of Psychiatry 151*, 1137–1139.

Bauer, M.S. *et al.* (1991) 'Independent assessment of manic and depressive symptoms by self rating.' *Archives of General Psychiatry 48*, 807–812.

Beach, S.R.H., Sandeen, E.E. and O'Leary, K.D. (1990) *Depression in Marriage.* New York: Guilford Press.

Beauchemin, J.M. and Hays, P. (1995) 'Prevailing mood, mood changes, and dreams in bipolar disorder.' *Journal of Affective Disorders 35*, 41–49.

Beck, A.T. and Greenberg, A.L. (1974) *Coping with Depression.* Available from The Centre for Cognitive Therapy, Room 602, 133 Smith 36th St, Philadelphia, PA 19104, USA.

Beck, A.T. *et al.* (1979) *Cognitive Therapy and Depression.* New York: Guilford Press.

Blackburn, I.M. (1987) *Coping With Depression.* Edinburgh: Chambers Press.

Carlson, G.A. *et al.* (1974) 'Follow up of 53 bipolar manic-depressive patients.' *British Journal of Psychiatry 124*, 134–139.

Cohen, S. and Dunner, D. (1989) 'Bipolar affective disorder: review and update.' In J.G. Howells (ed) *Modern Perspectives in the Psychiatry of the Affective Disorders: Modern Perspectives in Psychiatry, Vol. 13.* New York: Brunner/Mazel Inc.

Cooper, P. *et al.* (1982) 'Evaluation of a modified self report measure of social adjustment.' *British Journal of Psychiatry 141*, 68–75.

Cosmides, L. and Tooby, J. (1992) 'Cognitive adaptions for social exchange.' In J.H. Barkow, L. Cosmides, and J. Tooby (eds) *The Adapted Mind: Evolutionary Psychology and the Generation of Culture.* New York: Oxford University Press.

Coyne, J.C. and Calarco, M.M. (1995) 'Effects of the experience of depression: application of focus group and survey methodologies.' *Psychiatry 58*, 149–163.

Depue, R.A. and Monroe, S.M. (1978) 'The unipolar-bipolar distinction in the depressive disorders.' *Psychological Bulletin 85*, 1001–1029.

Derogatis, L.R. and Cleary, P.A. (1977) *SCL-90, Administration, Scoring and Procedure, Manual 1 for the R (Revised) Version.* Baltimore: Johns Hopkins University School of Medicine.

Gardner, R. (1982) 'Mechanisms of manic-depressive disorder: an evolutionary model.' *Archives of General Psychiatry 39*, 1436–1441.

Gardner, R. (1988) 'Psychiatric infrastructures for intraspecific communication.' In M.R.A. Chance (ed) *Social Fabrics of the Mind.* Hove: Lawrence Erlbaum Associates Ltd.

Gilbert, P. (1989) *Human Nature and Suffering.* Hove: Lawrence Erlbaum Associates.

Gilbert, P. (1992) *Depression: The Evolution of Powerlessness.* Hove: Lawrence Erlbaum Associates Ltd and New York: Guilford Press.

Gilbert, P. (1993) 'Defense and safety: their function in social behaviour and psychopathology.' *British Journal of Clinical Psychology 32*, 131–154.

Gilbert, P. (1995) 'Biopsychosocial approaches and evolutionary theory as aids to integration in clinical psychology and psychotherapy.' *Clinical Psychology and Psychotherapy 2*, 135–156.

Gilbert, P. (1996) 'Working with the depressed person.' In R. Bayne, I. Horton and J. Bimrose (eds) *New Directions in Counselling.* London: Routledge.

Goodnick, P.J. *et al.* (1987) 'Inter-episode major and subclinical symptoms in affective disorder.' *Acta Psychiatrica Scandinavia 75*, 597–600.

Goodwin, F.K. and Jamison, K.R. (eds) (1990) *Manic Depressive Illness.* New York: Oxford University Press.

Graves, J.S. (1993) 'Living with mania: a study of outpatient group psychotherapy for bipolar patients.' *American Journal of Psychotherapy 47*, 113–126.

Greenberg, D. and Padesky, C.A. (1995) *Mind Over Mood: A Cognitive Therapy Treatment Manual for Clients.* New York: Guilford Press.

Hawton, K. *et al.* (1990) *Cognitive Behaviour Therapy for Psychiatric Problems.* Oxford: Oxford University Press.

Healey, D. and Williams, J.M.G. (1989) 'Moods, misattributions and mania: an interaction of biological and psychological factors in pathogenesis of mania.' *Psychiatric Developments 1*, 49–70.

Jackson, S.W. (1986) *Melancholia and Depression: From Hippocratic Times to Modern Times.* New Haven: Yale University Press.

Klerman, G.L. and Weissman, M.M. (eds) (1994) *New Applications of Interpersonal Psychotherapy.* Washington, DC: American Psychiatric Press Inc.

Kraepelin, E. (1921) *Manic Depressive Insanity and Paranoia.* (trans. R.M. Barclay; ed. G.M. Robertson) Edinburgh: E & S Livingstone (Reprinted New York: Arno Press 1976).

Leonhard, K. (1959) 'Aufteilung der endogenen Psychosen.' As quoted in J. Becker (1974) *Depression: Theory and Research.* New York: Winston Wiley.

Mulhall, D.J. (1976) 'Systematic self-assessment by PQRST.' *Psychological Medicine 6*, 591–597.

Newman, C. and Beck, A.T. (1993) *Cognitive Therapy of Rapid Cycling Bipolar Affective Disorder – Treatment Manual.* Centre for Cognitive Therapy, University of Pennsylvania, Philadelphia.

Palmer, A.G., and Williams, H. and Adams, M. (1995) 'CBT in a group format for bipolar patients.' *Behavioural and Cognitive Psychotherapy 23*, 153–168.

Perris, C. (1966) 'A study of bipolar (manic depressive) and unipolar (recurrent depressive) psychoses.' *Acta Psychiatrica Scandinavia 42*, (Suppl. 194), 1–189.

Post, R.M. *et al.* (1989) 'Dysphoric mania: clinical and biological correlates.' *Archives of General Psychiatry 46*, 353–358.

Price, J.S. (1972) 'Genetic and phylogenetic aspects of mood variations.' *International Journal of Mental Health 1*, 124–144.

Ray, J.C. and Sapolsky, R.M. (1992) 'Styles of social behavior and their endocrine correlates among high-ranking wild baboons.' *American Journal of Primatology 28*, 231–250.

Rehm, L.P. (1988) 'Self-management and cognitive processes in depression.' In L.B. Alloy (ed) *Cognitive Processes in Depression.* New York: Guilford Press.

Sapolsky, R.M. (1990a) 'Adrenocortical function, social rank and personality among wild baboons.' *Biological Psychiatry 28*, 862–878.

Sapolsky, R.M. (1990b) 'Stress in the wild.' *Scientific American* January, 106–113.

Sapolsky, R.M. (1994) 'Individual differences and the stress response.' *Seminars in the Neurosciences 6*, 261–269.

Scott, J. (1995) 'Psychotherapy for bipolar disorder.' *British Journal of Psychiatry 167*, 581–588.

Sedler, M.J. (1983) 'Falret's discovery: the origin of the concept of bipolar affective illness.' *American Journal of Psychiatry 140*, 1127–1133.

Shapiro, M.B. (1961) 'A method of measuring psychological changes specific to the individual psychiatric patient.' *British Journal of Medical Psychology 34*, 151–155.

Smith, J.A. and Tarrier, N. (1992) 'Prodromal symptoms in manic depressive psychosis.' *Social Psychiatry and Psychiatric Epidemiology 27*, 5, 245–248.

Teasdale, J.D. and Barnard, P.J. (1993) *Affect, Cognition and Change.* Hove: Lawrence Erlbaum Associates.

Vasile, R.G. *et al.* (1987) 'A biopsychosocial approach to treating patients with affective disorders.' *American Journal of Psychiatry 144*, 341–344.

Weissman, M.M. and Bothwell, S. (1976) 'Assessment of social adjustment by patient self report.' *Archives of General Psychiatry 33*, 1111–1115.

Weissman, M.M. *et al.* (1978) 'Social adjustment by self report in a community sample and in psychiatric out patients.' *Journal of Nervous and Mental Disease 166*, 317–326.

Williams, J.M.G. (1992) *The Psychological Treatment of Depression (2nd Edition).* London/New York: Routledge.

Wolpe, J. (1979) 'The experimental model and treatment of neurotic depression.' *Behaviour Research and Therapy 17*, 555–565.

Yalom, I.D. (1986) *The Theory and Practice of Group Psychotherapy. Third edition.* New York: Basic Books.

Further reading

Padesky, C.A. and Greenberg, D. (1995) *A Clinician's Guide to Mind Over Mood.* New York: Guilford Press.

Appendix 1

Outline of the structure of sessions

Session 1: Introduction

- Aims, objectives and description of the structure of the sessions.
- Confidentiality and commitment.
- The nature of bipolar affective disorder.
- Brief overview of cognitive behavioural therapy.
- Exercise to link thoughts, feelings and behaviour.
- How to monitor mood state changes.
- Introduce Action Plan.
- Homework: read handouts about bipolar disorder and Manic Depression Fellowship literature; Action Plan; Mood Charts.

Session 2: Overview of the cognitive model of depression

- Review of homework.
- Participants' experiences of depression.
- Cognitive model of depression – flow chart.
- Cognitive triad of depression.
- Thoughts, feelings and behaviour as early warning signs of depression.
- Homework: read Beck and Greenberg (1974); Action Plan; Mood Charts.

Session 3: Medication

- Review of homework.
- Talk from chief hospital pharmacist.
- Homework: read pharmacy handout; Action Plan; Mood Charts.

Session 4: Life events and stressful situations

- Review of homework.
- Stressful situations.
- Effects of disruptions in routine.
- Misattributions.

- ○ Positive activities – mastery and pleasure.
- ○ Homework: flow chart showing circadian rhythm disorganisation, adapted from Healey and Williams (1989). Read example of completed activity chart from Hawton *et al.* (1990). Activity Charts; Action Plan; Mood Charts.

Session 5: Awareness of negative automatic thoughts (NATS)

- ○ Review of homework.
- ○ Characteristics of NATs and illustrative examples.
- ○ Card sort of examples of NATs.
- ○ Three-column thought record.
- ○ Homework: read handout on NATs; thought recording; Action Plan; Mood Charts.

Session 6: Challenging NATS

- ○ Review of homework.
- ○ Cognitive distortions.
- ○ Challenges.
- ○ Homework: read handout and example sheet on challenging NATs; work on challenging NATS; Action Plan; Mood Charts.

Session 7: Vulnerability factors and identification of beliefs

- ○ Review of homework.
- ○ Review of cognitive model of depression flow chart.
- ○ Describe and illustrate the importance of sensitising events in childhood and temperament.
- ○ Give definition, description and themes of beliefs with examples.
- ○ Homework: read 'Factors in Childhood History Leading to Depression' handout taken from Williams (1992). Checklist of examples of beliefs, taken from Blackburn (1987); Action Plan; Mood Charts.

Session 8: Identification and modification of beliefs

- ○ Downward chaining to identify beliefs.
- ○ Pros versus cons for holding beliefs.
- ○ Methods of modifying beliefs.
- ○ Homework: identify and list pros versus cons for holding a belief; Action Plan; Mood Charts.

Session 9: Relationship of behaviour to beliefs, and review

- ○ Review of homework.
- ○ Old belief and new belief plans of behaviour.
- ○ Review of strategies and skills for depressed mood state.
- ○ Review of Action Plan for depression.
- ○ Homework: try out a new behaviour which cannot be accommodated into existing beliefs; Action Plan; Mood Charts.

Session 10: Overview of cognitive model of hypomania

- ○ Review of homework.
- ○ Participants' experiences of hypomania/mania.
- ○ Cognitive model of hypomania.
- ○ Cognitive triad of hypomania.
- ○ Early warning signs of hypomania including hyper-positive thinking.
- ○ Homework: Action Plan; Mood Charts.

Session 11: Life events and stressful situations

- ○ Review of homework.
- ○ Stressful situations.
- ○ Effects of 'breaks in routine'.
- ○ Disturbances in sleep and increases in activity.
- ○ Importance of pacing.
- ○ Homework: read handout about central clock disorganisation (adapted from Healey and Williams (1989)); Action Plan; Mood Charts.

Session 12: Consequences of hypomanic behaviours

- ○ Review of homework.
- ○ Family, friends, work and intrapersonal effects.
- ○ Homework: Action Plan; potential gain versus destructive risk of one aspect of manic behaviour (Newman, personal communication); record reminder of the things 'you promised yourself you never want to happen again'; Action Plan; Mood Charts.

Session 13: Strategies for hypomania

- ○ Review of homework.
- ○ Review cognitive method flow chart.
- ○ Describe strategies.
- ○ Activity reduction.

- Homework: read handout about strategies; choose personally acceptable strategies; Action Plan; Mood Charts.

Session 14: Overall review

- Review of homework.
- Feedback from participants.
- How to deal with setbacks in both mood states.
- Help-seeking behaviour for both mood states.
- Check Action Plans are complete.
- Plan follow-up sessions.
- Homework: read relapse handout; keep a record of any problems for follow-up session; Mood Charts.

Appendix 2: Summary of Main Techniques Used

Type	Purpose
Symptom checklist	Breakdown mood state into thoughts, feelings and behaviour
	Link thoughts, feelings and behaviour
	Use of thoughts, feelings and behaviour as early warning signs
Dysfunctional thought records	Recognising NATs and hyper-positive thoughts
	Noting cognitive distortions
	Challenging NATs and hyper-positive thoughts
Automatic thoughts card sort	Recognising NATs from examples
Activity schedules	Re-planning activities – increase or decrease
	Achievement of balance between mastery and pleasure in depressive phase
Charts to monitor mood state	Becoming alert to variations in current mood state
	Prime use of skills and strategies
	Visible reminder
Belief cards sort/downward chaining, analysis of advantages and disadvantages of beliefs	Aid awareness of beliefs
	Modification of beliefs
Cognitive model flow charts	Understanding cognitive model
	Apply model to self
New belief plans	Modification of existing dysfunctional beliefs by acting against
Self-instruction	Production of self-generated reminders
Behavioural techniques for hypomanic phase (Newman and Beck 1993)	To make own choice of coping techniques ahead of time

CHAPTER 5

What Social Work Can Do To Help

Jean Nursten

Part I: The background

It has long been held that people need many kinds of provision, ranging from food to shelter, education, friendship, employment and recreation. But as attitudes – that is, thoughts and feelings – have a part to play in getting these basic needs, there can be no such thing as social work that does not take them into account. As Reynolds (1934) wrote: 'I am... sure that no (social) work can succeed in isolating a person's attitudes and treating them apart from the conditions of life in which they find expression'.

Such a psychosocial approach holds within it a methodology and an application that addresses the needs of people who have practical problems, difficulties in their personal relationships, and within themselves. It can be a way of helping people with mood disorders and the situation within which they live.

It is part of human experience to feel unhappy in times of trouble, but in this chapter the concern is to do with a person's change of mood to depression manifested by reduced energy; pessimistic thoughts about the past, present and future; hopelessness; helplessness; and low self-esteem. Elation, too, may be part of human experience at times of good fortune but here the consideration is to do with mood change in the direction of mania which brings with it over-activity, irritability, grand ideas and self-importance. Mood changes, expressed through depression and mania, may be brought together. The swings of mood may be seen as bipolar depression. Such a diagnostic term is used on the grounds that a manic phase cloaks a depressive disorder.

The case of Mrs Dobson, discussed in detail in Part II, demonstrates components of a bipolar depression. Many social workers will see service-users who show features of mild depression, the unipolar state, in the face of loss, deprivation, disruption and adversity. Many studies show that depression may affect children, adolescents, adults, and particularly the elderly. It may descend on people who suffer from Parkinson's disease, Alzheimer's or AIDSs and other illness; descend post-operatively after hysterectomy or post-natally; descend on the homeless, the unemployed or on populations displaced and on the move; and it may descend after loss sustained by divorce, and by death. (For comprehensive coverage see Social Work Abstracts 1994 onwards and Seebohm Report 1968.) Depressed people are seen in any setting of social work, whether local authority social services, hospitals, probation, education welfare departments, and in voluntary organisations. Carers may be affected, too.

Recently, social work practitioners and care managers in social services have had attention drawn to depression as a major health problem which may become chronic (Hervey 1995). Psychosocial origins of chronic depression have been reviewed (Brown and Moran 1994), and an understanding of pharmacological relief, which may be given alongside psychosocial intervention, has been offered by Montgomery (1994). Apart from the relief of symptoms, it is well recognised that the quality of life should be addressed. A multidisciplinary approach is consistently advocated (Department of Health 1995; Kennedy 1995). Within this approach the quality of life is seen as particularly relevant to the condition of the elderly as this group shows higher rates of prevalence than younger people and high levels of recurrence. The effectiveness of psychosocial approaches as a therapeutic mode has been considered by Fielden (1992), particularly in relation to older people.

Apart from work with the elderly, social workers have children and families on their caseload and the needs of this group in relation to depression has recently been considered afresh. During the 1960s, the family was the focus of study when detailed consideration of the effects of physical separation of mother and child was undertaken. Emotional and psychological separation were also viewed as happening when a parent, being depressed, turned feelings and thoughts inwards and away from the child (Walzer 1961).

This understanding was drawn upon by psychiatric social workers in clinical settings in multidisciplinary teams, in both child guidance clinics and psychiatric hospitals. Following Winnicott's (1963) constructive paper on the value of depression, a spate of papers appeared relating to work with a family member's depression and its effect on other members, both in the UK (among others see Jackson 1964 and Leonard 1964) and in the USA. Winnicott put across the idea that within depression there is 'the germ of recovery'. This phrase enabled social workers to face the condition in others and counteract the feelings of hopelessness and helplessness within themselves, mirroring the client's state.

However, in the 1970s and 1980s, following the amalgamation of professional social work groups into the British Association of Social Workers, and with the reorganisation of social services following the Seebohm Report (1968), there were relatively fewer publications dealing with this specific client group. This happened, too, in a climate against labelling and fixing people in a set position. During this time, professional identity and competence was being established, and a multidisciplinary approach awaited further development as a model of practice. A few classic papers, such as that on a depressed woman and her rebellious adolescent (Weissman and Siegel 1972), and one considering the recognition of mental health problems by doctors and social workers (Cohen and Fisher 1987) are still drawn upon, for instance, in contemporary work on maternal depression, child care and social work (Sheppard 1994a).

Concern now centres on mental health problems: 'A minimum of 50% of *all* people on social workers' caseloads, irrespective of whether individuals are accepted by mental health services, other specialist (e.g. elderly, children) or generic teams, have mental illness' (Department of Health 1995, p.84). And further, there is specific mention of the treatment of depression and the ensuing risk of suicide which could have impact on, 'appropriate referral to social workers and other sources of social support' (Department of Health 1995, p.84).

What has led to this renewed focus on mental health – and in this case to depression – and the social work approach to it? An answer may be found within recent legislation and in the perception of the value of social workers' use of the psychosocial approach. The approach is helped by the campaign to increase the awareness of depression and in the change in social work education.

Legislation

There is a requirement that social service departments undertake duties and responsibilities to facilitate mental health. A service is provided to all age groups, in their own homes or elsewhere. This means assessing need, agreeing on a care plan and providing social work support. The Mental Health Act (HMSO 1983) led to the employment of approved social workers in order to provide an assessment and emergency service throughout the week. This in turn led to the improvement of training, and these particular social workers became able to provide group and family work, for instance, in relation to severe depression and the risk of suicide.

The Children Act (HMSO 1989) provides the remit to anticipate and take preventive action in relation to children at risk, whether physically or mentally. Post-natal depression had led to children under one year of age being taken into the care of the local authority (Bebbington and Miles 1989). Prevention is now sought. Other provision and support is needed at later stages, too, since a mother's depressed state during a child's middle years is a risk in relation to his/her later development of depression. Daughters are especially at risk of depression during adolescence (Fergusson, Horwood and Lynsky 1995); alternatively behaviour problems may occur (Cummings and Davies 1994; Philips and O'Hara 1991). Back-up support of significant others such as a spouse or partner is important, too (Sheppard 1994b, p.37), as it is for other carers whether managing sheltered accommodation or providing a service through family centres.

The Criminal Justice Act (HMSO 1991) requires certain prisoners to be supervised by the probation service on release from custody. Some will be depressed.

Perception of psychosocial approaches

Apart from the shift, determined by policy, from hospital care to community care, there has also been a change in the perception of the contribution that may be made by social workers who adopt a psychosocial mode of practice. This is noted by community psychiatrists:

> The use of support and social networks, early intervention in crises, work with families, attention to employment and rehabilitation, and admission to community day care or residential resources are part of everyday treatment. Supportive contact and ventilation of problems for mild depression...are probably among the most powerful therapeutic influences available. (Paykel and Marshall 1991, p.239)

Psychiatric opinion firmly concludes that a multidisciplinary approach, that is, prescription of antidepressants for symptoms and psychosocial approaches for functioning, is the effective treatment of choice for the depressed person (Paykel and Marshall 1991, p.262).

Campaigns to increase recognition of depression

Several organisations have launched campaigns in relation to the recognition and treatment of depression and the management of suicidal risk. The Department of Health, in urging inter-agency working, particularly addresses social workers. Similarly, the Royal College of Psychiatrists in *Defeat Depression* (1993) has pointed out that depression is a major factor in the 4000 suicides in the UK each year, which in turn causes damage to the remaining family. The National Children's Bureau, too, is concerned specifically about teenage suicide (NCB 1994). Organisations in the voluntary sector such as the Samaritans have widened their remit to give service to the depressed as well as to the more overtly suicidal. Booklets by MIND (1994) include one on manic depression. Individuals, too, particularly Libby Purves in *The Times* (16 February 1994) encourage the recognition of depression and its treatment. Each campaign increases awareness.

Change in social work education

The education and training of social workers now includes the requirement that the subject of mental health be part of the curriculum for the award of the Diploma in Social Work (Central Council for Education and Training in Social Work 1995). This faces the fact that deserves repeating, that a minimum of 50 per cent of *all* people on a social worker's caseload have a mental illness (Department of Health 1995, p.84). Many of this number will be depressed. The curriculum also includes new emphasis on using and understanding research. There are well-founded sources to draw on in sociology, psychology and psychiatry, as well as social work, to gain an understanding of mental health and approaches to depression. The requirements also include a focus on gender which leads to the consideration of the impact and frequency of depression in women.

Managing depression

When a depressive disorder is moderate or severe, the first consideration is the likely need for inpatient or day-patient care, taking into account the risk of suicide or likely harm to family members, particularly children. An assessment by the social worker attached to a ward, or as a practitioner within a social services mental health team, will add to the picture of life events, stress, family relationships and absence of support figures. This would go towards the overall assessment by the general practitioner or psychiatrist. But social work practitioners, or approved social workers, may need to act at once in relation to a client's suicidal threats (or attempts) in order to preserve life (Pritchard 1995; Smith and Nursten 1995; Vaughan and Badger 1995, Chapter 4). A next step for the psychiatrist would be to consider admission or the prescription of antidepressant drugs, as described in Chapter 8.

There are costs as well as benefits to hospital admission. This brings the benefit of assessment and treatment by a multidisciplinary team of doctors, nurses, occupational therapists, psychologists and social workers, along with respite, even though brief, from outside stress. It may bring relief to the family. On the other hand, admission means breaking family ties, possibly with those of young children. Change of this nature will interrupt employment or daily occupations; alter self-image and lower self-esteem in being seen as mentally disturbed, and increase helplessness and dependency. Placing a person in hospital, in turn, leads to the outside world being seen as large, daunting and complicated. Hence, following hospitalisation, the social worker has a role in helping the person back into the community and preventing further depressive episodes by addressing social problems and social relationships. A discharged patient would be little helped by returning to an unchanged situation at home.

When depression is mild and more clearly seen as a reaction to life events and circumstances, then help is based on a psychosocial approach which may be short term in relation to being task-centred or problem-solving, aimed at relieving the person in a situation that is eroding and weighs heavily. Crisis intervention and support may be needed when matters cannot be changed and the person faces an unchangeable reality. But longer-term work is needed in many instances, as Mrs Dobson's case will illustrate. Serial contacts with a variety of different social workers do not go sufficiently towards containing such a fragile state as hers. Continuity within the professional relationship is itself of value to people who have had discontinuities in their lives, and such a relationship is of special worth to depressed people who have no one in whom to confide.

However, writing in this way does little to identify the ingredients in the methods used. As Huxley (1991) says: 'In many…studies reported in the literature, the approaches used by (social) workers are not described adequately'. In response to this observation a case study is now presented showing a social worker's approach to Mrs Dobson, a depressed person who also exhibits some manic behaviour. A commentary is given on the nature of the work, on points of choice and the moments missed. The case study is also offered as the use of live or fictitious cases is strongly advocated as a form to draw upon in training professional workers in the field of mental health (Department of Health 1995).

Mrs Dobson, at the time of referral, was not seen as severely depressed. There was no evidence of delusions, hallucinations or risk to life. However, she was having recurrence of episodes of mild to moderate depression for which help was being sought by the health visitor and GP. She herself obliquely seeks help. Names and places are disguised. The case is presented as representative of those in a social worker's case load.

Part II: The case of Mrs Dobson, aged 23 years

The original referral was made to the local authority social services department by a health visitor nearly a year ago. The concern centred on Mrs Dobson's depression and her inability to cope following a recent abortion. At the time, Mrs Dobson was living in a neat and tidy council house with Mr Shaw, who had been her partner since she left her husband three years before. Living with them were her daughters, Christine Dobson, four-and-a-half years, and Jean Dobson, three years. In addition, there was her son, Jamie, one-and-three-quarter years, fathered by Mr Shaw.

The Care Manager in Social Services allocated the case to the Family Centre for short-term help. Mrs Dobson was seen a few times until the care worker left the Centre.

Eleven months later Mrs Dobson approached the Centre herself asking for someone to visit to help her with financial problems. A Care Manager would take several factors into account when the Centre alerted him/her to this self-referral. Thought would be given to Mrs Dobson's expressed need as a service-user and to the possibility of an immediate practical response to her financial difficulties. But this would also be seen in the context of Mrs Dobson's previous depression and the continuing needs of three young children. Would day care or nursery school address their needs, as well as the service-user's needs, and reduce the likelihood of care proceedings? Questions would also be in mind about finding care-figures in the family or neighbourhood who could support Mrs Dobson. Existing links with the health visitor would be revived and the use of provision in the voluntary sector – such as the Citizen's Advice Bureau – would be considered. Should Mrs Dobson's case be taken on once again, the Care Manager would also arrange for later assessment and review, and ensure that the social worker to whom Mrs Dobson was assigned would have support through supervision. Resources would be a factor in deciding the outcome of Mrs Dobson's request for help.

Apart from functions inherent in the role, the Care Manager would need to take into account the vulnerability factors in cases of depression that are known to be apparent in Mrs Dobson's history. Several of these impinge on Mrs Dobson and her situation. She has the care of young children, in fact three children under 14 years of age (Brown and Prudo 1981) and no work outside the home. In addition, she sustained the loss of her own mother before the age of 11 years (Brown and Harris 1978) with doubtful quality of care following this loss (Bifulco, Harris and Brown 1992), and has no one in which to confide. Further research is being undertaken to clarify vulnerability factors, but in many instances, when added to a person's current adverse circumstances, such as Mrs Dobson's disrupted marital/partner relationships and her financial difficulties, the likely outcome is to experience feelings of hopelessness, low self-esteem and, ultimately, depression.

Mrs Dobson's history

Mrs Dobson's background was further known from the original care worker's records. She was the youngest of nine children and described her father as violent to her mother as well as to the children. An occasion was vividly recalled when she intervened on her mother's behalf, hitting her father with a brass candlestick, knocking him out and thinking she had killed him. When she was ten years old her mother died and it was stated that this was from natural causes. Following this bereavement, she was moved to live with a married sister, moving from this household at 17 years of age to marry in order to gain, as she saw it, 'security and a home of my own'.

However, her husband (Mr Dobson) drank heavily and, in her own words, 'beat her up'. She left him after her second daughter's birth and went to live with Mr Shaw, which worked out well for a time but, following her abortion, she became depressed and fearful that Mr Shaw would leave her. He, himself, was unemployed and began to gamble with their joint income from state support, which led to growing debts and arrears in rent.

During the short-term work with a care worker, Mr Shaw found a job and Mrs Dobson became less depressed. However, after the care worker left, Mrs Dobson got in touch with her GP about her concern of further pregnancy or termination of pregnancy. The GP was concerned that either would lead to a recurrence of depression. Hence, Mrs Dobson underwent sterilisation. A few weeks later, Mr Shaw was again without work.

The Care Manager's decision to re-assign the case to the Family Centre was taken following a conference with the GP, health visitor and relevant social work colleagues. It was decided that a social worker would visit Mrs Dobson, with thought being given to Mrs Dobson and Mr Shaw being seen as a couple at a later stage. A strength was seen in Mrs Dobson having asked for help, and in the new family unit still being together. The Centre's drop-in facilities and the mothers' group work could be drawn upon later.

The case was given to a woman social worker in training who would be able to see Mrs Dobson over a period of four months, from October to February. A social worker in training would have frequent and regular supervision of her work. In supervision, there would be reflection on the social worker's activity in this particular case within the psychosocial approach. Relevant areas for discussion are mooted here in order to show what it is that a social worker's supervisor or practice teacher would consider.

First, the *socioeconomic* situation which led to Mrs Dobson's self-referral, that is, the threat of eviction, debts, arrears and the lack of employment would be discussed.

Second, that the 'financial difficulties' are happening to a young mother of three children, subject to depression, whose life has held many losses, that is, there has been the *psychological impact* of losing her mother through death; her father in moving from him to her sister's household; her husband through leaving him; her unborn child through abortion; and the idea of herself as a future mother through sterilisation. She has also lost financial security through her husband's drinking and her partner's gambling. In addition, she has lost her original, and helpful, careworker. Losses in themselves are important factors but it is the response to such eroding events, with the ensuing feelings of hopelessness, that is relevant to depression. Hopelessness attached to such specific events, as listed above, may become generalised and features of depression become manifest.

Third, the *family relationships* – the social situation and the psychological state experienced by Mrs Dobson within the context of her family, where she faces the needs and demands of three children and fears the absence of her partner – need to be discussed.

Finally, *the social worker's own thoughts and feelings* about her work with Mrs Dobson, and others, would be part of the supervisory process. She would also need to be aware of the meaning to her client that there is in the timing of her visit. A month has elapsed since Mrs Dobson contacted the Centre. It is now a year since her abortion, an anniversary which could hold meaning.

A selection from the social worker's records follows. The commentary on the work undertaken is given by the author, who also summarises some of the interviews.

Social worker's record: 23 October – initial contact

> An appointment was made by letter but Mrs Dobson was out when I visited. She 'phoned the agency, apologising for her absence and I arranged another appointment.

> As I approached the house a young-looking woman asked who I was and introduced herself as Mrs Dobson, putting a key into my hand. She told me to let myself in, she was just going to the shop. I opened the door, saw the baby, Jamie, asleep in a tidy, well-furnished room, then went outside and talked with Christine, four-and-a-half years, who chatted brightly and unreservedly.

> Returning, Mrs Dobson talked briefly about the children before opening a box of letters, saying she wanted to show me some. They were a variety of threats: reminders of gas and electricity arrears, a notice to quit and two summonses from the fine default court. Mrs Dobson was embarrassed, saying she was the worst client ever. I asked about their general financial situation and then with Mrs Dobson looked at each debt separately, working out realistic repayments on their social security income. She wanted me to make decisions but I put the decision back to her each time.

> Once her immediate financial worries seemed clearer and more manageable, she expanded on their troubles. She saw Mr Shaw as the culprit and felt that left to herself she could cope with their financial commitments, since she liked 'things to be straight'. He gambled, however, and when 'anything happened' he 'blew all the money'.

> Mrs Dobson mentioned the previous social worker, saying 'I bet she's forgotten all about us'. She had not written as promised. She continued

to express feelings of being abandoned – no one ever came to see her; she became depressed sitting in the house with the children. I asked if she had any relatives nearby, and she told me how her mother-in-law (Mrs Dobson snr) visits to look after the children.

As she spoke, Jean, three years, and Jamie, one-and-three-quarter years, sought her attention constantly. Jean clung to her mother and moaned quietly; Jamie was more vociferous and received most cuddling. Mrs Dobson was extremely loving and obviously very proud of him, playing loud peek-a-boo games with him. She spoke of her abortion and sterilisation very rationally; she now felt that it was a good thing, she need fear pregnancy no longer and could plan ahead. 'Jamie's lovely though, he's my baby son' – she repeated this several times, telling him what a good boy he was. By contrast Jean's whimpering annoyed her, and when Christine, four-and-a-half years, ran out after being told off, Mrs Dobson complained she was cheeky and 'too clever by half'.

Drawing the visit to a close I arranged to visit weekly and to make enquiries on her behalf about financial payments.

26 October

Mrs Dobson 'phoned the Centre distraught; Mr Shaw had left with all their money. A worker visited (I was unavailable) to find her calmer, and her mother-in-law present.

COMMENT ON THE INITIAL CONTACT, 23 OCTOBER

At the start the social worker is left holding the baby! When Mrs Dobson returns from shopping, after a brief exchange about the children, she opens a box of letters revealing a notice to quit and summonses to court. Mrs Dobson's view of herself is that she was 'the worst client ever'. The social worker has a choice here. Should she draw on cognitive therapy and counteract Mrs Dobson's negative view which indicates her low self-esteem? Such a negative picture of herself would be part of her depression. But the social worker holds back from exploring this view. She stays with the Pandora's box of letters, neither blaming nor condemning. Nor does she feed into 'learned helplessness' (Miller, Rosellini and Seligman 1985) by taking the debts off Mrs Dobson's hands. Rather than take over, as in her surprise she found herself doing when Mrs Dobson left her with the children while shopping, she partialises the problems and helps keep Mrs Dobson functioning. It is as though the social worker knows of the 'germ of recovery' in depressed people (Winnicott 1963).

In response to this, Mrs Dobson expands, moving from the trouble with money to trouble with people. Mr Shaw, in her opinion, is the culprit. In addition, the previous care worker is seen as remiss, too, in having forgotten the family. No one comes to see her, she says. The social worker does not seek an elaboration of this view but instead searches for figures of support and discovers the mother-in-law. Networks of relatives, neighbours, teachers, and so on, need to be found for anxious and depressed people, especially when those in such a network have a 'capacity for equanimity' (Hollis and Woods 1981).

The social worker also notices Mrs Dobson's interaction with the children and sees the close relationship with Jamie, one-and-three-quarter years, who is the last of her children. Jamie holds the position she, herself, held in her childhood, and Jamie is her partner's child.

In this first contact, the social worker does not press Mrs Dobson to open up too much. The abortion and sterilisation are each mentioned. The cool, rational way in which these are mentioned could well cover more feeling, but releasing feelings too soon could overwhelm a client. Instead, at this stage, the interview ends with a plan. A structure begins to appear in the planned weekly visits. However, Mrs Dobson's fears of being left could have been taken into account. The frequency of visits is stated, but not the length of time that they will continue.

30 October

Before the next planned visit a week later, Mrs Dobson 'phoned the Centre to say that her partner, Mr Shaw, had left with their money – and that Jamie had been scalded. A care worker from the Centre responded to her pleas and, mindful of possible hurt to Jamie, called at the home. The key social worker was unavailable, but even so this demonstrated the ready support given by the Centre.

Later, at the arranged time for the second visit, Mrs Dobson talked freely about her mixed feelings and unhappiness in relation to Mr Shaw. He had now returned home, and Jamie was all right, but she felt 'grey and hopeless'. After talking in this way she then asked the social worker to go with her to the Housing Department. They went together and Mrs Dobson paid off some rent arrears, this being done with, rather than for, her.

6 November

On this third visit, the house looked even more neat and tidy, and Mrs Dobson talked of her need to have everything 'just so', even though it exhausted her. She felt very down when the housework remained undone. Mr Shaw would laugh at her, she said, calling this her 'mania'.

Following this discussion, the social worker helped Mrs Dobson look ahead. First, she helped her face the summons to appear before the court in a week's time, and offered to go with her. Second, she introduced the forthcoming interruption to the planned visits over Christmas, being sensitive to Mrs Dobson's reaction to being left by key figures. In her own words, Mrs Dobson in such circumstances felt 'abandoned', 'hopeless' and 'went to pieces'. The social worker let her know that the Centre would be open, apart from three days, and mentioned activities, such as the mothers' group, which are held there. As the Centre had a known location, and as members of the team had responded to her need some ten days ago, the hope was that there would be sufficient support should she seek it.

Social worker's record: 13 November – court appearance

Mrs Dobson arrived breathless and late at court asking nervously if I had thought she wouldn't turn up. I said that I trusted her to do so because she had said she would come. The Clerk of the Court expressed surprise at her presence. Giving evidence she sat wet and bedraggled (it was a rainy day), clutching Jean and Jamie, looking small and pathetic. At one point she cried, as her debts were enumerated. The court put her under a Fine Supervision Order and reduced her fine payments.

Afterwards I suggested we went for a drink in Safeways and we talked in a deserted coffee shop. Mrs Dobson's anxiety was very high; Mr Shaw had lost the week's money and broken into the gas meter; because of this and existing arrears she feared gas disconnection. Everything was unpaid, and they had eaten little all week. The court experience had emphasised what a load of debts she had. She said she felt exhausted and at her 'wits end'. During our conversation she ranged from initial hopelessness and despair, to bitterness and finally resignation, all directed against Mr Shaw – 'it's plain where the trouble lies'. She didn't know why she endured him; she ought to 'throw him out' and pay off the debts herself. She asked me several times what she should do. I told her I could give her no simple answer; to leave him after three years was a big step to take. She would have to think hard before such a step and feel that she had made the right decision in her own time.

I said that when things were bad, she seemed to see leaving him as the solution to her difficulties, yet in better times she perhaps felt very differently about him. Mrs Dobson took this up immediately and spoke of her difficulties in making decisions and sticking to them. She linked these ideas up with those of responsibility and 'being adult', and said wistfully that she didn't seem to know her own mind. She felt she was too 'soft'.

While still very upset, she had talked of running away as the solution, or alternatively of 'getting put away'; it would release her from her commitments. I asked her gently how she would feel leaving her children. She took this without comment, then started to talk of her life. It had been one of unhappy drudgery since her mother had died. She had married Mr Dobson to escape from the restricted life with her sister; from him she had escaped to Mr Shaw and now she felt like escaping again. I reflected that she felt she had spent much of her life running away. She agreed emphatically, it was a case of 'out of the frying pan and into the fire'. Mrs Dobson said that Mr Shaw's way was that if he ignored things for long enough they would go away. I replied that everyone thought this way sometimes, but unfortunately things usually got worse if left, which makes it even harder to tackle them when eventually you have to deal with them.

By the end of the interview Mrs Dobson was considerably more composed. As a parting remark she said that if the gas were cut off she would not panic, but would tell Mr Shaw to pack his bags.

COMMENT ON 13 NOVEMBER

The social worker supports her client during their fourth contact by being in court with her. The previous joint visit to the Housing Department, having demonstrated the social worker's commitment, may have helped Mrs Dobson to turn up in court. Many hard-pressed social workers would have felt satisfied with the morning's work and parted from the client. But there is more to do than addressing financial problems alone, and being aware of this the social worker stays on to talk with Mrs Dobson in the supermarket coffee shop while the children play in the supermarket crèche.

At this point, Mrs Dobson could well have been given more credit for turning up in court and facing difficulties. Self-esteem needs to be built up. In fact, self-esteem is of greater relevance in treating depression than the feelings of helplessness (Harris and Bifulco 1991). However, she readily moves from financial issues to interpersonal problems, revealing the fear that she has of Mr Shaw leaving her, which runs alongside her wish to throw him out. She reveals a basic human conflict, that is, to be dependent or independent.

The social worker helps her see what is involved in her dilemma and in decision-making – there are no easy answers, hard thinking is needed, there are different ways to solve problems and a decision involves family members other than Mr Shaw and herself. This is an attempt to help her think through, rather than act out, and cognitive processes are addressed with the aim that control be gained over impulsive behaviour. The social worker avoids being seen as a harsh figure. She neither condemns Mrs Dobson for running away, nor criticises Mr Shaw for ignoring problems.

19 and 26 November

Such themes aired in the previous interview need working and re-working, as the next summary of interviews shows. Crises continue, advice is still sought and ambivalence is still apparent. But some movement takes place. First, Mrs Dobson is able to share her fear of harming the children, which had not been openly faced when Jamie was scalded. Although she had 'phoned (26 October) for help she quickly turned the episode into a 'storm in a tea cup'. Second, Mr Shaw has become part of some sessions, speaking more positively, too, about returning to work.

The next six weeks up to mid-February

These weeks were reported as better for the whole family. The social worker prepared them for the break in her visits over Christmas, and when seeing Mrs Dobson in the new year she found her less depressed, the family relationships less fraught and the financial difficulties eased through Mr Shaw having found employment. Bearing these factors in mind, and the reality that her time at the Centre was nearly up, the social worker broached the matter of ending her sessions with Mrs Dobson.

The social worker began the visit of 12 February by discussing the gains with Mrs Dobson that had been achieved over the past weeks. Mrs Dobson then summed up the difference between her previous care worker's approach and the present social worker. In her eyes, the former just focused on money matters whereas the latter treated her as a person, acknowledging this with a rare smile.

The social worker then opened up the question of ending the contract, to which Mrs Dobson immediately flared – 'look what happened before... debts, arrears, eviction notices, unemployment...'. She immediately became jumpy and talked of her 'nerves' and 'mania'.

Talk of her 'nerves', 'mania' and fears of being left by Mr Shaw continued on 19 February. She did not know what she would do without the Centre.

The social worker had known back in October that she would be leaving for further training at the end of February. Rather than face Mrs Dobson with this fact at such a late stage it would have been appropriate to let her know this at the start. The frequency of regular visits was known but the length of time was not discussed. To Mrs Dobson, it would seem that when events, and mood, settle she then loses an important figure. Endings in her life have been sudden and disruptive.

Termination is hard on social workers, too, and the subject is often delayed. In this instance, there could be uncomfortable feelings about the opportunities available to the one when denied through circumstances of the other.

Three days after this session, Mrs Dobson is in greater difficulties. A full account of the record follows of the social worker's penultimate visit prior to ending.

Social worker's record: 25 February and home visit on 26 February

> Message to the Family Centre from the social services locality office: Mrs Dobson had been caught trying to shoplift childrens' coats on 22 February. She had confessed to the store manager who had sent her home in a taxi and then contacted them. No charges were being made. Next day I visited the home. Mrs Dobson was downstairs with the children but immediately I arrived she decided to do some frantic cleaning upstairs. I followed. She talked angrily, with little interruption from me, about two things. First, Mr Shaw: she couldn't stand the way he behaved any longer. She hated him. She ought to get some rat poison and watch him die slowly. Second, her loneliness: she was 'fed up' of sitting in the house thinking, it made things worse.
>
> Mrs Dobson repeated that 'it' was getting worse and she couldn't stand it much longer. She felt she was reaching the point where she had to know definitely one way or the other: Would he stay and did he love her? The uncertainty was torturing her; it was constantly 'gnawing at her mind'.
>
> Downstairs again, she sent the children out to play. I broached the subject of her shoplifting. I said I felt she should know I had been informed. Not to tell her would be unfair, and I wanted her to know that I was concerned for her. Mrs Dobson sat down, clasped her hands and, with eyes cast downwards, began to talk quietly, sadly and intensely. She had wanted to tell me but it was difficult; she was so ashamed of herself she did not know how to. I acknowledged that she must have felt bad and asked did she think I would be angry with her? She reacted immediately – oh yes, because it was such a terrible, bad thing to have done, like assassinating the Queen. She had thought of nothing else all weekend. Mr Shaw did not know. She recounted that she had taken the coats and felt so scared that she could neither put them back nor leave with them. She had seen the manager and told him. He had reprimanded her but understood that her nerves were bad. Later that afternoon she had bought Jamie an anorak elsewhere. I said that I wasn't a policeman; I hadn't come to tell her off, I'd come to help.
>
> A serious, musing reverie followed for about half an hour in which she expressed feelings of overwhelming badness... 'I can't say I'm honest now – I'm a stealer. Nobody will want to have anything to do with a

thief. I feel as if everyone knows and I can't face them with the shame inside me'. I said quietly that not everyone knew. Furthermore, she was not a 'failure' in my eyes. She was the same person whom I had got to know. I didn't know why she had done it, but I did not think it was because she was a 'criminal'. I pointed out that it wasn't a sensible act; she knew the consequences possible from her actions. She began to think aloud; why had she done it? She had £30 in her pocket at the time. She felt afraid to trust herself now. I remarked that she had been shopping since without incident. Using the same attempt to understand herself as before, she concluded that it must have been a plea for help or attention; she was sick of the house. They might take her away. Mr Shaw would think she was mad... but perhaps she might tell him now.

She brought the subject back to the original theme of certainty/ uncertainty. Would I see Mr Shaw and ask him if he was going to stay? I questioned whether this would be helpful. Mrs Dobson was resentful: 'Why didn't I know the answer, wasn't I trained?'. I replied that she knew I was still in training, and moreover there were no simple answers. She felt she 'definitely needed help' but would not talk about marriage counselling. I asked whether she would talk to her doctor – but, no 'he's a man'. She thought that freedom (when all the children were at school) was the answer. Then she said in a subdued voice that she would like to do things together with Mr Shaw; she always seemed to be either alone or in a crowd. I said we had talked for a long time, perhaps we should look at the kind of help she wanted next week. She agreed.

COMMENT ON THE PENULTIMATE INTERVIEW, 26 FEBRUARY

When the two meet, Mrs Dobson readily shows the angry feelings she has for Mr Shaw. Does he want her, or not? She releases her feelings of uncertainty. This would be a place for the social worker to ask whether Mrs Dobson is feeling this way about her and the Centre, too? Uncertainty reinforces the idea that she is of little worth. It is now 'torturing her', and 'gnawing at her mind'.

A shift takes place – literally – in the interview when the two come downstairs and the children go out to play. The social worker opens up the subject of shoplifting and Mrs Dobson talks about her shame in detail. She sees herself as a thief, feels bad and fears the social worker's anger. The social worker counteracts this negative self-image. For instance, she is not a failure in her eyes, and Mrs Dobson is given credit: she did tell the shop manager and she has been shopping since without incident.

A number of women who shoplift are known to have depressive disorders, especially when there are difficulties in their backgrounds and when there has been a recent upsetting life event (Gibbens, Palmer and Prince 1971). Mrs

Dobson has numerous difficulties and her action may be associated with the sudden realisation of losing her social worker and the support she provides.

Before the end of the interview, Mrs Dobson recognises, or rather re-affirms, her continued need for help, but rejects 'marriage counselling' or a talk with her doctor. The social worker apparently has not mentioned continued contact with the Centre, but she says the next week they will look together at the kind of help wanted.

The social work approach – current and future

Mrs Dobson in her depressed state and in her difficult social situation has been helped by the social worker over some 16 weeks but progress has been put in jeopardy by the way in which the proposed ending of the professional relationship was handled.

Nevertheless, there is still much to be built upon. The social worker, maintaining a psychosocial approach, has offered Mrs Dobson a better view of herself. She is seen as a person to be trusted, neither is she taken to be a thief, nor seen as a failure, and gains have been made. Financial difficulties have been handled by Mrs Dobson herself, and learned helplessness avoided. She has also been given space and time to talk about her feelings to a person to whom she is able to confide.

The relationship formed with this depressed person is a central ingredient in the mixture of work. Within the relationship, the social worker has provided essential components needed by Mrs Dobson. Together they have reflected on bills, found an order of priority for dealing with them and taken action. Between them, they have explored decision-making where there are no easy answers and talked of different ways of solving problems. Sufficient trust was built up for Mrs Dobson to tell of her fear of harming the children, the venom she felt towards her partner and the badness experienced within when she shoplifted. She has voiced violent feelings and shame at her actions and now needs continued help so that she no longer has to run from her situation or fulfil her partial wish to be put away. The aim would be to help her have other adaptive modes to draw on in the face of difficulties – whether experienced within or without. The aim would be to increase her self-esteem, lessen the feelings of depression, enhance her maternal role and enable the family unit to stay together.

What could now be offered following the social worker's departure? What range of services and resources would address the needs of the Dobson/Shaw family? Once again, the Care Manager as purchaser within social services would take funds into account and be constrained by the structure in which he/she operates. Cohen (1995) aptly notes: 'Even if our Social Services were better resourced their structure is now so misconceived that they could still only support the most superficial personal service'. He further points out that long-term work is less possible to undertake, yet to hold back from this is not cost-effective. Without long-term work, clients return again and again and, when endings are imminent, problems arise. Long-term work is known to be necessary (Kanter (1995) substantiates this view).

But should a new plan of care be designed what could it hold? The management would need to take into account the work being offered by other disciplines through the health visitor and GP, by other agencies such as the Housing Department and Social Security, and by networks in the neighbourhood, in the family (Mrs Dobson snr) and through the school. Purchasing help from other professions would be considered, for instance, counselling, but this therapeutic mode for Mrs Dobson might lead to self-examination and introspection that could increase guilt and hopelessness. As Sheppard (1994a p.46) notes: 'Intervention which is directed at [the] psychological state, but which does not at the same time address social circumstances and capacity to manage problems, may in the end go nowhere'.

It is continuity and support from a social worker who is able to give attention to social needs as well as to psychological components that Mrs Dobson, and others depressed like her, need. In looking specifically at maternal depression, Sheppard (1994a, p.46) places the mother, 'firmly within the social work domain, where social workers' profession-specific skills would be appropriate to the circumstances of the client'. Moreover, in advocating the psychosocial approach there are echoes of Reynold's (1934) statement of more than 60 years ago.

Continued work with the client would also mean having in mind the possibility of depression in a mother leading to insecure attachment between her and the two-and-three-year-olds. There would also be a further preventive function. Supposing recurrence of depression was experienced by Mrs Dobson during the children's middle years: treatment at that time would counteract the chance of future depression, particularly in her daughters, during their adolescence (Fergusson et al. 1995).

A service-user's own ideas need consideration. Mrs Dobson was right in seeing the need for help with financial problems last October. She could well be right now, in February, in seeing that freedom from the children would lighten her load once they are in school. A newly assigned social worker could begin to explore with her a school for Christine, nursery school for Jean and partial day care for Jamie, while having the skills to respond to the affective and cognitive components in relation to depression within Mrs Dobson. After all, Mrs Dobson was putting into words a vulnerability factor which Brown and Harris (1978) identified, but the record does not acknowledge the association between a mother's depression and the fact that she has three young pre-school children. Their attendance at school would give her relief. This change would address a further vulnerability factor by releasing her for work outside the home, or at least allowing her to consider it. Work brings social contacts, money and respite from over-familiar surroundings. It can reduce helplessness and increase self-esteem.

The use of the case study

In the presentation of this detailed case study, the aim has been to show aspects of what a social worker may do in the use of the psychosocial approach when working with a depressed woman who shows manic features. The intention has been to draw out material which may be used and developed in other instances of professional work. Further initiatives are needed in order to clarify and evaluate different ways of treating different levels of depression. The use of a case study is offered to enhance discussion, as it has been advocated as a preferred mode (Department of Health 1995). Different perspectives will emerge both from within the social work profession and from other mental health professionals. The case of Mrs Dobson gives one view of what it is that a social worker does.

References

Bebbington, A. and Miles, J. (1989) 'The background of children who enter local authority care.' British Journal of Social Work 19, 5, 349–369.

Bifulco, A., Harris, T. and Brown, G. (1992) 'Mourning of early inadequate care? Re-examining the relationship of maternal loss in childhood with adult depression and anxiety.' Development of Psychopathology 4, 433–449.

Brown, G. and Harris, T. (1978) Social Origins of Depression. London: Tavistock.

Brown, G. and Moran, P. (1994) 'Clinical and psychosocial origins of chronic depressive episodes.' British Journal of Psychiatry 165, 447–56.

Brown, G. and Prudo, R. (1981) 'Psychiatric disorder in a rural and urban population. i. Aetiology of depression.' Psychological Medicine II, 581–99.

Central Council For Education And Training In Social Work (1995) Paper 30: Rules and Requirements for the Diploma in Social Work. London: CCETSW.

Cohen, A. (1995) 'A note protesting the betrayal of our social work heritage.' Practice 7, 4, 7.

Cohen, J. and Fisher, M. (1987) 'Recognition of mental health problems by doctors and social workers.' Practice 3, 225–40.

Cummings, E. and Davies, P. (1994) 'Maternal depression and child development.' Journal of Child Psychology and Psychiatry 35, 1, 73–112.

Department of Health (1995) Building Bridges: A Guide to Arrangements for Inter-Agency Working for the Care and Protection of Severely Mentally Ill People. Wetherby: Department of Health.

Fergusson, D., Horwood, L. and Lynsky, M. (1995) 'Maternal depressive symptoms and depressive symptoms in adolescents.' Journal of Child Psychology and Psychiatry 36, 7, 1165.

Fielden, M. (1992) 'Depression in older adults; psychological and psychosocial approaches.' British Journal of Social Work 22, 3, 291–307.

Gibbens, T., Palmer, C. and Prince, J. (1971) 'Mental health aspects of shoplifting.' British Medical Journal iii, 612–615.

HMSO (1983) The Mental Health Act. London: HMSO.

HMSO (1989) The Children Act. London: HMSO.

HMSO (1991) *The Criminal Justice Act*. London: HMSO.

Harris, T. and Bifulco, A. (1991) Chapter 13. In C.M. Parkes, J. Stevenson-Hinde and P. Marris (eds) *Attachment Across the Lifecycle*. London: Routledge.

Hervey, N. (1995) 'Abstracts, psychology and psychiatry.' *British Journal of Social Work 25*, 529–536.

Hollis, F. and Woods, M. (1981) *Casework – A Psychosocial Therapy*. New York: Random House.

Huxley, P. (1991) 'Social work.' In D. Bennett and H. Freeman (eds) *Handbook of Community Psychiatry*. Edinburgh: Churchill Livingstone.

Jackson, G. (1964) 'Depression in the family.' *British Journal of Psychiatric Social Work VIII*, 4.

Kanter, J. (1995) *Clinical Studies in Case Management*. San Francisco: Jossey-Bass.

Kennedy, G.J. (1995) 'The geriatric syndrome in later-life depression.' *Psychiatric Services* (formerly *Hospital and Community Psychiatry*) *46*, 1, 43–48.

Leonard, P. (1964) 'Depression and family failure.' *British Journal of Psychiatric Social Work viii*, 4.

Miller, W., Rosellini, R. and Seligman, M. (1985) 'Learned helplessness and depression.' In J. Coyne (ed) *Essential Papers on Depression*. New York and London: New York University Press.

Mind Publication (1994) *Manic Depression*. London: Mind Mail Order, Granta House E15 4BQ.

Montgomery, S.A. (1994) 'Long term treatment of depression.' *British Journal of Psychiatry*, (Suppl. 26) 447–56.

National Children's Bureau (1994) *Teenage Depression and Suicide*. London: NCB Publication.

Paykel, E. and Marshall, D. (1991) 'Depression: social approaches to treatment.' In D. Bennett and H. Freeman (eds) *Handbook of Community Psychiatry*. Edinburgh: Churchill Livingstone.

Philips, L. and O'Hara, M. (1991) 'Prospective study of post-partium depression: four and a half year follow up of women.' *Journal of Abnormal Psychology 100*, 2, 151–155.

Pritchard, C. (1995) *Suicide – The Ultimate Rejection*. Buckingham: Oxford University Press.

Purves, L. (1994) 'Depression.' *The Times*, 16 February.

Reynolds, B. (1934) 'Environmental Work.' In F. Hollis and M. Woods (1981) *Casework: A Psychosocial Therapy*. New York: Random House.

Royal College of Psychiatrists (1993) Defeat Depression. London: Gaskell Press.

Seebohm Report. Report of the Committee on Local Authority and Allied Personal Social Services. (1968) London: HMSO.

Sheppard, M. (1994a) 'Maternal depression, child care and the social work role.' *British Journal of Social Work 24*, 33–51.

Sheppard, M. (1994b) 'Postnatal depression, child care and social support.' *Social Work and Social Sciences Review 5*, 1, 24–26.

Smith, M. and Nursten, J. (1995) 'Murder, suicide and violence.' *Journal of Social Work Practice 9*, 1, 15–22.

Social Work Research and Abstracts. (1994 onwards) Washington: National Association of Social Workers.

Vaughan, P. and Badger, D. (1995) *Working with the Mentally Disordered Offender in the Community*. London: Chapman and Hall.

Walzer, H. (1961) 'Casework treatment of the depressed parent.' *Social Casework XLII*, 10, December, 505–512.

Weissman, M. and Siegel, R. (1972) 'The depressed woman and her rebellious adolescent.' *Social Casework 53*, 9, 563–70.

Winnicott, D.W. (1963) The value of depression. Address to the general meeting of the Association of Psychiatric Social Workers, September.

Further Reading

Parker, G. (1992) 'Early environment.' In E.S. Paykel (ed) *Handbook of Affective Disorders*. New York: Guilford Press.

CHAPTER 6

What Nurses Can Do To Help

Paul Needham

Margaret is a qualified psychiatric nurse working on a rehabilitation unit within a large mental hospital. She is also diagnosed as suffering from a manic depressive disorder. Margaret traces her illness back to a time when she was 23 years old. She had been married for a year and had recently given birth to her son. She was compulsorily admitted to an acute admission ward at another mental hospital when she became severely depressed and voiced suicidal intentions. After one week, however, Margaret's mood changed dramatically from apathy and despair to elation and frenetic activity; she was unable to rest or sleep and she chased around the ward lecturing loudly, reorganising and interfering with any hapless person she came across. It took several weeks for Margaret's manic behaviour to subside and for her to be discharged.

Over the next 12 years Margaret experienced several similar episodes. Although her periods of depression were never as severe, her manic eruptions proved to be devastating, resulting in a broken marriage, debt, a poor employment history and numerous admissions to hospital.

She was able to maintain her job as a psychiatric nurse largely due to sympathetic support from her colleagues. Margaret's ward manager was able to detect a pattern to Margaret's illness; first she would become depressed for a period of a week to ten days, followed by a rapid shift to mania. It was speculated that if Margaret could be persuaded to seek inpatient care during this initial phase of depression her manic phase might be averted or minimised and, of equal importance to the ward, disruption and risk to patients might be avoided.

This hypothesis proved largely correct but called for careful management which was only possible through a close collaboration between the ward staff, the hospital managers, Margaret's husband (before their separation), social worker, consultant psychiatrist and, of course, Margaret herself.

Manic depression

The course of Margaret's illness proved to be fairly consistent over time and between episodes, but there is enormous variability in the patterns experienced by people with manic depressive illness. The frequency, duration and severity of both depressive and manic phases and the gaps in between can differ greatly between sufferers, and it seems the only consistent requirement for this diagnosis is that the patient must have shown elements of both depression and mania at some time in his or her life (American Psychiatric Association 1994). Ironically, while it is the depressive phase which often causes the most distress to the patient, it is the manic phase which causes the most concern for others and is more likely to lead to hospitalisation.

The risk of self-neglect and profound sadness associated with depression is obviously cause for concern to relatives and carers, and the threat of suicide cannot be underestimated. In a review of 30 studies between 1936 and 1988, Goodwin and Jamison (1990) calculated suicides among depressed patients as 18.9 per cent. In a Finnish study, Isometsä et al. (1994) found that 79 per cent of suicides among manic depressive patients occurred during the depressed phase.

Although the risk of suicide may be much lower in the manic phase the patient, experiencing euphoria, increased energy and a sense of invulnerability, may engage in risk-taking, extravagant or disruptive behaviours which can result in injury, promiscuity, debt, crime or conflict with others; problems which may have considerable long-term consequences for the patient (American Psychiatric Association 1994). Indeed, these consequences, combined with the stigma of mental illness, the lowering of self-esteem, the fear of recurrence and the strain on the patient's personal relationships, may be responsible for further depression (Beach, Sandeen and O'Leary 1990; Coryell et al. 1993).

The nurse's role

Nurses are adept at giving medication, providing physical care and ensuring the safety of vulnerable patients. These skills have been handed down through generations of nurses for a number of historical reasons:

- the predomination of the medical model with its emphasis on the biological causes of disease and cure has created a tradition of reliance on drugs as the mainstay of psychiatric care (Olsen 1992)

- the legal, social and organisational expectations of nurses to ensure the safety of the patient and the dire consequences for those nurses who have failed (Abrams 1978; Darcy 1978)

- the difficulty nurses have experienced in setting goals and outcome measures for intangible social and psychological problems (Green 1992).

Nurses are not alone in believing that comprehensive (or holistic) care must incorporate an equal focus on the patient's environment, social relationships, coping skills and internal thoughts and feelings if he or she is to be helped towards optimum health. These concepts have been drawn from humanistic psychotherapies such as that espoused by Carl Rogers (1951) and incorporated into a variety of conceptual models which are important elements of current nurse training (Pearson and Vaughan 1986) and are slowly and gingerly finding their way into nursing practice, albeit with some reservations (Allmark 1992; Cash 1990; Huckabay 1991).

Of course, mental health nurses have long known that talking with patients can be helpful. They have been trained to work in a variety of clinical settings both in hospitals and the community, using a number of different roles within their repertoire: the sociotherapeutic role within therapeutic community settings; the psychotherapeutic role using counselling skills; the behavioural role developed for psychiatric rehabilitation, and the behaviour nurse therapist role described by Marks (1985) as well as the doctor's assistant and administrator roles (Cormack 1983).

More recently there has been growing recognition of the plight of the mental health patient or 'consumer of mental health services' who has been disempowered by an iniquitous system of social prejudice, legal and medical paternalism, and a general lack of control over resources. Wallcraft (1994) argues that for centuries people who have been labelled as mentally ill have been silenced by denial of their human rights, the shame of the stigma of madness, their routine invalidation as self-determining human beings, the fear of punitive and damaging treatment, and the effects of treatment itself. Nurses have responded over the last decade by debating their roles as advocates and how they might empower patients. It is argued that nurses are in a unique position to defend the rights of the patient by giving information, fostering independence and protecting the patient from all kinds of physical and psychological abuse (Needham 1988).

Not surprisingly perhaps, the debate among nurses as to how they might empower patients has been largely academic. It is the radical changes in social policy that have revolutionised the patient's standing in the scheme of their health care. The British government White Papers *Working for Patients* (Cm 555 1989) and *Caring for People* (Cm 849 1989) laid the foundations for care provision to be accountable to, and purchased by, external agencies such as GP fundholders. This was made law with the passing of the National Health Service and Community Care Act (1990) and although funding is still remote from the patient, the purchasers are able to set the criteria for the quality of care. The government's policy guidance (Department of Health 1990) gives the following objectives:

- ○ to restore and maintain independence by enabling people to live in the community wherever possible

- ○ to achieve equal opportunities for all

- ○ to promote individual choice and self-determination and to build on existing strengths and care resources

- ○ to promote partnerships between users, carers and service providers in all sectors.

The implications of this for nurses are that they must work collaboratively with the patient and other carers and justify their own existence.

Other recent changes have also had a considerable impact on nurses. Care patterns are changing rapidly to embrace new technologies, new ways of organising care and more advanced treatments. There have, for example, been major innovations in psychological interventions, and community psychiatric nurses in particular are being urged to develop their skills from a broad base of training to acquire knowledge and skills at greater depth. A number of innovative training initiatives, such as the Thorn Programme at Manchester University and the Institute of Psychiatry in London and a masters level programme at Middlesex University, are currently preparing nurses to use contemporary research-based case management and psychosocial interventions for clients with enduring mental illnesses (Gournay 1995). The basic nursing diploma courses are now almost entirely based at universities such as Thames Valley University in London, which also offers a number of practice-based modules in advanced care practice at diploma and first degree levels.

The nurse–patient relationship

The nurse's close contact with the patient gives him or her a unique position to develop a lasting relationship based on trust and empathy. Through sensitive communication the nurse can help the patient to understand the implications of health problems and the treatment alternatives. An understanding of the health care system, terminology and the nurse's partnership with other professional carers allow the nurse to help the patient through education (Needham 1988). Kennet (1986) suggests that nurses have the communication skills and often the time to engage in a meaningful, two-way flow of information which may promote a trusting and sensitive relationship with the patient.

Community psychiatric nurses have a particular advantage in establishing a meaningful relationship since they can step into the patient's world. The patient is more likely to desire interactions with a carer who is able to understand how personal health problems affect the patient in the real world outside the treatment or consultation setting (Dillon 1990).

The therapeutic relationship between the carer and the manic depressive patient is of critical importance. In depression the patient is likely to be swamped by low self-esteem and self-deprecation (Beck 1967) and may benefit from some affirming, positive regard, a listening ear and supervision to ensure safety. The manic patient may be particularly vulnerable to exploitation or abuse from others and may require protection and control. In the intervals between, the carer may be able to help the patient to resolve problems created during episodes of dysfunction and to negotiate ongoing prophylactic care and contingency plans to reduce either the prospects of future relapse or the domestic, social and financial damage which may occur with future episodes (American Psychiatric Association 1994; Townsend 1993).

Pilette, Berck and Achber (1995) argue that the therapeutic relationship has boundaries which need to be effectively managed: 'While the consequences of mishandling a social relationship may result in uncomfortable feelings and some degree of psychological and interpersonal conflict, violations of professional boundaries carry the additional toll of shifting the relationship into non-thera-peutic dynamics' (Pilette *et al.* 1995). Violations might include blatant exploi-tation of the patient for the nurse's personal gratification or may be inadvertent and subtle such as being too helpful and thus promoting an unhealthy dependence. Boundaries become blurred when the relationship slips into a social context or when the nurse's behaviour is influenced by her own needs rather than those of the patient (Pilette *et al.* 1995). Patients exhibiting mania are particularly susceptible to violations of relationship boundaries. Their quick wit, comic antics, boundless humour, generosity and flirtatiousness, as well as their aggression and the capacity to manipulate others, make them both target and *agent provocateur*. Once therapeutic boundaries have been breached it may be difficult for the nurse to put the relationship back on track.

Miller (1990) advocates a simplified version of Eric Berne's (1966) transac-tional analysis model to help guide the nurse's interactions. Figure 6.1. shows the three positions of parent, adult and child represented by circles. On the left of the circles are some of the positive and healthy characteristics of these positions and on the right are some of the negative and unhelpful characteristics. Berne argued that people can switch between parent, adult and child very quickly depending on their need to be authoritative, belligerent, nurturing (parent conditions), tactful, considered, objective (adult conditions), playful, petulant or sulking (child conditions). These transitory roles can be seen as strategies designed either to make gains within a relationship or to express feelings. The relative positions are also reciprocal, depending on the position adopted by the other person in the relationship. For example, if confronted with a belligerent *parent* it would be a natural reaction to adopt a *child* position either by cowering or protesting.

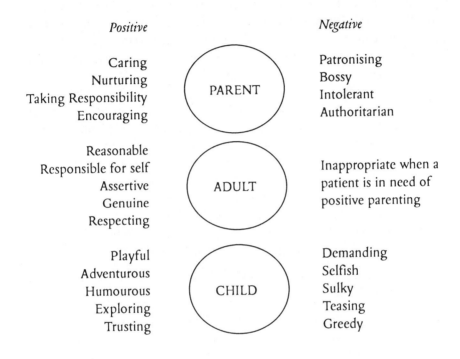

Positive		Negative
Caring Nurturing Taking Responsibility Encouraging	PARENT	Patronising Bossy Intolerant Authoritarian
Reasonable Responsible for self Assertive Genuine Respecting	ADULT	Inappropriate when a patient is in need of positive parenting
Playful Adventurous Humourous Exploring Trusting	CHILD	Demanding Selfish Sulky Teasing Greedy

Figure 6.1 The parent, adult and child roles with some of their positive and negative qualities

The positive characteristics of parent, adult and child can all be used effectively at certain times within a therapeutic relationship. There are times when the nurse needs to be a caring and nurturing parent and other times when child humour and play can be used effectively. However, the nurse can force the patient to adopt a reciprocal role; either a child to the nurse's parent or a parent to the nurse's child, both of which may be unhelpful and untherapeutic. An awareness of these dynamics can help the nurse to avoid pushing the patient into an inappropriate position. The aim is for both nurse and patient to adopt adult roles with mutual respect and a reasoned collaboration.

The acute care of the manic patient

The acute care of a patient with mania presents a considerable challenge for nurses in inpatient settings. During this phase the patient may be extremely vulnerable to his or her own risk-taking, poor judgement and abuse by others who may wish either to take advantage of the patient's generous or promiscuous behaviour, or to hit back at the patient's manipulative, interfering or overtly aggressive behaviour. The nurse is charged with maintaining the patient's safety under these conditions and to protect those who may be at risk from the manic patient. The patient may also be at risk from malnutrition and dehydration as he or she burns off calories through constant activity but is unable to spare the time to eat regular meals (Townsend 1993).

An added complication is that the patient is often delighted with his or her condition and would not wish to comply with any treatments that might take away his or her euphoria and grandiose goals (Gutheil 1982; Jamison 1991). Sometimes the patient may exhibit psychotic symptoms, namely delusions and, to a rarer extent, hallucinations. The delusions, often grandiose in nature, may contain paranoid features which make the patient suspicious, defensive or aggressive towards others. In extreme mania the patient may also display considerable agitation and pressure of speech, with rapidly changing ideas or incomprehensible gibberish, unable to keep pace with his or her own thoughts.

The nursing strategy with the manic patients involves:

- reducing background stimulation as much as possible with the aim of helping the patient to achieve rest

- maintaining the safety of the patient by removing hazards, maintaining supervision and ensuring that there are adequate staff on hand to restrain the patient if it becomes necessary

- providing suitable physical activity as an outlet for frustration if it becomes necessary

- assisting the patient to take medication which will help to reduce his or her activity levels

- monitoring changes in the patient's mood or behaviour that might indicate added risks or treatment responses

- using a calm but firm approach that instils confidence but also establishes firm boundaries on acceptable behaviour

- keeping high protein food and drink available and encouraging the patient to eat and drink regularly

- giving the patient praise and encouragement for acceptable behaviour and generally to boost his or her self-esteem.

Achieving rest is the ultimate aim of reducing the background stimulation. Tranquillising drugs may be prescribed for this purpose. Sleep deprivation has been implicated in the onset of mania and, interestingly, has been used with some success by Wehr (1992) to help treatment-resistant depressed patients lift out of their depression.

The risk of harm to the patient is more likely to arise from reckless behaviour but suicide during manic episodes accounted for 11 per cent of all suicides in Isometsä's study in Finland (Isometsä et al. 1994) and some precautionary supervision is necessary.

The acute care of the depressed patient

Depression is described as being characterised by the 'Triad of Depression' (Bech 1992, p.3) involving depressed mood, decreased motor activity and negative beliefs. The depressed mood is expressed in terms of helplessness and hopelessness, and negative beliefs include low self-esteem and feelings of guilt (Beck 1967). The patient may tire easily and become preoccupied with bodily sensations, interpreting them as signs of serious physical illness. In manic depressive disorders there can be a great deal of variation between the severity, duration and frequency of depressive episodes. Margaret (in the case vignette at the beginning of this chapter) experienced a mild form of depression for just a week or two before her mood swung to mania. Other sufferers may experience more debilitating forms of depression for longer periods.

Adolescents are a group particularly at risk of undiagnosed manic depression since their changes in mood are often attributed to the stresses of growing up, exams and new relationships (Goodwin and Jamison 1990). The difference between reactions to adolescent adjustment and the onset of manic depressive disorder is the persistent and uncharacteristic nature of mood changes in the latter.

There is also a distinct association between manic depression and drug and alcohol abuse which often blurs the clinical picture and creates considerable additional problems (Ghadirian and Roux 1995; Winokur et al. 1995). Regier et al. (1990), from the US Epidemiological Catchment Area project, estimate a 56 per cent lifetime rate for substance abuse in manic depressive patients.

Hospital admission during the depressed phase is less common, largely because it is less socially and domestically disruptive. However, it may be considered necessary if the patient is thought to be at risk of self-harm or where the patient is not likely to adhere to treatment.

The risk of suicide is particularly high in depression, which sometimes means that carers and care agencies feel compelled to limit the patient's freedoms. This is ultimately disempowering and has further implications for the patient's independence and self-esteem, raising some difficult ethical issues and highlighting the need for frequent and thorough risk assessment with the goal of handing back autonomy to the patient as soon as possible.

The nursing strategy with depressed patients involves:

- assessing the risk of suicide, removing environmental hazards and maintaining supervision of the patient

- providing opportunities for the patient to verbalise feelings and providing acceptable ways of venting anger, such as through physical exercise, art or drama

- using listening skills and giving affirming, non-judgmental communication

- helping the patient to examine and review relationships, loss and, possibly, religious beliefs

- teaching the patient assertiveness and communication techniques

- involving the patient in domestic and self-care activities

- allowing the patient to participate in the assessment and planning process and discussing the progress that has been made

- encouraging the patient to participate in group activities that may promote feelings of acceptance and self-worth

- promoting compliance with prescribed medication and observing for side effects.

The nurse's affirming interactions with the patient can be helpful. Listening is probably the most important element of these interactions. Throwing advice at the patient is generally considered unhelpful, as is offering the nurse's own experiences of coping. The patient has almost certainly developed a hard kernel of dysfunctional beliefs about him or herself as a worthless person and tends to seek evidence to support these beliefs, assisted in this task by distorted thinking involving a tendency to exaggerate, set unrealistic expectations and find hidden meanings in innocuous events (Stern and Drummond 1991). Testimony of other people's successes is likely to offer the patient yet more evidence of their own failure. Counselling and cognitive psychotherapies are highly skilled processes that attempt to unravel these dysfunctional, negative thoughts and systematically challenge them. While this may be beyond the scope of most nurses, an increasing number are developing these skills in post-basic courses. Nevertheless, the nurse's art of listening can be immensely useful in allowing the patient to verbalise his or her problems.

Suicide

Suicide poses a significant threat to depressed patients. Hawton and Cohen (1990) assert that 50 per cent of all suicides are committed by people with a diagnosis of depression. Predicting which patients are likely to commit suicide is difficult. Although male gender, living alone, previous suicide attempts and voiced suicidal intentions are among the likely indicators, a number of authors (reviewed in Wolfe 1994) claim that a false positive prediction error might result in one hundred to two hundred people being predicted to be suicidal for every one person who actually would have committed suicide. This obviously holds implications for cost and resources, and the denial of patients' freedoms (Wolfe 1994).

While validity problems affect all of the published risk assessment scales, the 18-item scale published by Pallis, Gibson and Pierce (1984) offers a method which is relatively easy to use. However, Wolfe (1994) suggests that clinicians should not depend on risk assessments alone. Diagnosis must also include clinical judgement based on experience and an understanding of the patient's environment and support networks.

Townsend (1993) suggests that a therapeutic contract might be negotiated where the patient would give a written undertaking not to attempt suicide or to cause self-harm. In my own experience I have been able to negotiate such contracts with depressed patients in exchange for some liberty that they would otherwise have been denied.

Mood assessment

During the acute and ongoing care of the patient in all phases of the disorder, the patient may be able to use a self-rating scale employing subjective units of mood on a 12-point scale (see Figure 6.2). This type of scale is often used by anxious patients to describe and record their levels of distress in anxiety-provoking situations (Stern and Drummond 1991), but this simple scale has been customised to represent the two extreme mood poles with 'no significant mood inclination' at the mid-point. Unfortunately the customised scale has not been tested for reliability, and differentiating degrees of mania can be difficult for the patient who is concurrently anxious or angry, or he or she may simply refuse to co-operate. While patients are often able to identify mild depression, their reporting of mild mania is rare (American Psychiatric Association 1994). My own anecdotal experience of this tool involved asking all the nurses on one acute ward to rate simultaneously and independently a manic patient's mood. The scale used the terms 'high' and 'low' at each pole. Results showed a surprisingly high level of agreement.

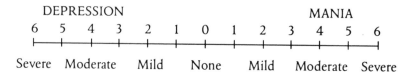

Figure 6.2 Subjective mood rating scale

Another, more reliable assessment method used in inpatient settings is interval sampling, which relies on the observation and recording of all the patient's behaviours during brief intervals of, say, five minutes every hour (Barker 1982). The assessments are more reliable since they record objective activity associated with mood rather than on subjective impressions of mood. The interval times must be pre-set and followed strictly to avoid bias creeping into the assessment. If, for example, the nurse is permitted to decide what five minute period within the hour she will sample, she may be prompted to grab her clip-board when the patient commences activity after a long period of relative quiet. This will distort the overall picture and become misleading when compared with readings from other intervals.

For any assessment to give predictive power for future episodes of depression and mania, it needs to plot progress and events over a period of time so that patterns and cycles can be identified. Post, Roy-Byrne and Uhde (1988) describe a system for graphically plotting the life course of a patient's manic depressive illness which takes account of mood changes, significant life events and treatments. Figure 6.3. shows a presentation of how a section of Margaret's chart would have looked.

Graphic charting makes it possible to identify seasonal relationships with relapse, as well as the possible influences of life stresses and the longer-term effects of treatment. This has possible benefit in allowing the planning of contingencies for future care, negotiated with the patient when he or she is stable in mood and retains some insight.

Drugs

Nurses have a natural central role in giving medication or encouraging the patient to take it safely and in the doses and at the times prescribed (Gournay 1995). Drug treatments for manic depressive disorders generally fall within three distinct schemes: mood stabilisers such as lithium, valproate and carbamazepine which have all been shown to ameliorate mood extremes (Goodwin and Jamison 1990; Janicak *et al.* 1993; American Psychiatric Association 1994); adjunctive medication for the treatment of acute or protracted depression or mania; and antipsychotic drugs where psychosis is involved. Despite claims for

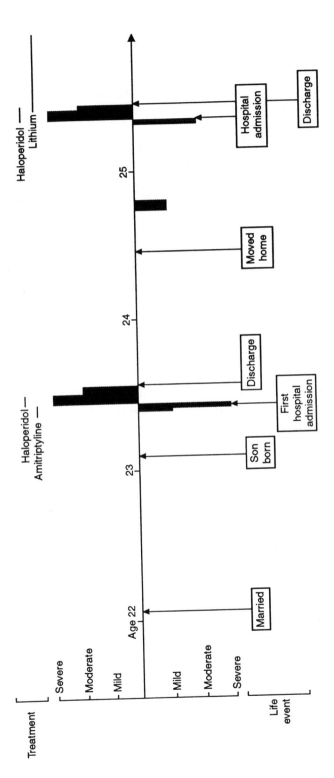

Figure 6.3 Section of the life chart plotting the course of Margaret's illness (adapted from Post , Roy-Byrne and Uhde 1988)

the effectiveness of these drugs they cannot be said to cure manic depressive illness.

Unfortunately, patients' failure to comply with prescribed drug regimes is a well-documented problem (Gutheil 1982; Jamison 1991) which has been blamed for the recurrence of episodes of disordered mood (Goldberg, Harrow and Grossman 1995; Jamison and Akiskal 1983). There are a number of understandable reasons why patients may be reluctant to continue to take medication; they may deny that they have a psychiatric problem, and they may become disenchanted with the lack of immediate results, the burden of following the regime (which may also involve regular donations of blood samples for monitoring blood drug levels and blood cell anomalies) and finally, the numerous common side effects which accompany these drugs. It is, therefore, essential that the nurse involved in the ongoing support of the patient encourages drug compliance by emphasising their potential benefits in terms of future mood stability and their positive influence on the patient's social and functional well-being. The nurse may be tempted to ignore or skirt around the inconveniences of medication taking and their side effects in the vain hope that the patient will not notice, or attribute any distressing side effects to other causes, but this will lead ultimately to the patient questioning the nurse's integrity, jeopardising the nurse-patient relationship.

The problem of side effects cannot be ignored. Goodwin and Jamison (1990) suggest that 75 per cent of patients prescribed lithium (the most popular of the mood stabilising drugs) experience one or more of the many reported side effects. These include increased urination, increased thirst, weight gain, impaired memory and concentration, muscle tremors, lethargy, nausea, vomiting, diarrhoea, hair loss, white blood cell anomalies, acne and oedema. Schou (1991), however, argues that most side effects are minor and can be relieved by reducing the dose. By keeping an eye open for these effects and working with the patient frankly and honestly the nurse may be able to suggest dose changes with the prescribing doctor that may reduce or eliminate these problems.

Drug and alcohol abuse has been associated with manic depressive illness, especially in the manic phase when the patient becomes impulsive with an expansive lifestyle and poor judgement (Goodwin and Jamison 1990; Winokur et al. 1995). The dual diagnosis of substance abuse and serious mental illness is now considered a problem throughout the world (Smith and Hucker 1994). The American Psychiatric Association (1994) suggests that treatment of drug and alcohol problems should be tackled concurrently since they can complicate the clinical picture and treatment outcomes of the primary mood disorder.

Psychosocial interventions

Despite the success claimed for modern drug therapy, the risk of further episodes of severe mood disturbances among manic depressive patients is around 50 per cent (Perry, Tarrier and Morriss 1995), and less than 50 per cent of patients are able to maintain adequate functioning in all areas of their social, domestic and occupational lives (Goldberg *et al.* 1995). While the broad aims of psychosocial interventions are to alleviate distress, reduce the frequency of episodes of mood disorder and maximise the patient's functioning (Kahn 1993), the more specific goals for working with patients and their families are to:

- identify the early warning signs of recurrence (or relapse) so that medical and social contingency plans might be introduced

- identify life events or stresses that may trigger recurrence and to maintain healthy life patterns where these stresses might be avoided

- increase the patients' capacities to cope with their problems

- provide ongoing support and education to patients and families struggling to come to terms with the illness and its consequences.

Recent studies suggest that most patients have a period of two to four weeks when early (prodromal) signs and symptoms occur before the onset of mania or depression. Over 85 per cent of patients are able to report these prodromal signs (Molnar, Feeney and Fava 1988; Smith and Tarrier 1992). Perry *et al.* (1995) claim that each individual patient may have a 'relapse signature' which consists of tell-tale signs such as racing thoughts, poor concentration, changes in energy levels, changes in sleeping patterns, heightened sensitivity or irritation. While Perry *et al.* (1995) used a five-stage procedure to identify prodromal signs, the community psychiatric nurse, working closely with the patient and his or her family, occupies an ideal position to discover these signs and to test them over time in order to establish predictive validity. Once this has been achieved a contingency plan may be implemented, involving changes to the patient's routine, reduction of stress, changes to medication, and proactive changes to the patient's domestic and occupational circumstances to limit future damage through reckless or negligent behaviour. Perry, Tarrier and Morriss 1995) suggest that it is imperative to act at an early stage while the patient retains insight into the illness and its risks. In the case vignette at the beginning of this chapter, Margaret did not have the benefit of this structured procedure for detecting prodromal signs, but her nurse colleague was nevertheless able to predict the onset of Margaret's illness by her withdrawn behaviour on the ward. A word of warning from Perry *et al.* (1995) is that the patient may become so aware of mood changes that he or she may seek help during normal fluctuations in mood.

Pollack (1995) claims that manic depressive patients often complain that they are given little practical advice and information about their illness. She describes a highly evaluated group therapy programme in an inpatient setting which focused on patient self-management and included sharing information about manic depressive disorder and medication issues, improving interpersonal relationships and learning to solve problems in a supportive environment. The community psychiatric nurse also has an important role in educating the patient and family and can help them to accept the reality of the illness, gain co-operation with treatment plans and reduce stress. Community psychiatric nurses with appropriate training in family therapy may also provide treatment programmes such as those described by Falloon, Boyd and McGill (1984) and Miklowitz and Goldstein (1990).

Future directions

Nurses, because of their breadth of training and the intimacy of their relationships with patients, have a considerable contribution to make to the care of patients with manic depressive disorder. They are, however, just one part of a team of health care professionals with a variety of specialised skills. Case management (described by Onyett (1992)) provides models for organising individually tailored care based on a comprehensive assessment of patients' needs and effective management of services. In the UK and Australia, where case management systems have been developed, the majority of case managers who negotiate and manage the care packages with patients are mental health nurses (Gournay 1995). Although they have a natural advantage in developing this role, it requires skills which are not part of current basic nurse training. The importance of training in these skills has been highlighted by Muijen et al. (1994), who concluded that community psychiatric nurses were unlikely to make a significant impact on care unless their skills and the back-up services available to them were developed. The need to develop case management and psychosocial intervention skills among community psychiatric nurses has also been recognised in the Butterworth Report (Butterworth 1994). These challenges are being met by a growing number of advanced courses for nurses (mentioned earlier) and may be assisted by the compulsory requirement for all nurses to undergo regular updating and further training in order to maintain their nursing registration (United Kingdom Central Council for Nursing, Midwifery and Health Visiting 1990).

References

Abrams, N.A. (1978) 'The contrary view of the nurse as patient advocate.' *Nursing Forum* *17*, 3, 256–267.

Allmark, P. (1992) 'The ethical enterprise of nursing.' *Journal of Advanced Nursing 17*, 1, 16–20.

American Psychiatric Association (1994) 'Bipolar disorder.' *American Journal of Psychiatry 151*, 12, 2–36.

Barker, P.J. (1982) *Behaviour Therapy Nursing*. London: Croom Helm.

Beach, S.R.H., Sandeen, E.E. and O'Leary, K.D. (1990) *Depression in Marriage*. New York: Guilford Press.

Bech, A.T. (1992) 'Symptoms and assessment of depression.' In E.S. Paykel (ed) *Handbook of Affective Disorders*. London: Churchill Livingstone.

Beck, A.T. (1967) *Depression: Clinical, Experimental and Theoretical Aspects*. New York: Harper and Row.

Berne, E. (1966) *Games People Play*. New York: Grove Press.

Butterworth, T. (1994) *Mental Health Review*. London: HMSO.

Cash, K. (1990) 'Nursing models and the ideas of nursing.' *International Journal of Nursing Studies 27*, 3, 249–256.

Cm 555 (1989) *Working for Patients*. London: HMSO.

Cm 849 (1989) *Caring for People*. London: HMSO.

Cormack, D.F.S. (1983) *Psychiatric Nursing Described*. London: Churchill Livingstone.

Coryell, W. *et al.* (1993) 'The enduring psychosocial consequences of mania and depression.' *American Journal of Psychiatry 150*, 5, 720–727.

Darcy, P.T. (1978) 'Psychiatric nursing today: 1. protecting the patient.' *Nursing Mirror* 13 July, p.31.

Department of Health (1990) *Community Care in the Next Decade and Beyond*. London: HMSO.

Dillon, J.T. (1990) *The Practice of Questioning*. London: Routledge.

Falloon, I.R.H., Boyd, J.L. and McGill, C.W. (1984) *Family Care for Schizophrenia: A Problem-Solving Approach to Mental Illness*. New York: Guilford Press.

Ghadirian, A.M. and Roux, N. (1995) 'Prevalence and symptoms at onset of bipolar illness among adolescent inpatients.' *Psychiatric Services 46*, 4, 402–404.

Goldberg, J.F., Harrow, M. and Grossman, L.S. (1995) 'Course and outcome in bipolar affective disorder: a longitudinal follow-up study.' *American Journal of Psychiatry 152*, 3, 379–384.

Goodwin, F.K. and Jamison, K.R. (1990) *Manic Depressive Illness*. New York: Oxford University Press.

Gournay, K. (1995) 'Mental health nurses working purposefully with people with serious and enduring mental illnesses: an international perspective.' *International Journal of Nursing Studies 32*, 4, 341–352.

Green, S. (1992) *Measuring Outcomes in the Mental Health Services*: Discussion Paper 29. Birmingham: Health Service Management Centre.

Gutheil, T.G. (1982) 'The psychology of pharmacology.' *Bulletin of the Menninger Clinic 46*, 4, 321–330.

Hawton, K, and Cohen, P. (1990) *Dilemmas and Difficulties in the Management of Psychiatric Patients*. Oxford: Oxford University Press.

Huckabay, I. (1991) 'Nursing models and theories: do they work in practice?' *Nursing Administration Quarterly.* Spring, 15, 3, v–80.

Isometsä, E.T. *et al.* (1994) 'Suicide in bipolar disorder in Finland.' *American Journal of Psychiatry 151*, 7, 1020–1024.

Jamison, K.R. (1991) 'Manic-depressive illness: the overlooked need for psychotherapy'. In B.D. Beitman and G.L. Klerman (eds) *Integrating Pharmacotherapy and Psychotherapy.* Washington, DC: American Psychiatric Press.

Jamison, K.S. and Akiskal, H.S. (1983) 'Medication compliance in patients with bipolar disorder.' *Psychiatric Clinics of North America 6*, 1, 175–192.

Janicak, P.G. *et al.* (1993) *Principles and Practice of Psychopharmacotherapy.* Baltimore: Williams & Wilkins.

Kahn, D.A. (1993) 'The use of psychodynamic psychotherapy in manic depressive illness.' *Journal of the American Academy of Psychoanalysis 21*, 3, 441–455.

Kennet, A. (1986) 'Informed consent: a patient's rights?' *Professional Nurse 2*, 3, 75–77.

Marks, I.M. (1985) *Psychiatric Nurse Therapists in Primary Care.* London: Royal College of Nursing.

Miklowitz, D.J. and Goldstein, M.J. (1990) 'Behavioral family treatment for patients with bipolar affective disorder.' *Behavior Modification 14*, 4, 457–489.

Miller, R. (1990) *Managing Difficult Patients.* London: Faber and Faber.

Molnar, G., Feeney, M.G. and Fava, G.A. (1988) 'Duration and symptoms of bipolar prodromes.' *American Journal of Psychiatry 145*, 12, 1576–1578.

Muijen, M. *et al.* (1994) 'Community psychiatric nurse teams: intensive versus generic care.' *British Journal of Psychiatry 65*, 2, 211–217.

National Health Service and Community Care Act (1990) London: HMSO.

Needham, P. (1988) 'Can nurses make effective advocates for psychiatric patients?' (Unpublished paper for the ENB 655 behaviour therapy course) Salford School of Nursing.

Olsen, M.R. (1992) 'Measuring effectiveness in psychiatric care.' In S. Green (ed) *Measuring Outcomes in the Mental Health Services.* Discussion Paper 29. Birmingham: Health Service Management Centre.

Onyett, S. (1992) *Case Management in Mental Health.* London: Chapman & Hall.

Pallis, D., Gibson, J.S. and Pierce D.W. (1984) 'Estimating suicide risk among attempted suicides: 2. efficiency of the predictive scales after the attempt.' *British Journal of Psychiatry 144*, 2, 139–148.

Pearson, A. and Vaughan, B. (1986) *Nursing Models for Practice.* London: Heinemann.

Perry, A., Tarrier, N. and Morriss, R. (1995) 'Identification of prodromal signs and symptoms and early intervention in manic depressive psychosis patients: a case example.' *Behavioural and Cognitive Psychotherapy 23*, 4, 399–409.

Pilette, P.C., Berck, C.B. and Achber, L.C. (1995) 'Therapeutic management of helping boundaries.' *Journal of Psychosocial Nursing 33*, 1, 40–47.

Pollack, L.E. (1995) 'Treatment of inpatients with bipolar disorders: a role for self-management groups.' *Journal of Psychosocial Nursing 33*, 1, 11–16.

Post, R.M., Roy-Byrne, P.P. and Uhde, T.W. (1988) 'Graphic representation of the life course of illness in patients with affective disorder.' *American Journal of Psychiatry 147*, 7, 844–848.

Regier, D.A. *et al.* (1990) 'Co-morbidity of mental disorders with alcohol and other drugs of abuse.' *Journal of the American Medical Association 264*, 19, 2511–2518.

Rogers, C. (1951) *Client-Centered Therapy, Its Current Practices, Implications and Theory.* London: Constable.

Schou, M. (1991) 'Relapse prevention in manic depressive illness.' *Canadian Journal of Psychiatry 36*, 7, 502–506.

Smith, J. and Hucker, S. (1994) 'Schizophrenia and substance abuse.' *British Journal of Psychiatry 165*, 1, 13–21.

Smith, J.A. and Tarrier, N. (1992) 'Prodromal symptoms in manic depressive psychosis.' *Social Psychiatry and Psychiatric Epidemiology 27*, 5, 245–248.

Stern, R.S. and Drummond, L.M. (1991) *The Practice of Behavioural and Cognitive Psychotherapy.* Cambridge: Cambridge University Press.

Townsend, M.C. (1993) *Psychiatric Mental Health Nursing: Concepts of Care.* Philadelphia: F.A. Davis.

UKCC (1990) *The Report of the Post-Registration Education and Practice Project.* London: United Kingdom Central Council for Nursing, Midwifery and Health Visiting.

Wallcraft, J. (1994) 'Empowering empowerment: professionals and self-advocacy projects.' *Mental Health Nursing 14*, 2, 6–9.

Wehr, T.A. (1992) 'Improvement of depression and triggering of mania by sleep deprivation.' *Journal of the American Medical Association 267*, 4, 548–551.

Winokur, G. *et al.* (1995) 'Alcoholism in the manic-depressive (bipolar) illness: familial illness, course of illness, and the primary-secondary distinction.' *American Journal of Psychiatry 152*, 3, 365–372.

Wolfe. J. (1994) 'Suicide risk assessment'. Unpublished paper for the MSc mental health interventions course'. Middlesex University.

CHAPTER 7

What Relatives and Friends Can Do To Help

Eia K. Asen

Illness and the family

Serious illness – whether physical or psychological – can be a threat to family stability as it inevitably affects all its members and may completely upset the functioning of the family machinery.

How families and the individuals within them adapt to the serious illness of one of its members can in fact vary a great deal, and this in turn will affect the sick person's functioning. It could be argued that families possess the characteristics of systems: there are some (unwritten) rules which govern the family's functioning and different members have different roles and ways of inter-relating. If one person falls ill, some of the specific roles and functions of particular family members need to be redefined or even reallocated. In some families, however, this may not be acknowledged because they can only operate as though the illness does not exist. Such denial can become so powerful that everyone is caught up in it: however strange or fraught their feelings and behaviour may be, they will resolutely declare that all is normal. It may suit some families, or the individuals within them, to believe that all is 'normal', but in other families shock turns into general paralysis with other members developing stress-related symptoms: everybody seems to be ill one way or another, with a covert competition as to who is worst off. Thankfully, when it comes to coping with serious illness most families lie somewhere between these two extremes and, with the help of friends, tend to establish a new equilibrium.

Major domestic and work changes usually result from severe or chronic illness as the ill person needs to take time off work convalescing at home. This means that family members tend to be more exposed to each other, more than they are used to and, perhaps, too much! Not surprisingly, therefore, this is a testing time which can disrupt the family for good or ill. How those near and dear, no matter whether family or close friends, respond to serious illness does have a major impact on the ill member in its midst. Common sense tells us that hostile responses are likely to make things worse while sympathetic handling of the ill person is likely to be helpful. Yet we also know that too much sympathy can all too easily turn into over-protectiveness and render the unwell person more helpless, which might hinder the recovery process. Once permanently wrapped in cotton wool the person feels increasingly like a 'patient', with the helping responses reinforcing this status.

Illness can and does cause crises in families, but the consequences can be both positive as well as negative. It can contribute to uniting family and friends and it can also tear them apart. While illness is usually initially an unwelcome visitor it can, over time, become a valued family friend. The 'illness bond' is a common phenomenon: families become closer through the joint experience of illness, and relationships which would otherwise fall apart can be 'glued' together. For example, some shaky marriages can apparently be saved when one person falls ill. It seems so much more difficult to leave an ill partner: the guilt of deserting someone close at a time of need can be overwhelming and pressure from extended family and friends can prove unbearable. To outsiders it may at times seem impossible to determine whether illness has produced family dysfunction or whether family dysfunction has produced illness. There is little doubt that these are closely interconnected and this, as we shall see, is very important.

Manic depressive illness and family response patterns

The responses of families to physical and psychological illness are generally quite different. The latter still carries a stigma in many families and the fact that there are often no visible causes for the person's suffering makes psychological illness much more difficult to accept. The aetiology of manic depressive disorder is highly complex: genetic and constitutional factors interact with life events and social factors. There is also the 'family factor' which definitely affects the course of the illness. Viewing the illness in interactional terms does not ignore complex aetiologies. It is one complementary way of viewing illness in context: the focus is widened from the ill persons's mind and brain to his or her immediate living context, namely family and friends.

Deinstitutionalisation and the policy of community care has led to relatives and friends becoming the primary carers for patients suffering from serious mental illness. This has produced high levels of distress and psychological disorder in carers. Reducing care-giver distress or 'burden' is an important task in supporting seriously mentally ill patients in their homes. It is a frequent observation that the key relatives' 'expressed emotion' changes, particularly with a reduction of criticism. Research has demonstrated that a reduction in critical comments is positively related to a significant decrease in the relapse rate of schizophrenics (Leff *et al.* 1982). Similar findings have not yet been scientifically established for affective disorders, but it is very likely that there are similar pressures at work.

The family's response to the illness of one of its members is not only determined by family issues but also by the nature and course of the particular illness. When comparing families containing a schizophrenic with those containing a bipolar patient, a number of significant differences can be found (Miklowitz and Goldstein 1990): families of manic depressive patients are of a higher socioeconomic status and tend to be more psychologically minded. Generally speaking, their interactions are more spontaneous, more affective and more fast-paced – in contrast to families of schizophrenics. They are also more likely to challenge and resist a didactic approach to treatment. When it comes to looking at the individual characteristics of bipolar as compared with schizophrenic patients some other significant differences emerge: manic depressive patients are less severely ill between episodes; they tend to be more overtly emotional, dependent and demanding in family interactions; and they are particularly sensitive to being labelled and stigmatised (Miklowitz and Goldstein 1990).

The experience of families containing an individual with bipolar disorder is characterised by ambiguity and uncertainty (Moltz 1993). Much of the time the patient's affect appears controlled, thinking seems logical and a semblance of rationality, self-control and responsibility is maintained. Yet during hypomanic episodes judgement is severely impaired and during depressive spells the patient can seem so paralysed that other family members feel they have to take over responsibility and decision-making temporarily, often very much against the patient's own wishes.

Family members often refer to 'personality changes' in their manic depressive relative and seem at times puzzled about what the 'real self' is – given that there seem to be sometimes three different ones: one low, one high and one presumed 'normal'. Relatives ask themselves whether certain personal characteristics are 'real' or simply evidence of illness. These seemingly unanswerable questions can undermine the fundamental base of reality from which the family operates, causing ambiguity and confusion (Moltz 1993).

The episodic aspects of manic depressive disorder create fears of relapse among friends and relatives of the affected person. It is precisely the illness's apparent unpredictability which makes the threat of relapse so ever-present, affecting family life profoundly. Watching the signs of onset in the hope of averting an episode can become an intensive preoccupation, if not an obsession, all round. At times it may be difficult to distinguish 'ill' and 'normal' behaviour: increased self-confidence, enthusiasm or a high level of energy may be misread as prodromal signs of mania. Irritability or anger may be appropriate expressions of feelings related to specific family dynamics, but could be misinterpreted as early symptoms of a psychotic episode. In their often well-meaning efforts to detect and hopefully avert another episode of illness, family members may become overly cautious. They, more so than the affected individual, may be on constant 'red alert'. However, living with such hypervigilance can take its toll: families can develop a kind of 'siege mentality' and live constantly on the look-out for the next disaster, with the danger of this becoming a self-fulfilling prophecy. While the process of being on the watch may well have protective aspects during an acute phase, over time it can become repressive and therefore problematic. Any strong emotion may cause alarm, with the danger that normal emotions become disqualified as being the prodromal signs of yet another episode. For example, any hint of anger may evoke neutralising responses, any initiative may be curbed in case things 'get out of hand'. Constraints are imposed on the range of acceptable behaviours in the family: because of a learned association with illness any intense or unusual behaviour is avoided (Moltz 1993). Moreover, family members are often afraid that any confrontation could lead to another episode of illness. Needless to say, such distrust of emotional intensity can result in a stifling, overcontrolled home environment, with persistent avoidance of emotional expression and denial of strong feelings.

Relapse, remission and family mood swings

Bipolar affective disorder characteristically follows a relapse–remission course in which patients experience on average some 12 episodes over a 25 year period (Goodwin and Jamison 1984). While modern medication affects the relapse rate significantly, lithium appears to be a better prophylactic agent for hypo-mania than for depression. Apart from the limited efficacy of psychotopic medication there is also the major problem of non-compliance: roughly 50 per cent of all bipolar patients discontinue lithium in their first year of treatment, and many more become non-compliant at a later stage with an increased risk of relapse.

It could be argued that lithium is a 'family drug' in that it regulates not only the patient but also the family. As it decreases the likelihood of relapses it acts as a 'sedative' to the whole family who put their trust and hope in its magic. Sometimes the regular taking of this medication is supervised by a key relative or close friend. This is not unproblematic as the home might be at risk of being gradually transformed into a hospital ward, thereby reinforcing illness behav-iour which feeds the belief that the 'patient' cannot be trusted to be in charge of his or her own medication. The fact that manic depressives feel subjectively 'well' during a hypomanic phase and therefore often stop the medication poses a major dilemma for relatives and friends: if they intervene they face the accusation of making the sufferer worse by insisting on medication and exposing him or her to the unwanted side effects of the prescribed drug(s).

However, not intervening in this situation may mean exposing the ill person to the very real possibility of financial, physical or emotional ruin. Characteristically, families will adopt 'trial and error' strategies, temporarily experimenting with either leaving the medication issue to their ill member or controlling it – and eventually settling down somewhere in the middle – until the next crisis occurs.

In this context the phenomenon of 'family mood swings' may be mentioned: some families tend to alternate between 'highs' when the patient is low to 'lows' when the patient is high. It is particularly during a hypomanic episode that despair among family and friends sets in: exhausted by the ill person's level of activity, inappropriate behaviour and major spending sprees, they all wish for this spell to be over as quickly as possible. However, once he or she has sunk into a deep depression worries about the general apathy and possibly suicidal preoccupations produce another set of horrendous worries and anxieties. Families of manic depressives can go through these ups and downs in regular intervals, which are characterised by high emotionality, raised voices, lively interactions, continuous interruptions – and humour. Denial is not an uncommon feature, as the ill person's 'highs' can be quite infectious, so much so that nobody wants to think about the immediate future.

Anyone living with a chronically depressed person will know about the all-pervasive power of depression: it can severely affect the family atmosphere – 'his illness is getting us all down' is a common complaint made by relatives. Insisting on getting an answer to what it actually is that is getting the ill person down is unlikely to yield results. Often the person is genuinely quite unable to pinpoint the 'cause' of his or her suffering. This may get family members to give up in frustration, seemingly at a loss as to how to help. Soon the ill person is blamed and criticised for being so unforthcoming. When suicidal ideas are expressed, relatives tend to be overtly anxious and quietly resentful as they feel controlled by the ill person. Characteristically, relatives fluctuate between feeling sorry and being fed up.

Suppression of anger by relatives is a common feature. During a manic episode, in the knowledge that the disinhibited social and financial behaviours are largely attributable to illness over which the patient has relatively little control, the relative feels guilty about expressing anger directly. The patient, on the other hand, will feel increasingly guilty about the consequences of their out-of-control behaviour and, when depressed, become dependent on the spouse or other key relative, with fears of being abandoned (Bloch *et al.* 1994). This cycle of mutual suppression of anger becomes a relational issue, resulting in indirect expression of anger or inauthentic interactions. After the acute episode is over, there are difficulties of discussing what happened. The ill person can feel consumed by guilt and shame and the relatives may be too hurt or angry to discuss their feelings openly – if only to avoid further confrontations.

Managing acute crises

During an acute crisis the family and close friends are immediately affected. They are often so worried that it comes as a relief when the psychiatric services take over and when the ill person gets admitted to hospital. Everyone can take a short rest. Yet it is only a question of time until relatives become critical of ward regimes or staff and when they feel bad about leaving the ill person in the sole care of the psychiatric team.

From a clinical point of view it is very important to involve family and friends in the management of the patient: they need to be helped to help. Family work can start at any time and, if at all possible, during the inpatient period. The clinician's task when conducting a family session is to facilitate a calm, non-blaming atmosphere, avoiding emotional escalations and keeping the session to a 'business' type of level, by looking at concrete problems and finding ways of helping the family to solve these. Sometimes separate meetings between clinician and affected person may be necessary. Relatives also may need their special time and assistance in making decisions regarding the person's and their own safety.

At the outset of family work the emphasis is on making a good connection with all members and forming a working relationship. Clinicians want to make an assessment of the skills of the family in managing the illness effectively, communicating productively and being able to solve problems (Miklowitz and Goldstein 1990). More specifically, attention is paid to frequencies, timing and delivery of positive and negative feedback, as well as to listening and communication skills (Miklowitz et al. 1987). Clinicians will also want to understand the social network of the ill person and create a map of his or her relationships with family, friends and significant others. This will produce valuable information as to the various resources available and can lead to planning how and when family and friends can be helpful. In order to understand the ill person's current life context, a variety of 'circular questions' (Selvini Palazzoli et al. 1980) are asked to map out family and other environmental pressures that may have triggered the recent episode, as well as examining the family's adaptation to illness behaviours. Through this process of interviewing, family members are invited to reflect upon each other's positions and examine their belief systems regarding their relative's illness. The emergence of different perspectives highlights the relative nature of each position.

One particular area that clinicians need to help family and friends with is denial. Denial of illness is a common feature of hypomanic episodes, particularly when followed by periods of apparent 'normality'. If this denial is not addressed the affected person might be prematurely forced into his or her prior roles and functions and the family may collude. Many bipolar patients want to return to work as quickly as possible and, as if to prove their point, stop taking medication. It is known that lithium can reduce the frequency of hypomanic episodes by some 50 per cent and tackling medication non-compliance is therefore a major task for clinicians who need to enlist the help of family and friends. This is easier said than done: non-compliance is a complex phenomenon and can have different causes and functions – we have already mentioned denial mechanisms. Non-compliance can also be a 'rebellion' against the family, who are perceived as wishing to control the mood of the patient, 'spying' on them so as to ensure that the medication is taken regularly. What can families and friends do? The right balance needs to be found, allowing the affected person to feel both autonomous and cared for. In families which have struggled with the disorganising effects of bipolar illness, a particularly high value is often placed on strong boundaries, continuity and cohesion (Moltz 1993). This may make any move for autonomy become a loaded issue as it may have connotations of disinterest or disloyalty.

Living with manic depressive illness

For many families the experience of living with a relative who is suffering from manic depressive disorder is like living with a time bomb: it can go off at any moment and with devastating consequences. One of the major features of the disorder is its apparent unpredictability and often relatives report that it tends to come 'out of the blue', with little or no warning. However, retrospectively it is usually possible to identify specific signs. Unpredictability can produce feelings of insecurity and associated anxieties, but there is also another side: spontaneity and impulsiveness. Unpredictability becomes a way of life for 'bipolar families', with disadvantages and some advantages, such as spicing everyday life with both anxiety and excitement. When well-meaning clinicians introduce too much predictability by working out tight schedules and response plans with families, they are likely to be met with considerable resistance, not only from the affected person but also from relatives.

Families and their individual members need to adapt to the illness in its midst, for example by reallocating roles. Families and friends may at times need to be helped so that they can become helpful to the affected person. For example, family and friends need to keep in mind that all role reallocations following illness need to be reviewed regularly so as to avoid 'institutionalisa-tion': the family can become a 'total institution' with all the rules and constrictions often only encountered in mental hospitals or prisons. How can families guard themselves against this? Flexible responses to changing circum-stances have as their precondition a regular planned review of arrangements and strategies. This includes deciding on what jobs can be handed back to the ill person. For instance, for a man, both father and husband and seen as the 'head of the family', it can be particularly depressing to discover that the family machinery is ticking over without him. He can suffer a secondary 'reactive' depression, seriously denting his self-esteem. Different members of the family may have quite diverse responses, ranging from totally accepting to denying the illness and the limitations this may cause for this man's professional and domestic career. Awareness of these and other dynamics will enable relatives and friends to be helpful to the sufferer in their midst.

There are some very practical tasks that need to be tackled: for example, making plans for money management and dealing with the unusual hours and sleeping times of the hypomanic person. Talking about the manic episode is an important step. Family and friends, particularly after a first episode, feel traumatised by what has happened and may be frightened that it could all start again without any warning. Finding the right time is not easy and this is often best done in the presence of a neutral person, such as a sensitive and unbiased family friend. Acknowledging the trauma is not an easy task as emotions may be runnning high with everyone being frightened that talking about it will set off unhealthy blame or self-blame. A family conference may need to be held, conducted in a low key manner so as not to refuel any of these strong emotions prematurely. There are occasions when a clinician, such as a family therapist, needs to be brought in to help things move on.

When a manic patient has been sectioned with the agreement of the family, he or she is often full of a sense of betrayal, feeling that the relatives can never be trusted again. In family meetings, possibly attended by close friends and preferably conducted by a family therapist, these complex feelings can be explored slowly. This can include the posing of hypothetical scenarios by speculating about what would have happened if the ill person had not ended up in hospital. Going over the whole episode in some detail can also help to identify warning signs and encourage reflection on what could be done next time round.

Family therapists tend to ask questions about the illness and its effects on the family, as well as questions on how family and friends may affect the illness itself. Such questions are not simply information-gathering but interventions in their own right as they stimulate self-reflection. Here are some examples:

- What is the effect of the illness on each family member?

- How do the family members talk to one another about the illness?

- What explanations and expectations do they each have?

- How does the family adapt to the illness – how do roles and functions become reallocated?

- How would things change if the person was cured, once and for all, of his or her illness? What would be better? What would change for the worse?

○ Are any family members doing anything to maintain the patient in the 'ill role'?

○ What, if anything, could anybody have invested in the illness persisting?

One of the aims of asking these kinds of question is to increase the family's understanding of the nature and treatment of bipolar disorder. Being informed helps to combat the illness, and most families are very keen to discuss the possible causes of manic depressive illness and issues regarding its genetic transmission. It is here that the drawing up of a family genogram might provide some clues for the identification and understanding of family patterns of illness. Relatives are not infrequently concerned that they, or others in the family, may share a disposition to affective disorders and monitor themselves or others for any possible signs. This can lead to an anxious look-out for symptoms. Children in particular can be very vulnerable if parental concerns get projected on to them. Becoming increasingly aware of parental 'monitoring' while being confused about its reasons has the effect of getting children to wonder about what is wrong with them to warrant their parents' worried looks and actions. Children pick up this anxiety and get slowly 'infected' by it, with the risk of parental concerns turning into a self-fulfilling prophecy.

Often it is difficult to discuss prognosis and management of the disorder within the family without all sorts of processes being set in motion. This is where friends – and professionals – come in: they provide a neutral ground and allow new perspectives to prevail from which not only the patient's predicament but the whole family's response system can be viewed.

Chronic illness and chronic relationships

Manic depressive illness can pose diagnostic problems: different clinicians can be in disagreement as to whether a particular 'episode' is evidence of manic depressive disorder or just a difficult patch for a person and the family. Subsequently the family is given contradictory advice. Medication may be a reminder that the person is 'ill' and a dance around the regular taking of medication can ensue, involving part of the professional network. For example, if a husband feels that his wife, diagnosed by one doctor as suffering from manic depressive disorder, is too argumentative he may wish to put this down to another outbreak of the illness and ask for the medication to be increased. However, if another family member believes the woman's symptoms to be the frank and therefore healthy expression of her position in relation to her husband's unreasonable behaviour, then another professional, say a family therapist, could be drawn in to support that view. It is conceivable that this clinician reframes the husband as 'manipulative' in that he encourages his wife to take the pills to 'calm down', disqualifying her behaviour as 'ill' just because it does not suit him. While either professional view might be correct, the ill person is rarely helped by becoming caught up in the midst of such a war of opinions. Enlisting professionals to confirm or challenge a 'diagnosis' can become a complex manoeuvre in which there are usually some casualties.

Illness can be used as a tool, for example to communicate something important that cannot be communicated in any other way. There are those who develop a 'taste for illness' and the indirect benefits that can be derived from it. There are occasions when certain family members appear to be playing 'patient and nurse' games – often without being consciously aware of this. Partners who turn into (unpaid) 'nurses' often have themselves learned that one way of conducting relationships is to look after another person. It provides some kind of 'security' and perhaps the only tolerable focus in a specific relationship. Being a heroic 'nurse', sticking with the 'patient' come what may, earns a lot of admiration from friends, family – and even the medical profession. In the unlikely event that the 'patient' recovers permanently, the 'nurse' becomes 'unemployed' and this 'redundancy' may change the relational game, so much so that the roles become reversed. The question arises: is there anything other than the illness bond that keeps the partners together? If the answer is 'no' then the couple may be condemned to terminal relay races of patient and nurse routines. Many professionals have referred to the 'symbiotic' nature of 'manic depressive marriages', with both partners having a high degree of mutual influence (Bloch *et al.* 1994). However, in reality the divorce rate among bipolar patients is very high (over 60 per cent).

What can relatives and friends do to help? At times they may find themselves hopelessly and helplessly embroiled in chronic relationships centring around the bipolar illness. By virtue of this position they are quite unable to see the contribution they themselves make in maintaining the dysfunctional relationships. Friends can be helpful here by encouraging the partners or whole family to seek professional help.

Preventing relapse

It is important to train families to detect warning signs of depression or hypomania. This allows additional medication and psychological and systemic intervention to be introduced at potential crisis times, with the likelihood of increased compliance. When a person has relapsed many times, particularly with hypomanic episodes that have resulted in potential financial ruin for the whole family, then relatives and friends surely need to institute an 'early warning' and 'quick response' system.

The first step is to help the family acknowledge that the illness is a 'reality' which may come back and for which therefore emergency plans need to be made. The ill person, family members and important friends can each be asked to list one major warning sign suggestive of an imminent manic or depressive episode. A family discussion can then be held to compare notes on what possible action could or should be taken. This discussion needs to involve the affected person centrally: if he or she consents to this 'rehearsal' it is more likely that the plan will be followed during a real emergency. Going through each of the possible actions, weighing up the advantages and disadvantages, hopefully helps patient and family to make a joint plan that can be activated at a time of crisis.

Such family discussions can establish what does and what does not constitute 'danger signs'. Similarly, discussions should also address situations that may be unusual or emotional but are not deemed to be 'dangerous': defining what is part of the illness also means deciding what is not. The next step is to come to some agreement on how and when the 'early warning system' should be activated and what actions are to be followed. Involving the ill person in a discussion as to what changes need to be made so that relapse becomes less likely gives him or her some responsibility, they are an agent, rather than just the passive victim of some uncontrollable illness called manic depressive disorder.

It is through discussions with family and friends that the ill person remains involved in his or her management, rather than being treated as a 'mad patient', incapable of acting responsibly. In this way family and friends are a vital part of the rehabilitation process. At times the help of a systemic family therapist may be required to allow this process to go ahead in a more measured way or for new and different perspectives and views to emerge. However, in the end it is family and friends who are not only affected by the person's illness, but who are also instrumental in affecting his or her recovery.

References

Bloch, S. *et al.* (eds) (1994) *The Family in Clinical Psychiatry.* Oxford: Oxford University Press.

Goodwin, F.K. and Jamison, K.R. (1984) 'The natural course of manic depressive illness.' In R.M. Post and J.C. Ballenger (eds) *Neurobiology of Mood Disorders.* Baltimore, MD: Williams and Wilkins.

Leff, J. *et al.* (1982) 'A controlled trial of social intervention in the families of schizophrenic patients.' *British Journal of Psychiatry 141,* 121–134.

Miklowitz, D.J. and Goldstein, M.J. (1990) 'Behavioral family treatment for patients with bipolar affective disorder.' *Behaviour Modification 14,* 457–489.

Miklowitz, D.J. *et al.* (1987) 'The family and the course of recent-onset mania.' In K. Hahlweg and M.J. Goldstein (eds) *Understanding Major Mental Disorder: The Contribution of Family Interaction Research* New York: Family Process Press.

Moltz, D.A. (1993) 'Bipolar disorder and the family: an integrative model.' *Family Process* 32, 409–423.

Selvini Palazzoli, M. *et al.* (1980) 'Hypothesizing, circularity, neutrality: three guidelines for the conductor of the session.' *Family Process 19*, 3–12.

CHAPTER 8

What Drugs Can Do To Help

Jill Rasmussen and Cosmo Hallström

Effective clinical management of bipolar disorders is as important as management of other serious diseases. It is estimated that one in four patients with bipolar disorder can be expected to attempt suicide, a risk surpassed only in schizophrenia and schizo-affective disorder (Weissman, Leaf and Livingston 1982). By epidemiological standards, the 1.2 per cent morbid risk associated with bipolar disorder places it among the more lethal of common disorders (Weissman *et al.* 1988). Inadequate treatment may contribute to the more aggressive course of the disease known as 'rapid cycling', wherein patients have four or more episodes of mania or depression in one year. This was initially described by Dunner and Fieve in 1974, who also predicted that such patients were less likely to respond to standard drug therapy.

The critical issues in effective management of bipolar disorders are early recognition, careful differential diagnosis and persistent clinical management together with social support.

Epidemiological studies in recent years have highlighted the need for early detection, aggressive intervention and long-term maintenance therapy in bipolar disorder. It has long been known that inadequate treatment is associated with a high risk of recurrent mania (Winokur, Clayton and Reich 1969), accelerated deterioration in a patient's overall condition (Prien and Gelenberg 1989) and an increasing risk that subsequent episodes may respond less well to standard treatment, such as lithium (Gelenberg *et al.* 1989; Post 1993). The phenomenon of kindling may occur where each previous episode actually increases the risk of the next, even if the episode is mild or subclinical. More recent data suggest that repeated episodes of mania and depression may lead to deterioration of brain tissue (Altshuler 1993).

Diagnosis is not necessarily straightforward. As Kraepelin (1921) recognised in his descriptions of 'manic depressive insanity', it is a familial condition with multiple clinical presentations of widely varying severity from temperamental to psychotic. In the modern nosology, Kraepelin's spectrum of related disorders has been separated into such categories as dysthymia, cyclothymia, recurrent unipolar depression, simple mania and others, even though it is still recognised that one of these forms can readily substitute for another. As a consequence, the underlying bipolar disorder may remain undiagnosed and inadequately treated until it presents finally in florid form. It is essential, therefore, when considering any of the related affective disorders that close attention be given to any suggestive family history.

Evidence from epidemiological and twin studies supports the view that bipolar disorder has strong familial (genetic) links, and that environmental stressors also influence the disease (Gershon *et al.* 1987; Nurnberger and Gershon 1992). However, the precise effects of these stressors and the mode of inheritance of the disorder are uncertain. It could be anticipated, and is confirmed by clinical experience, that the disease is likely to have a lifelong and deteriorating course. Certainly no 'cure' for all cases has yet been discovered, so the objectives of management are to reduce insofar as possible the severity and number of episodes experienced; to extend the euthymic intervals; to delay or eliminate progression to the malignant, rapid-cycling form; to decrease the psychosocial consequences of episodes, and to improve the psychosocial functioning between episodes. In addition, it is vital that treatment strategies are continually reviewed and reassessed as new information becomes available and/or the patient's clinical status changes. A mutual understanding of bipolar disorder and how it affects an individual patient and family is critical to the development of rapport, confidence and trust between patient and clinician. It is also important to ensure compliance with treatment, to assist with the early identification of relapses, and to avoid the complications of the disease.

These objectives demand treatment not only of the acute manic or depressive phases, but also long-term, prophylactic maintenance therapy coupled with the social support necessary to ensure compliance with treatment and to minimise environmental factors which may trigger relapse. For both acute and prophylactic therapy, a variety of drugs has proved of value. It is, however, critical to recognise that no drug is equally effective against the manic and depressive phases and that some drugs or combinations of drugs can precipitate an episode. For example, depressive episodes may be induced by reserpine or α-methyl 3,4–dihydroxyphenylalanine (DOPA) (Goodwin and Jamison 1990), while antidepressants and corticosteroids may precipitate a manic phase.

Because all drugs presently used in the management of bipolar disorders have limitations of efficacy as well as varying risk of toxicity or adverse effects, the search for the 'magic bullet' continues. Notwithstanding their limitations, however, drugs provide the best means for controlling the acute phases of the disease, for minimising their potentially devastating personal, social and vocational consequences and for preventing recurrence. Moreover, by controlling the more florid symptoms of depression and, particularly, mania, drug therapy improves the potential for social and psychological support to ameliorate further the impact of the disease.

Lithium, the most venerable of drug therapies for bipolar disorders, remains the first-line treatment in most cases. However, anticonvulsants, antidepressants, antipsychotics, certain benzodiazepines and augmentation strategies can also be of value. Electroconvulsive therapy (ECT) may give the most rapid control of the most severe and psychotic episodes of either the manic or the depressive phases of the disease.

Lithium was used clinically as early as the mid-19th century in a variety of conditions, and its prophylactic efficacy in recurrent depression was already noted late in the same century (Lenox and Watson 1994). However, it was not until the seminal observations of Cade, subsequently confirmed in placebo-controlled clinical studies, indicated that lithium was effective not only in controlling the symptoms associated with acute mania, but also in prophylaxis (Cade 1949) that the drug took its pre-eminent place in the management of bipolar disorders.

Acute mania

An extensive body of both comparative and placebo-controlled data supports the efficacy of lithium in acute mania. In four placebo-controlled studies, the overall response (remission or 50 per cent decrease in symptoms, Young's Mania Scale) rate to lithium was 78 per cent (Goodwin and Jamison 1990). Comparisons of lithium with antipsychotics (the mainstay of treatment for an acute manic episode before lithium) showed an average 74 per cent response to lithium (Johnson, Gershon and Hekimian 1968; Shopsin et al. 1975). However, in cases where rapid control of over-activity is required, the addition of antipsychotics to lithium therapy has been found useful because their sedative effects compensate for the delayed onset of action of lithium.

Patients with pure mania are those most likely to show a good response to lithium, in the order of 80 per cent, but as with any condition, there is a group of patients who do not respond to conventional treatment. Predictors of poor response to lithium include rapid or continuous cycling, mixed states or dysphoric mania, substance abuse, personality disturbance and three or more prior episodes (Prien and Potter 1990). It was only recently realised that some anticonvulsants, carbamazepine and valproate, overlapped with lithium in their ability to treat certain aspects of the spectrum of bipolar disorders, and that these drugs were also effective in some patients unresponsive to lithium.

The idea that carbamazepine could be of value in bipolar disorder originated from a number of sources, including a theory based on preclinical observations that drugs which inhibit kindling in models of epilepsy should be effective in bipolar disorder (Post *et al.* 1987), and from observations of improvements in mood in epileptic patients (Dalby 1971; Dalby 1975).

Carbamazepine possesses a broad spectrum of effects, any number of which could be related to its potential for efficacy in bipolar disorders. Therefore, carbamazepine's ability to increase acetylcholine in the striatum (Consolo, Bianchi and Ladinsky 1976); decrease dopamine turnover (Maitre, Baltzer and Mondadori 1984; Post, Jimerson and Bunney 1980); decrease release of noradrenaline (Purdy, Julien and Fairhurst 1977); decrease cerebrospinal fluid (CSF) noradrenaline in mania (Post *et al.* 1985); decrease the activity of adenylate and guanylate cyclase (Bernasconi 1982); decrease gamma-aminobutyric acid (GABA) turnover (Bernasconi and Martin 1979); or its effects on potassium channel conductance via influence on the D3 receptor (Schwartz, Solokoff and Giros 1991), could all be relevant to its anti-manic effects.

A pooled analysis of six well-conducted, controlled clinical trials in acute mania showed carbamazepine to have comparable efficacy with lithium and antipsychotics (50 per cent, compared with 56 per cent and 61 per cent, respectively) (Ballenger and Post 1978; Grossi, Sacchetti and Vita 1984; Lerer *et al.* 1987; Okuma *et al.* 1979; Post, Ballenger and Uhde 1984; Small *et al.* 1991). The delay in onset of action of 7 to 14 days was similar to that seen with lithium. There is also evidence suggesting that oxcarbazepine, an analogue of carbamazepine, may be effective in acute mania. Early studies have shown superior efficacy compared with placebo, and comparable efficacy to lithium and haloperidol (Emrich 1990; Muller and Stoll 1984). Oxcarbazepine, although structurally similar to carbamazepine, has a more advantageous kinetic and pharmacological profile. It does not induce hepatic oxidative enzymes, nor is it metabolised to an epoxide metabolite with sedating effects (Houtkooper, Lammertsma and Meyer 1987; Kramer, Theison and Stoll 1985).

In the last three decades, there has been an increasing interest in the potential use of valproate in bipolar disorders, particularly for patients who show a poor response to lithium or carbamazepine due to poor efficacy or tolerability. Controlled studies in acute mania have shown valproate to be superior to placebo and comparable with lithium (Bowden *et al.* 1994; Brennan, Sandyk and Borsook 1984; Emrich, Dose and von Zerssen 1985; Freeman *et al.* 1992; Pope *et al.* 1991), with response occurring within 7–14 days of reaching a serum valproate level equal to or greater than 50μg/mL. Improvement in manic symptoms has been seen within three days of initiating treatment with valproate when loading doses of 20 mg/kg/day were used (Keck *et al.* 1993). Other uncontrolled data suggest that certain patients, who are resistant to the anti-manic effects of a single mood stabiliser, may benefit from the combination of valproate with lithium, valproate with carbamazepine or valproate with the new atypical antipsychotics, including clozapine (Keck, McElroy and Nemeroff 1992; Ketter, Pazzaglia and Post 1992; McElroy *et al.* 1991).

The value of the benzodiazepines, clonazepam and lorazepam in acute mania has also been studied alone and in combination with lithium. Chouinard (1987) reported that clonazepam had some advantages over lithium in the treatment of acute mania in a double-blind, cross-over study. Other workers have reported that benzodiazepines may be beneficial in difficult cases; for example, rapid cycling or patients with refractory affective symptoms (Aronson, Shukla and Hirschowitz 1989; Mander 1988). The availability of an intramuscular preparation of lorazepam (in contrast to other benzodiazepines) has proved to be of value in the management of agitated patients (Lenox *et al.* 1992). However, the majority of studies of benzodiazepines in acute mania have been difficult to interpret because of the small sample sizes, short duration of treatment and use of concomitant medications. The place of this class of drugs in the management of bipolar disorder remains to be determined in well-controlled clinical trials without the use of concurrent antipsychotic medication.

Diagnostic and Statistics Manual IV describes the essential features of Bipolar I Disorder as the occurrence of one or more manic episodes or mixed episodes, where the criteria for both manic and major depressive episode are met for at least one week. Often, individuals have also had one or more major depressive episodes. Episodes of substance-induced mood disorder (due to direct effects of medication, a drug of abuse or toxin exposure), or of mood disorder due to a general medical condition, do not count towards a diagnosis of Bipolar I Disorder.

For Bipolar II Disorder the clinical course is characterised by one or more depressive episodes, together with at least one hypomanic episode. Hypomanic episodes should not be confused with the several days of euthymia that may follow the remission of a major depressive episode.

The management of Bipolar II disorder or hypomania is essentially similar to that of Bipolar I except that in hypomania the symptoms are less pronounced. Therefore, patients are more likely to respond to mood stabilisers alone and are less likely to require additional antipsychotics or benzodiazepines (Figures 8.1 and 8.2). Evidence to date for the treatment of acute mania suggests that, although a significant number of patients may respond to lithium alone, patients with more severe mania, significant depression or dysphoria, a recent history of rapid cycling, a negative family history of mood disorder or EEG abnormalities are more likely to respond to anticonvulsants or antipsychotics either as adjunctive or monotherapy (McElroy *et al.* 1989; Calabrese and Delucchi 1990). Where other medical conditions or pregnancy complicate the picture, ECT should be considered the treatment of choice.

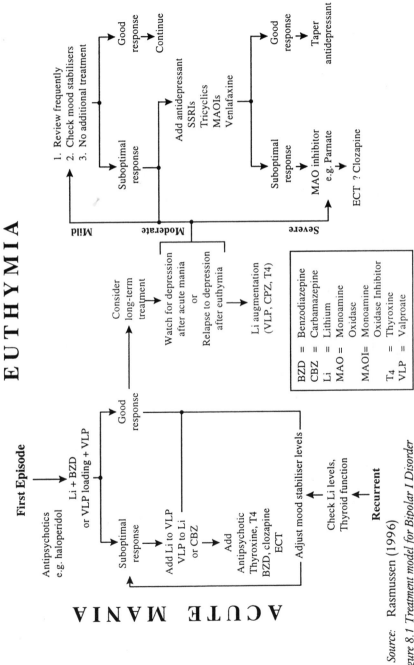

Source: Rasmussen (1996)

Figure 8.1 Treatment model for Bipolar I Disorder

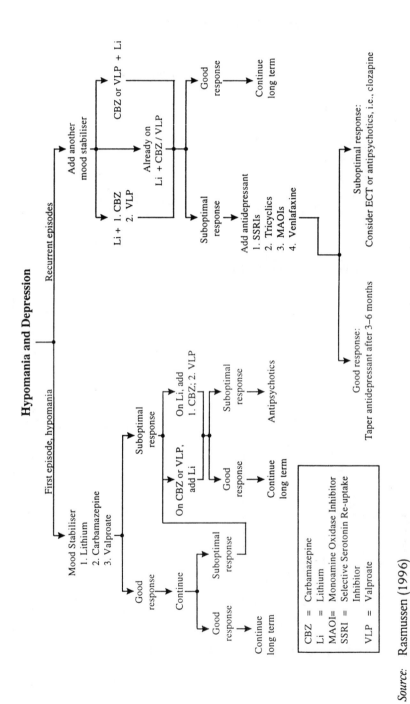

Source: Rasmussen (1996)

Figure 8.2 Treatment model for Bipolar II Disorder

Prophylaxis

The superiority of lithium over placebo in the prevention of recurrent mood disorders has been confirmed in ten, large, double-blind studies conducted between 1970 and 1978, in which a total of 514 bipolar patients were treated (Goodnick *et al.* 1989). The average relapse rate in these studies was 34 per cent for lithium-treated patients and 81 per cent for those who received placebo. When all patient data were reviewed, there was also evidence to show that lithium gave better protection from recurrent mania than from depression in bipolar disorder.

There is a high risk of recurrence in bipolar disorder if prophylactic lithium therapy is discontinued. This was very adequately illustrated by a meta-analysis of 14 studies involving a total of 257 patients with Bipolar I disorder (Suppes *et al.* 1991) which showed that the monthly risk of a recurrent bipolar episode following cessation of lithium was 28 times higher than when taking the medication. More than 50 per cent of patients who stopped lithium relapsed within six months and there was a highly significant decrease in mean cycle length following discontinuation of lithium. If a decision is taken to discontinue lithium prophylaxis, the risk of recurrence is diminished if a slow tapering of therapy is used (Faedda *et al.* 1993).

However, in a number of outcome studies in bipolar disorder where patients have been maintained on lithium, results have shown relapse rates in excess of 20 per cent despite adequate blood levels (Mander 1988; Miklowitz *et al.* 1986; O'Connell *et al.* 1985; Prien *et al.* 1984).

Studies of carbamazepine in the prophylaxis of bipolar disorder, although small and suffering from a lack of placebo-control, suggest carbamazepine may be effective in reducing the frequency and severity of episodes in some patients during a one year follow-up (Okuma *et al.* 1981; Prien and Gelenberg 1989). Interestingly, the majority of relapses in the carbamazepine group occurred in the first month of treatment, possibly as a result of lithium discontinuation (Post *et al.* 1992). In practice, carbamazepine is often combined with lithium. However, there have been no controlled trials of the combination with lithium, versus carbamazepine alone either in acute mania or in prophylaxis. The efficacy of sodium valproate in the prevention of recurrence of bipolar disorder has yet to be determined and the results of ongoing placebo-controlled studies are awaited with interest.

The combination of sodium valproate and carbamazepine is not recommended because of the potential for complex metabolic interactions. However, this combination has been reported in open treatment to be useful in the small percentage of patients with recurrent bipolar disorder who are resistant to all other therapies. Another treatment strategy which has been used in patients who are non-compliant, and/or resistant or intolerant of traditional drugs is depot neuroleptics. Naylor and Scott (1980), Ahlfors *et al.* (1981) and, more recently, Littlejohn, Leslie and Cookson (1994) have reported benefit in prophylaxis, and the control of mania and depressive episodes, when depot flupenthixol or fluphenazine is used alone or in combination with mood stabilisers or antidepressants.

Acute depression

The management of acute mania and prophylaxis has received most attention, and there are few data about the effectiveness of lithium and anticonvulsants either alone or in combination with other antidepressants, in the management of depression associated with bipolar disorder. Often lithium alone is not effective for acutely depressed bipolar patients, and evidence to date has suggested that both lithium and carbamazepine may be less effective in acute depression than in acute mania (Post et al. 1986). There are currently no data available for the efficacy of valproate in acute depression, and no one antidepressant or group of antidepressants has been shown to have greater effect than the others. The management of depressive symptomatology for both Bipolar I and II Disorder is very similar (Figures 8.1 and 8.2).

In open studies and/or case reports, the monoamine oxidase inhibitors, phenelzine and tranylcypramine; the reversible inhibitor of monoamine oxidase A, moclobemide; the selective serotonin re-uptake inhibitors, fluoxetine, paroxetine and sertraline; and the tricyclic antidepressants such as imipramine, as well as buproprion (only available in the USA) and trazodone have improved the depressive symptoms associated with bipolar disorder (Quitkin et al. 1981; Himmeloch et al. 1972; Baumhackl et al. 1989; Cohn et al. 1989; Zornberg et al. 1993; Prien et al. 1984). In one recent double-blind study tranylcypramine was associated with significantly better response than imipramine (Himmelhoch et al. 1991). All these drugs have been associated with mania or hypomania to a greater or lesser extent although the newer antidepressants, such as the selective serotonin re-uptake inhibitors, are significantly safer in this respect than the tricyclic antidepressants.

Where patients require a rapid response, where there are issues relating to tolerability of medications or where there are complicating features such as pregnancy, then, as in mania, ECT is the treatment of choice in the depressive phase of bipolar disorder. There are no known contraindications to ECT, it is safe when administered using modern methods, and adverse reactions related to the combination of ECT and lithium are rare. Other therapeutic approaches have included light therapy, which has been found to be helpful for some patients who have a seasonal pattern of depressive symptoms.

Rapid cycling and refractory bipolar disorder

There is preliminary evidence to suggest that hypothyroidism may lead to rapid cycling (Goodwin and Jamison 1990). An interesting association has also been described between long-term therapy and decreased thyroid function (Kramlinger and Post 1990). A study by Cho, Bone and Dunner (1979) found lithium-induced hypothyroidism in 31 per cent of rapid-cycling patients compared with 2 per cent in non-rapid-cycling bipolar patients. There is also preliminary evidence to suggest that hypothyroidism may lead to rapid cycling (Goodwin and Jamison 1990). Symptoms of mania and depression have improved when levothyroxine has been added to the treatment regimens of rapid-cycling patients who were unresponsive to treatment (Bauer and Whybrow 1990; Kusalic 1992). In some patients, the investigators noted that improvement in bipolar symptoms was not clearly related to thyroid status, that is, deficits may exist in the central nervous system when peripheral parameters are normal. As there are no double-blind studies of thyroid hormones in bipolar patients, it is difficult to draw any definite conclusions (Prudic, Sackeim and Devanand 1990; Bauer and Whybrow 1990; Beitman and Dunner 1982; McElroy et al. 1991).

Patients with refractory bipolar affective disorder have received far less attention in the clinical research environment, whether for acute or prophylactic treatment. A number of treatments, including ECT, thyroid augmentation, L-tryptophan and clozapine, have been tried with variable responses.

Seven patients with bipolar disorder and a well-documented history of treatment resistance to standard therapies (either alone or in combination), received the new antipsychotic clozapine for their manic episodes in doses ranging from 250 to 900 mg/day. All patients showed an improvement in symptoms, some within the first few weeks of treatment, which was maintained during a 3–5 year follow-up (Suppes et al. 1992). In a number of cases the concomitant lithium, anticonvulsant and/or antidepressant therapy was withdrawn slowly without precipitating a relapse. Considering the duration and severity of illness of this population, these results are quite remarkable, and indicate that clozapine deserves further study in this condition.

It is difficult to draw definitive conclusions from the studies that have been undertaken with these agents because of their methodological limitations, either of size, lack of control or duration. Nevertheless, it is important that even a few bipolar patients with a malignant history of rapid cycling or refractory depression have apparently shown improvement of symptoms which were resistant to traditional therapies.

Issues with currently available treatments

Significant numbers of patients find that drugs such as lithium or the anticonvulsants are too toxic or intolerable to continue treatment.

The side effects of lithium include tremor, weight gain, polyuria, polydipsia, sedation, poor concentration, gastrointestinal upset, hair loss, acne and oedema. There is often great concern about the risk of renal toxicity during long-term treatment with lithium. Although histological changes in the kidney can be found in up to 20 per cent of patients, they are seldom associated with changes in glomerular filtration or irreversible renal failure. Lithium-induced hypothyroidism, which occurs in up to a third of patients, is not a contraindication for continuing with the drug, but an indication for the need to add thyroid supplementation. The optimum serum level of lithium for efficacy is between 0.6 and 1 meq/L. The incidence of side effects and risk of toxicity is directly related to serum levels, and it may be difficult to maintain patients within the therapeutic range. Early signs of toxicity include tremor, nausea, increased confusion and blurred vision. The combination of lithium and haloperidol at high doses has been reported to cause long-term neurological damage.

One of the major issues with carbamazepine is the potential for clinically important interactions. On the one hand, levels of antipsychotics, benzodiazepines, tricyclic antidepressants, anticonvulsants and oral contraceptives are decreased because of the ability of carbamazepine to induce the metabolism of other drugs metabolised by the liver. On the other hand, drugs such as the serotonin re-uptake inhibitors, calcium channel blockers verapamil and diltiazem, and erythromycin inhibit the metabolism of carbamazepine, resulting in increased levels of the anticonvulsant and greater risk of tolerability and problems of toxicity.

The most frequently reported side effects with carbamazepine include fatigue, ataxia, diplopia, blurred vision and nausea. Rash, mild leucopenia, mild thrombocytopenia and a slight increase in liver enzymes occur less frequently. Carbamazepine may cause a decrease in thyroxine levels and increase free cortisol, but these are usually of little significance. Rare, but serious and potentially fatal effects include agranulocytosis, aplastic anaemia, hepatic failure, exfoliative dermatitis and Stevens–Johnson syndrome. Carbamazepine may also be fatal in overdose.

Evidence from the literature indicates that valproate is generally well tolerated and that it has a more favourable profile than lithium, antipsychotics and other traditional anticonvulsants. Patients frequently complain of gastrointestinal effects, which are dose-related and usually of short duration. Other associated effects include transient hair loss, increased appetite and weight gain. A variable degree of raised liver enzymes may occur, but this is usually asymptomatic. Rarely, irreversible hepatic failure may occur, usually within six months of starting treatment. Other important side effects associated with valproate include teratogenicity, and coma and death when taken in overdose.

Therapy with additional antipsychotics is often associated with sedation, which is an advantage in acute mania but a problem for many patients during longer-term treatment. Other side effects which often lead to tolerability issues include weight gain, sexual dysfunction, extrapyramidal symptoms and the risk of tardive dyskinesia.

Although benzodiazepines are very useful in controlling the symptoms of mania one must be very wary of their potential to cause dysphoria or disinhibition, and be alert to the risk of dependency.

Because of the tolerability and toxicity issues related to current treatments, the consequent risk of non-compliance and resulting relapse, and the recognition of the morbidity and mortality associated with bipolar disorders, the search for alternative treatment strategies, either as mono- or adjunct therapy, has become a priority.

New treatment possibilities

The ability of lithium and the anticonvulsants to treat bipolar disorders has led to a rethinking of the potential mechanisms of action of these compounds in affective disorders. Despite extensive work, the mechanism of action of lithium remains unclear. It has often been asked in what way such a relatively simple ion can affect neurotransmitter systems to produce a therapeutic benefit in both acute mania and prophylaxis. It is postulated that lithium could modulate over-active processes, whether they be inhibitory or excitatory. If each phase of the bipolar disorder is viewed as an over-activity, then lithium could stabilise these effects and, therefore, influence both manic and depressive symptomatology. Perhaps lithium's ability to influence adenylate cyclase and phosphoinositol turnover via secondary messenger systems is significant in dampening down over-active systems involved in bipolar disorder.

The phosphoinositol pathway is activated by a number of neurotransmitters, including acetylcholine, serotonin, histamine, glutamate, quisqualate, kainate and various neuropeptides (for example, substance P and thryrotrophin releasing hormone). This could also provide a mechanism for lithium's beneficial effects in both mania and depression, and a route by which a variety of drugs such as carbamazepine, valproate or lithium could have common effects in apparently opposite mood phases.

There is evidence from preclinical studies that valproate and carbamazepine exhibit cross-tolerance (Weiss et al. 1991). The fact that both drugs share anti-manic and prophylactic efficacy in bipolar disorder suggests that they may share some common mechanism of action that has not yet been recognised. However, differential response to one anticonvulsant has been observed, suggesting that response to one drug of this class does not necessarily predict a clinical response to the other. Cross-tolerance has been observed between valproate and benzodiazepines, but not between benzodiazepines and barbiturates (Gent *et al.* 1986). All these drugs are thought to influence the GABA complex. How this relates to their individual effects is unknown at present, but the cross-tolerance relationships may provide insights into their mechanisms of action.

Another interesting possibility for the mechanism of action of psychotropic drugs is the ability of G-proteins to couple receptors to second messenger and ion channels (Belmaker, Avissar and Scheiber 1991; Berridge 1989; Mander 1988; Taylor 1990; Wood and Goodwin 1987). Both lithium and carbamazepine have been shown to interfere with G-protein activity. In addition to these effects, lithium also has effects on calcium flux (Meltzer 1986; Meltzer *et al.* 1988; Okuma *et al.* 1981) and guanylate cyclase (Kanba *et al.* 1986), and competes with magnesium ions which are essential for binding guanosine triphosphate (GTP) to G-proteins. It has been reported recently that both lithium and carbamazepine inhibit cyclic guanylate monophosphate (cGMP) accumulation in lymphocytes, possibly by mechanisms involving the nitric oxide second-messenger system, which is stimulated by N-methyl-d-aspartate (NMDA) receptors (Schubert, Stoll and Muller 1991).

The rationale for the use of calcium antagonists in the treatment of mania is based on observation of increased calcium concentration in the CSF of bipolar patients during the depressed phase and decreased concentrations during the manic phase. Correction of these abnormalities has paralleled clinical improvement (Carman and Wyatt 1979; Carman *et al.* 1979). Verapamil at doses of 480 mg/day has been reported to be effective, compared with placebo, in the treatment of acute mania in a double-blind cross-over study (Dubovsky, Franks and Allen 1986). The patients included were all lithium-responsive, and other data suggest verapamil is less effective in patients who are unresponsive to lithium (Solomon and Williamson 1986). A preliminary report, from a double-blind, placebo-controlled trial of the calcium channel antagonist, nimodipine in patients with ultra-rapid-cycling affective disorder, found that five out of nine patients who completed the study had a good response (Pazzaglia *et al.* 1993). Nimodipine was associated with a significant reduction in the magnitude of mood fluctuations compared with the baseline placebo condition.

In addition to their calcium channel blocking potential, both verapamil and nimodipine possess a spectrum of pharmacological effects. Verapamil has effects on sodium, antagonises dopamine and acts as an anticonvulsant, while nimodipine has a unique profile of behavioural and anticonvulsant properties. It is hypothesised that verapamil's potential for anti-manic effects is more likely to reside with these other pharmacological activities rather than its effects on calcium.

The future

It will be interesting to see whether any of the group of new anticonvulsant drugs, which include felbamate, gabapentin and lamotrigine, have utility in management of the spectrum of bipolar disorders – acute mania, bipolar affective disorder and prophylaxis in refractory patients. Felbamate has been postulated to influence the NMDA receptor by antagonism at the glycine binding site (Young and Fagg 1990). Lamotrigine acts mainly to inhibit excitatory amino-acid (glutamate release), and stabilises neuronal membranes via blockade of voltage-operated sodium channels (Brodie 1992). Gabapentin, a GABA analogue, influences GABA release (Goa and Sorkin 1993). It appears that these drugs exert their effects when there is over-activity in a particular system, an interesting parallel with the actions of lithium referred to earlier.

The data on clozapine suggest that other new putative antipsychotics which are nearing the market – olanzapine, sertindole, seroquel, ziprasidone – are as yet untried and untested in bipolar disorder, but may yet prove to be of value in the management of this important condition. The potential for their efficacy against the primary negative symptoms of schizophrenia offers some parallel with the depressive phase of bipolar disorder.

Meanwhile, bipolar disorder continues to present a challenge to the caring professions. There are many avenues yet to be explored. One has to be alert to clinical observations, to the growing body of evidence of the pathophysiology of this disorder from technological and molecular investigations, and to the advances in our understanding of the possible mechanisms of action of drugs used in the management of this condition. It may be hoped that these endeavours will help to unravel the mysteries of this fascinating and important illness – bipolar disorder – and to assist in the discovery of more effective and more tolerable treatments.

References

Ahlfors, U.G. *et al.* (1981) 'Flupenthixol decanoate in recurrent manic depressive illness: a comparison with lithium.' *Acta Psychiatrica Scandinavica 64*, 226–237.

Altshuler, L.L. (1993) 'Bipolar disorder: are repeated episodes associated with neuroanatomic and cognitive changes?' *Biological Psychiatry 33*, 563–565.

Aronson, T.A., Shukla, S. and Hirschowitz, J (1989) 'Clonazepam treatment of five lithium-refractory patients with bipolar disorder'. *American Journal of Psychiatry 146*, 77–80.

Ballenger, J.C. and Post, R.M. (1978) 'Therapeutic effects of carbamazepine in affective illness: a preliminary report.' *Communications in Psychopharmacology 2*, 159–175.

Bauer, M.S. and Whybrow, P.C. (1990) 'Rapid cycling bipolar affective disorder: II treatment of refractory rapid cycling with high dose levothyroxine: a preliminary study.' *Archives of General Psychiatry 47*, 435–440.

Baumhackl, U. *et al.* (1989) 'Efficacy and tolerablity of moclobemide compared with imipramine in depressive disorder (DSM-III): an Austrian double-blind multi-centre study.' *British Journal of Psychiatry 155* (Suppl 6), 78–83.

Beitman, B.D. and Dunner, D.L. (1982) 'L-tryptophan in the maintenance treatment of bipolar II manic-depressive illness.' *American Journal of Psychiatry 139,* 1498–1499.

Belmaker, R.H., Avissar, S., Scheiber, G. (1991) 'Effect of lithium on human neurotransmitter receptor systems and G proteins.' In N.J. Birch (ed) *Lithium and the Cell: Pharmacology and Biochemistry.* London: Academic Press.

Bernasconi, R. (1982) 'The GABA hypothesis of affective illness: influence of clinically affective anti-manic drugs on GABA turnover.' In *Basic Mechanisms in the Action of Lithium – Proceedings of a Symposium Held at Schloss Ringberg, Bavaria, October 4–6, 1981.* Amsterdam: Elsevier Science Publishers.

Bernasconi, R. and Martin, P. (1979) 'Effects of anti-epileptic drugs on GABA turnover rate.' *Archives of Pharmacology 307,* R63-abstract, 251.

Berridge, M.J. (1989) 'Inositol triphosphate, calcium, lithium and cell signalling.' *Journal of the American Medical Association 262,* 1834–1841.

Bowden, C.L. *et al.* for the Depakote Mania Study Group (1994) 'Efficacy of divalproex vs lithium and placebo in the treatment of mania.' *Journal of the American Medical Association 271,* 918–924.

Brennan, M.J.W., Sandyk, R. and Borsook, D. (1984) 'Use of sodium valproate in the management of affective disorders: basic and clinical aspects.' In E.M. Emrich, T. Okuma and A.A. Muller (eds) *Anticonvulsants in Affective Disorders.* Amsterdam: Excerpta Medica.

Brodie, M.J. (1992) 'Drug profiles: lamotrigine.' *Lancet 339,* 1397–1400.

Cade, J.F.J. (1949) 'Lithium salts in psychiatric therapy and prophylaxis.' *Medical Journal of Australia. 36,* 349–352.

Calabrese, J.R. and Delucci, G.A. (1990) 'Spectrum of efficacy of valproate in 55 rapid cycling manic depressives.' *American Journal of Psychiatry 147,* 431–434.

Carman, J.S. and Wyatt, R.J. (1979) 'Calcium: bivalent ion in the bivalent psychoses.' *Biological Psychiatry 14,* 295–336.

Carman, J.S. *et al.* (1979) 'Increased serum calcium and phosphorous with the "switch" into manic or excited states.' *British Journal of Psychiatry 135,* 55–61.

Cho, J.T., Bone, S. and Dunner, D.L. (1979) 'The effect of lithium treatment on thyroid function in patients with primary affective disorder.' *Americal Journal of Psychiatry 136,* 115–116.

Chouinard, G. (1987) 'Clonazepam in acute and maintenance treatment of bipolar affective disorder.' *Journal of Clinical Psychiatry 48,* (10, suppl), 29–36.

Cohn, J.B. *et al.* (1989) 'A comparison of fluoxetine, imipramine and placebo in patients with bipolar depressive disorder.' *International Clinical Psychopharmacology 4,* 313–322.

Consolo, S., Bianchi, S. and Ladinsky, H. (1976) 'Effect of carbamazepine on cholinergic parameters in rat brain areas.' *Neuropharmacology 15,* 653–657.

Dalby, M.A. (1971) 'Antiepileptic and psychotropic effect of carbamazepine (Tegretol) in the treatment of psychomotor epilepsy.' *Epilepsia 12,* 325–334.

Dalby, M.A. (1975) 'Behavioural effects of carbamazepine in Complex Partial Seizures and their treatment.' *Advances in Neurology 11,* 331–343.

Dubovsky, S.L., Franks, R.D. and Allen, S. (1986) 'Calcium antagonist in mania: a double-blind study of verapamil.' *Psychiatry Research 18,* 309–320.

Dunner, D.L. and Fieve, R.R. (1974) 'Clinical factors in lithium carbonate prophylaxis failure.' *Archives of General Psychiatry 30*, 229–233.

Emrich, H.M. (1990) 'Studies with oxcarbazepine (Trileptal) in acute mania.' *International Clinical Psychopharmacology 5* (suppl), 83–88.

Emrich, H.M., Dose, M., and von Zerssen, D. (1985) 'The use of sodium valproate, carbamazepine and oxcarbazepine in patients with affective disorders.' *Journal of Affective Disorders 8*, 243–250.

Faedda, G.L. *et al.* (1993) 'Outcome after rapid vs gradual discontinuation of lithium treatment in bipolar disorders.' *Archives of General Psychiatry 50*, 448–455.

Freeman, T.W. *et al.* (1992) 'A double-blind comparison of valproate and lithium in the treatment of acute mania.' *American Journal of Psychiatry 149*, 108–111.

Gelenberg, A.J. *et al.* (1989) 'Comparison of standard and low serum levels of lithium for maintenance treatment of bipolar disorder.' *New England Journal of Medicine 321*, 1489–1493.

Gent, J.P. *et al.* (1986) 'Benzodiazepine cross-tolerance in mice extends to sodium valproate.' *European Journal of Pharmacology 128*, 9–15.

Gershon, E.S. *et al.* (1987) 'Genetics of affective illness.' In H.L. Meltzer (ed) *Psychopharmacology: The Third Generation of Progress.* New York: Raven Press.

Goa, K.L. and Sorkin, E.M. (1993) 'Gabapentin: a review of its pharmacological properties and clinical potential in epilepsy.' *Drugs 46, part 3*, 409–427.

Goodnick, P.J. *et al.* (1989) 'Lithium levels and inter-episode symptoms in affective disorder.' *Acta Psychiatrica Scandinavica 75*, 601–603.

Goodwin, F.K. and Jamison, K.R. (1990) *Manic-Depressive Illness.* New York: Oxford University Press.

Grossi, E., Sacchetti, E. and Vita, A. (1984) 'Carbamazepine vs. chlorpromazine in mania: a double-blind trial.' In E.M. Emrich, T. Okuma and A.A. Muller (eds) *Anticonvulsants in Affective Disorders.* Amsterdam: Excerpta Medica.

Himmeloch, J.M. *et al.* (1972) 'Treatment of previously intractable depressions with tranylcypramine and lithium.' *Journal of Nervous Mental Disorders 155*, 215–220.

Himmeloch, J.M. *et al.* (1991) 'Tranylcypromine versus imipramine in anergic bipolar depression.' *American Journal of Psychiatry 148*, 910–916.

Houtkooper, M.A., Lammertsma, A. and Meyer, J.W.A. (1987) 'Oxcarbazepine: a possible alternative to carbamazepine.' *Epilepsia 25*, 693–695.

Johnson, G., Gershon, S. and Hekimian, L.J. (1968) 'Controlled evaluation of lithium and chlorpromazine in the treatment of manic states: an interim report.' *Comprehensive Psychiatry 9*, 563–573.

Kanba, S. *et al.* (1986) 'Lithium ions have a potent and selective inhibitory effect on cyclic GMP formation stimulated by neurotensin, angiotensin II and bradykinin.' *European Journal of Pharmacology 126*, 111–116.

Keck, P.E., McElroy, S.L. and Nemeroff, C.B. (1992) 'Anticonvulsants in the treatment of bipolar disorder.' *Journal of Neuropsychiatry, Clinical Neuroscience 4*, 395–405.

Keck, P.E. *et al.* (1993) 'Valproate oral loading in the treatment of acute mania.' *Journal of Clinical Psychiatry 54*, 305–308.

Ketter, T.A., Pazzaglia, P.J. and Post, R.M. (1992) 'Synergy of carbamazepine and valproic acid in affective illness: case report and review of literature.' *Journal of Clinical Psychopharmacology 12*, 276–281.

Kraepelin, E. (1921) *Manic-Depressive Insanity and Paranoia.* Edinburgh: E&S Livingstone.

Kramer, G., Theison, M. and Stoll, K.D. (1985) 'Oxcarbazepine versus carbamazepine bie gesunden Probanden.' In K.R. Reinbeck (ed) *Studien zur Kinetik, zu Metabolismus und Vertaglick-keit. Epilepsie 84.* Enhorn.

Kramlinger, K.G. and Post, R.M. (1990) 'Addition of lithium carbonate to carbamazepine: hematological and thyroid effects.' *American Journal of Psychiatry 147,* 615–620.

Kusalic, M. (1992) 'Grade II and Grade III hypothyroidism in rapid cycling bipolar patients.' *Biological Psychiatry 25,* 177–181.

Lenox, R.H. and Watson, D.G. (1994) 'Lithium and the brain: a psychopharmacological strategy to a molecular basis for manic depressive illness.' *Clinical Chemistry 40,* 2, 309–314.

Lerer, B. *et al.* (1987) 'Carbamazepine versus lithium in mania: a double-blind study.' *Journal of Clinical Psychiatry 48,* 89–93.

Littlejohn, F., Leslie, F. and Cookson, J. (1994) 'Depot antipsychotics in the prophylaxis of bipolar affective disorder.' *British Journal of Psychiatry 165,* 820–829.

Maitre, L., Baltzer, V. and Mondadori, C. (1984) 'Psychopharmacological and behavioural effects of anti-epileptic drugs in animals.' In H.M. Emrich, T. Okuma and A.A. Muller (eds) *Anticonvulsants in Affective Disorders.* Amsterdam: Elsevier Science Publishers.

Mander, A.J. (1988) 'Use of lithium and early relapse in manic-depressive illness.' *Acta Psychiatrica Scandinavica 78,* 198–200.

McElroy, S.L. and Keck, P.E. (1993) 'Treatment guidelines for valproate in bipolar and schizoaffective disorders.' *Canadian Journal of Psychiatry 38* (3 supple 2), 562–566.

McElroy, S.L. *et al.* (1989) 'Valproate in psyiatric disorders: literature review and clinical guidelines.' *Journal of Clinical Psychiatry 50* (suppl) 23–29.

McElroy, S.L. *et al.* (1991) 'Clozapine in the treatment of psychotic mood disorders, schizoaffective disorders and schizophrenia.' *Journal of Clinical Psychiatry 52,* 411–414.

Meltzer, H.L. (1986) 'Lithium mechanisms in bipolar illness and altered intracellular calcium functions.' *Biological Psychiatry 21,* 492–510.

Meltzer, H.L. *et al.* (1988) 'Calmodulin-activated calcium ATPase in bipolar illness.' *Neuropsychobiology 20,* 167–173.

Miklowitz, D.J. *et al.* (1986) 'Expressed emotion, affective style, lithium compliance and relapse in recent onset mania.' *Psychopharmacology Bulletin 22,* 628–632.

Muller, A.A. and Stoll, K.D. (1984) 'Carbamazepine and oxcarbazepine in the treatment of manic syndromes: studies in Germany.' In H.M. Emrich, T. Okuma and A.A. Muller (eds) *Anticonvulsants in Affective Disorders.* Amsterdam: Exerpta Medica.

Naylor, G. and Scott, C. (1980) 'Depot injections for affective disorders.' *British Journal of Psychiatry 136,* 105.

Nurnberger, J.L. and Gershon, E. (1992) 'Genetics.' In E.S. Paykel (ed) *Handbook of Affective Disorders, 2nd edition.* New York: Churchill Livingstone.

O'Connell, R.A. *et al.* (1985) 'Social support and long-term lithium outcome.' *British Journal of Psychiatry 147,* 272–275.

Okuma, T. *et al.* (1979) 'Comparison of the antimanic efficacy of carbamazepine and chlorpromazine.' *Psychopharmacology 66,* 211–217.

Okuma, T. *et al.* (1981) 'A preliminary double-blind study of the efficacy of carbamazepine in the prophylaxis of manic-depressive illness.' *Psychopharmacolgia (Berl) 73,* 95–96.

Pazzaglia, P.J. *et al.* (1993) 'Preliminary controlled trial of nimodipine in ultra-rapid cycling affective dysregulation.' *Psychiatry Research, 49*, 3, 257–272.

Pope, H.G. Jr *et al.* (1991) 'Valproate in the treatment of acute mania: a placebo controlled study.' *Archives of General Psychiatry 48*, 62–68.

Post, R.M. (1993) 'Issues in the long-term management of bipolar affective illness.' *Psychiatr Ann. 23*, 86–93.

Post, R.M., Ballenger, J.C. and Uhde, T.W. (1984) 'Efficacy of carbamazepine in manic-depressive illness: implications for underlying mechanisms.' In R.M. Post and J.C. Ballenger (eds) *Neurobiology of Mood Disorders.* Baltimore: Williams and Wilkins.

Post, R.M. *et al.* (1980) 'Dopamine and mania: behavioural and biochemical effects of the dopamine receptor blocker pimozide.' *Psychopharmacology 67*, 297–305.

Post, R.M. *et al.* (1992) 'Lithium-discontinuation-induced refractoriness: preliminary observations.' *American Journal of Psychiatry 149*, 1727–1729.

Post, R.M. *et al.* (1985) 'Effects of carbamazepine on noradrenergic mechanisms in affectively ill patients.' *Psychopharmacology 87*, 59–63.

Post, R.M. *et al.* (1986) 'Antidepressant effects of carbamazepine.' *American Journal of Psychiatry 143*, 29–34.

Post, R.M., Uhde, T.W., Roy-Byrne, P.P. and Joffe, R.T. (1987) 'Correlates of antimanic response to carbamazepine.' *Psychiatry Research 21*, 71–83.

Prien, R.F. and Gelenberg, A.J. (1989) 'Alternatives to lithium for preventive treatment of bipolar disorder.' *American Journal of Psychiatry 146*, 840–848.

Prien, R.F. and Potter, W.Z. (1990) 'NIMH workshop report on treatment of bipolar disorder.' *Psychopharmacology Bulletin 26*, 409–427.

Prien, R.F. *et al.* (1984) 'Drug therapy in the prevention of recurrences in unipolar and bipolar affective disorders: report of the NIMH Collaborative Study Group comparing lithium carbonate, imipramine, and a lithium carbonate-imipramine combination.' *Archives of General Psychiatry 45*, 1096–1104.

Prudic, J., Sackeim, H. and Devanand, D.P. (1990) 'Medication resistance and clinical response to electroconvulsive therapy.' *Psychiatry Research 31*, 287–296.

Purdy, R.E., Julien, R.M. and Fairhurst, A.S. (1977) 'Effect of carbamazepine on the in vitro uptake and release of norepinephrine in adrenergic nerves of rabbit aorta and whole brain synaptosomes.' *Epilepsia 18*, 252–257.

Quitkin, F.M. *et al.* (1981) 'Prophylactic lithium with and without imipramine for bipolar I patients: a double-blind study.' *Archive of General Psychiatry 38*, 902–907.

Schubert, T., Stoll, I. and Muller, W.E. (1991) 'Therapeutic concentrations of lithium and carbamazepine inhibit cGMP accumulation in human lymphocytes: a clinical model for a possible common mechanism of action?' *Psychopharmacology 104*, 45–50.

Schwartz, J.C., Solokoff, P. and Giros, B. (1991) 'The third dopamine receptor.' *Society for Biological Psychiatry 29*, 18.

Shopsin, B. *et al.* (1975) 'Rebound phenomena in manic patients following physostigmine: preliminary observations.' *Neuropsychobiology 1*, 180–187.

Small, J.G. *et al.* (1991) 'Carbamazepine compared with lithium in the treatment of mania.' *Archives of General Psychiatry 48*, 89–93.

Solomon, L. and Williamson, P. (1986) 'Verapamil in bipolar illness.' *Canadian Journal of Psychiatry 31*, 442–444.

Suppes, T. *et al.* (1991) 'Risk of recurrence following discontinuation of lithium treatment in bipolar disorder.' *Archives of General Psychiatry 48*, 12, 1082–1088,

Suppes, T. *et al.* (1992) 'Clozapine in the treatment of dysphoric mania.' *Biological Psychiatry 32*, 270–280.

Taylor, C.W. (1990) 'The role of G proteins in transmembrane signalling.' *Biochemical Journal 272*, 1–13.

Weiss, S.R.B. *et al.* (1991) 'Cross-tolerance between carbamazepine and valproate in an amygdala kindled seizure paradigm.' *Society of Neuroscience Abstracts 497*, 6, 1256.

Weissman, M.M. *et al.* (1982) 'The epidemiology of dysthymia in the community rates, comorbidity and treatment.' *140th Annual General Meeting of the American Psychiatric Association.* Chicago: American Psychiatric Association.

Weissman, M.M., Leaf, P.J., Tischler, G.L., Blazer, D.G., Karno, M., Bruce, M.L. and Florio, L.P. (1988) 'Affective disorders in five United States cities.' *Psychological Medicine 44*, 141–153.

Winokur, G., Clayton, P.J. and Reich, T. (1969) *Manic Depressive Illness.* St Louis: CV Mosby.

Wood, A.J. and Goodwin, G.M. (1987) 'A review of the biochemical and neuropharmacological actions of lithium.' *Psychological Medicine 17*, 579–600.

Young, A.B. and Fagg, G.E. (1990) 'Excitatory amino acid receptors in the brain: membrane binding and receptor autoradiographic approaches.' *Trends in Pharmacological Sciences 11*, 126–133.

Zornberg, C.L. and Pope, H.G., Jr. (1993) 'Treatment of depression in bipolar disorder: new directions for research.' *Journal of Clinical Psychopharmacy 13*, 397–408.

Further Reading

Aldendoff, J.B. and Lux, H.D. (1985) 'Lithium slows neuronal calcium regulation in the snail *Helix pomatia.*' *Neuroscience Letter 54*, 103–108.

Coxhead, N., Silverstone, T. and Cookson, J. (1992) 'Carbamazepine versus lithium in the prophylaxis of bipolar affective disorder.' *Acta Psychiatrica Scandinavica 85*, 114–118.

Fieve, R.R., Kumbaraci, T. and Dunner D.L. (1976) 'Lithium prophylaxis of depression in bipolar I, bipolar II, and unipolar patients.' *American Journal of Psychiatry 133*, 925–930.

Souza, F.G.M. *et al.* (1991) 'Risk of recurrence following discontinuation of lithium treatment in bipolar disorder.' *Archives of General Psychiatry 48*, 1082–1088.

CHAPTER 9

What Hospitals Can Do To Help

Khaver Bashir and Malcolm Weller

Introduction

Manic depressive psychosis is a relapsing condition and sufferers often benefit from hospitalisation. We discuss the various advantages below, while recognising that very many patients are successfully treated in community settings. By 'hospital' we refer to inpatient treatment. No attempt will be made to discuss day hospitals, which are valuable in mild conditions and during convalescence.

Mania is characterised by reckless behaviour, for example, financial profligacy or irresponsible sexual activity. This sometimes catastrophic behaviour is associated with a lack of insight so that patients see no reason to curb their excesses. During the depressive phase there may be a high suicidal risk or self-neglect, which might reach such a dangerous degree that the patient eschews food and drink. Depression has adverse effects on social and physical functions, of the same order as medical illness such as diabetes and heart disease (Wells *et al.* 1989). More than 60 per cent of depressive disorders are compounded with some anxiety symptoms and 20 per cent have a concurrent anxiety condition or suffer from panic attacks (Clayton *et al.* 1991; Lydiard 1991). When anxiety co-exists with depression then the depression is usually more severe and the combination is particularly disabling (Lydiard 1991). The combination is associated with a greater family history of both depression and alcoholism (Clayton *et al.* 1991), the latter constituting an additional hazard for sufferers in a community setting, with restraint impaired in mania and alcohol consumption often increasing in depression. The consequences of the illness are thus potentially disastrous for the patients, their families and sometimes the community at large. Although milder episodes can be managed at home, admission to hospital (sometimes compulsorily) is the most appropriate course of action when the illness is severe.

Assessment

As manic depressive psychosis may compromise physical and social functioning in addition to the more obvious effects on mental health, a comprehensive assessment should be carried out in every patient. The following elements would ideally be part of this assessment:

- confirmation of the diagnosis of manic depression

- judging the severity of the condition, particularly risk to self and others

- detecting any psychiatric co-morbidity

- evaluation of the social situation, including the determination of precipitants and maintaining factors associated with relapse, adverse social consequences resulting from the illness and the level of support available to the patient from family and others

- a full physical examination and appropriate investigations to determine any evidence of self-neglect or underlying organic pathology.

In practice such a detailed assessment is most readily conducted while the patient is in hospital. In many cases of moderate or severe illness the assessment can only be carried out once the patient has been admitted.

Psychiatric assessment

Manic depressive psychosis may be difficult to distinguish from schizophrenia, illicit drug use or unipolar depression, especially at first presentation. The history from the patient may be unreliable due to lack of insight, or unobtainable if the patient's symptoms are severe. In such difficult circumstances admission to hospital offers a number of advantages:

1. Emergency treatment may be administered in a controlled environment prior to establishing a diagnosis. Once the patient's condition improves a more accurate appraisal will be possible.

2. While the patient is receiving initial treatment a collateral history may be obtained from family members, friends and the patient's general practitioner. Vital information may emerge which helps to clarify the diagnosis, for example details of previous episodes and how they were treated. Manic patients can suppress their symptoms for a short period and often do so while being interviewed by a doctor. A more accurate picture of the severity of the illness is obtained from another informant.

3. During admission the patient will be closely monitored by members of the psychiatric team. Such repeated observations from skilled staff may be particularly helpful in cases of diagnostic difficulty. In addition, previously undetected psychiatric co-morbidity and related difficulties such as drug and alcohol problems may be revealed.

Forensic issues

During manic and depressive episodes patients may break the law and, indeed, they may only come to medical attention after first going through the criminal justice system. Occasionally serious offences are committed. In such cases it is of paramount importance to clarify the relationship between the patient's mental illness and any illegal activity, as well as trying to establish the risk of a future offence, particularly where this may result in harm to others. Such a forensic evaluation is easier to carry out as an inpatient, where the response to treatment can be closely scrutinised. Hospitalisation also allows the community at large to be protected while the assessment is being made. Contracts which have been entered during the illness phase may be invalid because of a defect in testamentary capacity and legal advice may be desirable.

Social assessment

There is a complex relationship between social factors and mental illness which is interactive. Stressful life events may precipitate both manic and depressive episodes. The balance between social support and stress is important in determining the individual's vulnerability to depression, and chronic life difficulties may aggravate the condition and delay recovery (Brown and Harris 1978). The consequences of repeated relapses of manic depression may include loss of employment, inability to care for children and other dependants, financial distress (or even ruin) and impaired personal relationships. In a study of admissions from Heathrow Airport all eight divorced women with affective disturbance had hypomania (Jauhar and Weller 1982). Evaluation of the social situation is therefore an integral part of caring for people with this illness. Of course, much of this information can be obtained in outpatient settings as part of routine good clinical practice. However, admission to hospital enables more detailed assessment and often results in a higher priority being given to social problems. This has particularly been the case since the implementation of the care programme approach, which requires a systematic appraisal of the patient's immediate and long-term social care needs prior to discharge from hospital. Additionally, as admission is a marker of the severity of the illness it may be easier for patients to access scarce resources such as social worker input.

Case vignette 1

A divorced solicitor was visiting his ex-wife, with whom he remained on cordial terms. She felt that he was entering into a manic phase of his illness and contacted his psychiatrist, who agreed with her view. Unfortunately, a social worker could not be persuaded to make an application for compulsory admission, as had occurred in the past, and specifically objected on the grounds that the patient was a solicitor and might later attempt legal redress for an unwarranted application. The application could not be made by his ex-wife, who no longer stood in any formal relationship with the patient. A train of catastrophes ensued. The solicitor raided his clients' accounts and used the money to finance a trip to Paris with a girlfriend. His illness developed into a mixed affective state and he attempted to jump off the Eiffel tower. He was apprehended by the police because of criminal misuse of clients' funds and was struck off the register of solicitors. He developed a depressive downswing, and did not vigorously protest his mental state at the time of the trial for alleged theft of clients' funds, being hesitant to do so because of the uncertainty of disposal if there was a successful plea of insanity. He went to prison.

Physical assessment

The manic depressive patient may suffer from poor physical health for a number of reasons. The severely depressed individual may abstain from food and drink, leading to dehydration, weight loss and nutritional deficiencies. If the patient has other medical conditions such as diabetes or asthma, failure to take prescribed medications may have serious consequences. Self-poisoning and deliberate self-harm may be life-threatening. The manic patient may suffer injuries during destructive behaviour or while being restrained. Unprotected intercourse may result in unwanted pregnancy or sexually transmitted diseases, including potentially life-threatening conditions such as HIV infection and Hepatitis B. In addition, drugs given to treat the patient such as lithium and carbamazepine may have a number of toxic effects and the concentration of lithium in the plasma will be raised in dehydration. A thorough physical examination plus appropriate investigations is therefore required, and this also provides an opportunity to exclude organic pathology presenting with a similar clinical picture, for example thyroid dysfunction or even frontal lobe pathology, causing social disinhibition. Such a full assessment of an insightless or severely disturbed patient is rarely possible in outpatient settings. However, it is routine practice in most units when the patient is admitted.

Management

Full-blown relapses of manic depressive psychosis are psychiatric emergencies, requiring urgent and intensive measures such as physical containment and sedation, close observation to prevent suicide attempts and a variety of treatments aimed at stabilising mood. Inpatient units offer continuous 24-hour-a-day cover, skilled staff and a structured environment, which together provide a well-resourced setting for delivering such emergency care. In the following section the acute management of severe depression and mania will be considered separately in view of the major differences between the two.

Mania

Manic patients may thoroughly enjoy the euphoric experience and consequently are reluctant to avail themselves of treatment. This makes even mild episodes difficult to treat in the community. Stopping lithium prophylaxis when it is most needed may add a pharmacological rebound to an already deteriorating situation, with risks of the disastrous sequelae mentioned earlier.

Admission to hospital has the immediate advantages of:

1. Removing the individual from a stressful environment which may have precipitated the episode.

2. Protecting the patient from the consequences of their potentially reckless behaviour.

3. Preventing harm to others which may result from the irritability and irrascability erupting in violence.

4. Mania is often succeeded by depression. The transition can be sharp and provides a further reason for hospital monitoring.

The patient frequently fails to see these benefits and so must be detained in hospital for the purpose of assessment and treatment by using the appropriate section of the Mental Health Act of 1983.

After admission the first priority is usually to calm over-activity and aggressive irritibility. This requires a combination of skilled nursing care and appropriate medication. The design of the ward may facilitate this process by providing an area sufficiently large to allow some freedom of movement but at the same time secure enough to prevent the patient from absconding. If the patient is highly aroused he or she may have to be secluded, that is kept alone in a locked area, (or even in a room) with minimal furnishing, reducing the environmental stimuli and the risk of self-harm. Such seclusion is governed by local practice but typically limits the period and demands frequent checks. Staff can help to settle the patient by forming a trusting supportive relationship (often building on bonds forged during previous admissions) and by diverting energies into constructive, non-aggressive tasks such as occupational therapy.

Drug therapy is required to settle the acutely disturbed patient and has an important role in prophylaxis. Antidepressants have a tendency to aggravate mania and are often withdrawn at the outset of a manic episode. Antipsychotics and lithium both exert an anti-manic action but the latter takes approximately a week to act. Initial treatment is therefore typically with a sedative drug such as chlorpromazine (haloperidol may be preferred for the rapid control of acute mania but unfortunately can cause irreversible toxic encephalopathy when combined with lithium). Prevention of future episodes of mania (and depression) can be achieved by the introduction of a mood stabiliser such as lithium or carbamazepine. Hospitalisation facilitates drug therapy in mania for a number of reasons:

1. If the patient is very aroused or refusing oral medication the first few doses can be given by the parenteral route.

2. The stuttering compliance that is often a problem in outpatient settings can be largely remedied by careful nursing supervision.

3. As the patient is closely monitored higher doses can be administered with greater safety and confidence and finer adjustments made in relation to changes in mental state.

4. Lithium has a narrow therapeutic/toxic ratio so it is important to check renal function before commencing treatment and to monitor plasma levels of the drug closely in order to obtain therapeutic concentrations while avoiding the dangerous toxicity associated with overdosage. Lithium interferes in thyroid hormone synthesis and a baseline assessment of thyroid function is helpful. The introduction of lithium can easily and rapidly be achieved while the patient is in hospital but may be associated with practical difficulties in other settings.

Mania can also be successfully treated with electroconvulsive therapy (ECT) but in general adult psychiatry this is reserved for the rare situations where anti-manic medication is ineffective. (In the elderly it has the advantage of avoiding or minimising the troublesome side effects of medication.) Although it is possible to administer ECT to outpatients it is generally more practical to do this while the patient is in hospital, particularly when judgement is impaired, leading to concerns about the reliability of fasting before anaesthesia.

Depression

Mild to moderate depressive illnesses are for the most part successfully managed in community settings. However, more severely depressed patients require hospitalisation if there is a high suicidal risk or if a rapid response to treatment (usually ECT) is imperative, for example where the patient is failing to take sustenance. In all situations judgement is needed, but suicidal ideation has to be carefully evaluated and a 'safety first' approach has much to commend it with a willing patient. In hospital the level of nursing observation can be tailored according to the perceived suicidal risk. If the risk is thought to be high the patient can be 'specialled'. In other words, a nurse maintains close one-to-one contact with the patient all the time. As the patient improves the level of observation can be gradually relaxed. The close contact between patient and staff on the ward can also promote a therapeutic alliance. The patient receives general support, warmth and reassurance which may considerably assist recovery. Suicide attempts are most common when psychomotor retardation is lifting and initiative is returning, another reason for hospital care. As with mania, admission has the advantage of removing the depressed person from a stressful environment which might have been responsible for precipitating or maintaining the episode.

Drug treatment plays a key part in the management of depression. Typically in unipolar depression an antidepressant is introduced at a therapeutic dose and continued for at least six months if a response is obtained. In bipolar depression caution is required because antidepressants can precipitate mania. Either an antidepressant can be introduced in conjunction with a mood stabiliser such as lithium or the mood stabiliser can be used alone. Some sedative antidepressants, such as trimipramine and doxepin, can have mood-stabilising properties while being less inclined to cause a manic overswing, and so may be preferred to more traditional drugs in the treatment of bipolar depression. However, scientific justification for this clinical impression remains wanting. Whatever approach is used the patient must be closely monitored for signs of elation and this scrutiny is most easily achieved in hospital.

Tricyclic antidepressants (TCAs) may be preferred to selective serotonin re-uptake inhibitors (SSRIs) for two reasons. First, some clinicians believe that TCAs are more effective than SSRIs in the treatment of melancholia, even though published meta-analyses suggest no difference in efficacy between the two (Song *et al.* 1993). Second, the combination of SSRI and lithium is associated with a risk of central nervous system toxicity. The dose of TCAs has generally to be built up slowly in outpatient settings so that the patient can develop tolerance to side effects. Even so studies suggest that compliance is very poor in these settings. One general practice survey found that about two-thirds of patients were not taking the prescribed dose of antidepressant after four weeks (Johnson 1974). In hospital a full therapeutic dose can be established immediately and at the same time a much higher level of compliance is ensured. Furthermore, with some antidepressants the maximum recommended dose is greater for inpatients than for patients treated in other clinical settings. It is therefore possible to treat depression more vigorously in hospital than elsewhere with the added bonus of close supervision and monitoring of the patient's response.

In treatment resistance, lithium augmentation, the addition of L-thyroxine, the addition of three to six grams of L-tryptophan on a named patient basis, together with one gram of nicotinamide, all have their advocates, and dictate a special need for monitoring.

ECT is indicated where severe depression fails to respond to medication, or where a rapid response is needed, for example where the patient is not eating or drinking. Although ECT can be administered on an outpatient basis, many psychiatrists would take the view that if the patient is ill enough to need it admission is warranted in any case and compliance with pre-anaesthetic fasting can be assured.

Case vignette 2

A woman in her late 20s complaining of persistent sadness following the break-up of a relationship with an older man was prescribed an antidepressant by her general practitioner. Unfortunately this treatment triggered a switch into mania and she required inpatient care. A year later she became depressed again, this time without any obvious precipitant. She refused all medication and instead consulted a psychotherapist privately. The therapist suggested that the original manic episode represented anger over being sexually abused by her father, even though the patient could not recall any such interference. However, the explanation that the painful events had been completely suppressed from her conscious mind did seem convincing and she confronted her parents. Her father strenuously denied the allegations and her mother took his side. When the patient persisted her parents broke off all contact with her. This was unfortunate as her mother in particular had been a major source of support. Her depression worsened and she took an overdose of paracetamol which resulted in severe liver damage. She was transferred to a regional liver unit and only narrowly avoided a transplant. When medically fit she was moved to a psychiatric ward where appropriate medication and the supportive environment led to a rapid improvement in her mental state. Unhappily the patient's father suffered a fatal heart attack during this period, despite having no obvious risk factors. The consultant psychiatrist wrote to the psychotherapist suggesting that perhaps symbolically he had died from a broken heart.

Other benefits of hospital

Inpatient psychiatric care varies in differing units in this country and more so between units in different countries. Nevertheless, in trials of antidepressants, it is consistently found that between a quarter and a third of patients get better on placebo (Medical Research Council 1965). This is testimony to the beneficial effect of the therapeutic milieu created in hospital units throughout the world. This milieu has a number of components, an important one being removal from sources of stress, which include domestic commitments and business worries. Pressure from the family, which can be quite subtle, is also eased.

Sufferers from manic depressive illness often set high standards and are troubled by irrational feelings of guilt and unworthiness, which in many cases is predicated by high expectations. Inpatient care affords some relief and an opportunity for re-evaluation. Achievement, high standards and guilt with self-recrimination is a very uncomfortable and common combination. The respite of hospital care may provide better chances of recovery than a repeated cycle of attempt and failure. Furthermore, entry into a psychiatric unit affords legitimate recognition of illness and takes the sufferer out of a self-reinforcing cycle of impaired performance and repeated failure.

Resources such as occupational and industrial therapy, music and art therapy are generally more accessible to inpatients than their counterparts in the community. Such therapists, together with nursing staff, play a pivotal role in treatment and rehabilitation, turning restless energy to more constructive purposes, restoring confidence, promoting the acquisition of new skills, and offering support and advice to family members.

Many psychiatric wards hold regular group meetings. Although these groups may be constituted and run in a number of different ways, certain therapeutic factors are commonly present. Patients are helped to see that their problems are not unique (universality); they derive support and practical advice from their fellow sufferers; and improvement in other patients helps to boost optimism about their own recovery. These beneficial effects probably operate even in units which do not run formal groups.

Conclusion

We live in an era of reduced hospital facilities and a greater emphasis on community care for psychiatric illness. Nevertheless, we should not lose sight of the advantages of hospital care for severe psychopathology (Weller 1989). Manic depressive illness is a serious illness, generally persuing an episodic course, with a tendency for the frequency, severity and duration of episodes to increase with age (Angst and Grof 1977). It is a tautology that patients should not be needlessly detained in hospital but we hope we have shown that inpatient care continues to offer advantages in severe episodes. At the same time, dependence on an institutional setting can occur and has to be guarded against in cases of moderate severity, or in patients who are developing a neurotic attachment and fear of discharge.

References

Angst, J. and Grof, P. (1977) 'The course of unipolar and bipolar psychoses.' In A. Villeneuve (ed) *Lithium in Psychiatry: A Symposium.* Quebec: Presses del l'Universite Laval.

Brown, G.W. and Harris, T.O. (1978) *Social Origins of Depression.* London: Tavistock.

Clayton, P.J. *et al.* (1991) 'Follow-up and family study of anxious depression.' *American Journal of Psychiatry 148*, 1512–1517.

Jauhar, R. and Weller, M.P.I. (1982) 'Psychiatric morbidity and time zone changes. A study of patients from Heathrow Airport.' *British Journal of Psychiatry 140*, 231–235.

Johnson, D.A.W. (1974) 'A study of the use of antidepressant medication in general practice.' *British Journal of Psychiatry 125*, 186–192.

Lydiard, R.B. (1991) 'Coexisting depression and anxiety: special diagnostic and treatment issues.' *Journal of Clinical Psychiatry 52*, (suppl), 48–54.

Medical Research Council (1965) 'Report by Clinical Psychiatry Committee: clinical trial of the treatment of depressive illness.' *British Medical Journal 1*, 881–886.

Song, F. *et al.* (1993) 'Selective seratonin re-uptake inhibitors: meta-analysis of efficacy and acceptability.' *British Medical Journal 306*, 683–7.

Weller, M.P.I. (1989) 'Mental illness – who cares?' *Nature 399*, 249–252.

Wells, K.B. *et al.* (1989) 'The functioning and well-being of depressed patients.' *Journal of the American Medical Association 262*, 914–919.

CHAPTER 10

What Group Therapy Can Do To Help

Maurice Greenberg

Introduction

It is generally recognised that groups make a useful contribution to helping people in a wide variety of settings. These range from patient organisations which have established self-help groups where people come together in order to provide support and share information, to psychiatric units which offer a range of group treatments; from activity-based groups focused on particular activities such as art or drama, to discussion groups, to more insight-oriented groups. Yet despite the fact that so much help is offered through the medium of groups, there is relatively little empirical data to demonstrate their value for people with manic depressive disorder. However, it could be argued that group activity is helpful simply because so many of the problems facing people with a manic depressive disorder are psychological or social, and that an instrument which addresses these issues is bound to be useful.

There is often an uneasiness about applying group therapy to people with manic depressive disorder. This is exemplified by Yalom (1985) who described it as the worst disaster that can befall a group. Although this attitude seems to fly in the face of common practice and experience, many practitioners are only too aware of the dangers to which Yalom seemed to be referring. In particular, the manic patient who seems so involved, who contributes actively to the group and occasionally dominates it, is eventually recognised as being unable to reflect, and when they depart, generally leaves the other members feeling somewhat bemused, depleted and bruised.

This contrast between what sounds like a common sense approach to the use of groups in patients with manic depressive disorder, and an anxiety about its consequences, may in part be due to an imprecise use of various terms. Groups, for example, may differ considerably according to their membership, their style and their setting. Patients with manic depressive disorder also vary according to the stage of their illness, its severity and their particular personal and social needs. Some of these patient factors will inevitably influence the choice of group. Nevertheless, the range of combinations created by these, and other variables, demonstrates how difficult it is to answer simply a question about the usefulness of group therapy.

Other factors which can confuse this issue include the different ways in which manic depression can be used. In psychiatric terminology the term has now been replaced by 'bipolar disorder', a category of affective disorder which refers to disturbances of mood which are considered extreme enough to warrant treatment (American Psychiatric Association 1994). Bipolar disorder includes not only those people who suffer both manic and depressive swings, but also those who have only had a manic episode, on the assumption that eventually most of them will eventually experience a depressive one. The mood swings can include psychotic experiences and may be rapid and extreme. They may also be less severe, with a tendency to be more frequently depressed or manic. Another category which encompasses alternating moods is cyclothymic personality, which is a description of someone whose moods vary, and may be extreme, but not to the point of formal illness. These variations may be mild or severe, but there needs to be a continuity with an individual's normal character which sets them apart from bipolar disorder. It is also an inevitable part of the human condition to experience happiness and misery. These feelings usually relate to external events and are experienced as understandable and acceptable. If the stress is sufficient the mood change may be quite severe, and it is not uncommon for individuals to experience a fluctuating mood when subjected to either great distress or considerable happiness.

Review of the literature

In a recent review of psychotherapy for bipolar disorder, Scott (1995) pointed out that the consequences of bipolar disorder are extremely serious both in terms of morbidity and mortality. Despite the fact that psychosocial factors can contribute to nearly one-third of the outcome variants, and that sufferers recognise benefits from psychotherapy, biological models and treatments dominate the research agenda. Scott thought there were three reasons why psychosocial interventions have been ignored. First, because of the powerful genetic and biological arguments; second, the belief that people with bipolar disorder are well between episodes; and third, because psychoanalysts have tended to be more ambivalent about the suitability of psychotherapy for patients with manic depressive disorder than for those suffering from other severe illnesses. Historically this has been attributed to the inability of these patients to demonstrate introspection, their dependency and their tendency to play on their therapist's 'Achilles heel'.

Although Scott mentions that most of the discouraging views on psycho-therapy were published before the introduction of lithium, and contrasts this with the more positive attitude towards schizophrenia, she does not mention that advocates of psychotherapeutic treatment for schizophrenia published before the introduction of thenothiazines. The two major manuals on the diagnosis of psychiatric disorders, DSM-IV (American Psychiatric Association 1994) and ICD-10 (World Health Organisation 1992), follow a multiaxial approach which emphasises the importance of psychosocial and developmental correlates. The importance of 'stressful life events' and vulnerability factors in the causation of mental illness has been recognised (Brown and Harris 1986), and has resulted in psychotherapeutic interventions which have been re-searched, particularly in relation to family therapy and expressed emotion (Leff *et al.* 1985). Those authors who advocate psychotherapy consistently emphasise the importance of controlling biological manifestations of the disorder through medication, whereas much less weight is given to psychosocial aspects by those who promote biological treatments. It does, however, seem surprising that there has been so little empirical research into group therapy, an activity which provides an opportunity to address both internal psychodynamic and external, social factors.

Although there have been no controlled trials of group therapy, a number of open studies have been reported. Volkmar *et al.* (1981) described the results of a long-term psychotherapy group composed exclusively of manic depressive patients. Thirteen of the fifteen group members were men, the majority gave a history of poor co-operation with lithium therapy prior to entering the group, and most of them gave a family history of affective illness. They conducted their group using 'an interactional, interpersonal, here and now' approach, and focused on expression of affect, reality issues and immediate problems and concerns rather than on past history (Volkmar *et al.* (1981) p.229). Intellectu-alisation, superficiality and rationalisation were discouraged as far as possible. Lithium was dispensed monthly during a group meeting and was maintained within a therapeutic range. Occasionally patients who were not regular group members were allowed to attend a meeting, generally in response to their wish to meet other patients receiving lithium.

Most patients were characterised as following substantially the same clinical course during their participation in the group. Following an initial aloofness and diffidence, patients began to attend more regularly and showed an interest in the group itself after about ten sessions. When they started, new patients would focus on their treatment and their ambivalence about medication. After about six months the group members began to express their fear of relapse and its social consequences. Towards the end of the group they began to talk more about the effect of their illness on people close to them. The average inpatient stay before entering the group was about 16 weeks a year, and this fell to about three weeks a year. This change appeared to be associated with an improvement in their co-operation with lithium therapy.

A long-term outpatient support group for 14 patients, 13 of whom were men, was described by Kripke and Robinson (1985). This group had continued for 12 years and the patients were said to have fewer admissions and improved levels of functioning. Again, the patients appeared to prefer problem-solving rather than dynamic approaches.

Wulsin, Bachop and Hoffman (1988) reported a group which met on a monthly basis over four years. It contained 22 patients, of whom 10 were male. Medication was managed by other clinicians, and the group focused on interpersonal processes. Patients were asked to sign a contract before entering the group and the average number of members attending a session was four. Twelve of the members dropped out while the group was running. They found that the group was very preoccupied with the instability of relationships, a topic which had been raised during the pre-admission discussions. During conflicts within the group the wish to leave escalated and in two cases resulted in unplanned termination. The members described difficulties in maintaining relationships rather than in initiating them, and some of this was acted out during the sessions. The most intense and persistent interpersonal conflicts involved a man seeking, but not obtaining, the attention of a woman. After exploring a range of response styles, the therapists found themselves responding in a flexible way to information-seeking, and blended interpretation with fact-giving. Towards the end of the group the members focused more on their individual worth and the worth of the group itself. The authors concluded that the patients benefited from receiving practical and experiential information about their illness, in that they co-operated better with their medication and they learnt more about their interpersonal difficulties. The authors also re-marked on the relative cost–benefit effectiveness of treating people who have a chronic illness in a group setting.

The above reviews tend to emphasise the benefits of combining group therapy with lithium treatment. The style they recommend is much more of an interactional 'here and now' approach than a reflective analytic one, and they seem to encourage more openness and information-giving. Men predominate in most of the groups described, and the majority of patients had been hospitalised and seem to have been receiving additional neuroleptic medication. Although they generally argue that the rate and length of re-admission are reduced by group therapy, some of the groups had a very high fall-out rate. The impact of group therapy did not seem to depend upon whether the group therapists or an independent psychiatrist assumed responsibility for managing medication.

The dynamic process of the group and the style of treatment, rather than the practical aspects and outcome, such as co-operation with medication and re-admission rates, are addressed by Winther and Sorensen (1989). They described their experience of running a two year analytic group, in which all the patients had bipolar illness and were medicated by other clinicians. Their group showed a tendency towards splitting, idealisation and denial, which often started with the split between the biological and psychological aspects of the illness. For them this was illustrated by one patient who, when he became depressed, was unable to remember a recent episode of happiness, and needed numerous reminders by other group members before he could acknowledge this. They also described a clear narcissistic identification, whereby loss was transformed into a depressive reaction with guilt feelings and self-reproach, and they concluded that their patients were unable to make connections between outside events and internal mental experience. They believed that the shared group experience helped shift this sense of denial. They were also impressed by the intense orality of their patients, which confirmed observations made by previous observers. They described them sharing food, talking about it and demonstrating intense greediness. Like Wulsin *et al.*, they concluded by discouraging the use of a classical, neutral approach and recommended a more active and emotionally empathic one, working in the here and now and downplaying the importance of historical, developmental events.

Discussion

Most of the research described refers to group therapy for people with bipolar disorder who were being treated with lithium and who had been hospitalised, sometimes frequently. Since the criteria for embarking upon lithium include both the frequency and the severity of relapse, and most of their patients had been unwell for a long time, required neuroleptics and had been hospitalised, it is very likely that they were focusing on individuals at the more severe end of the spectrum. The groups were all homogeneous and outpatient-based, varied in frequency, and the majority of members were men. Attendance varied, but relapse seemed to be reduced for those who attended on a regular basis, both in terms of length of hospitalisation and its frequency. Most of the studies suggested that co-operation with lithium improved during the period of group therapy, and this may well have contributed to these improvements. There seems to have been universal agreement that the appropriate therapeutic style is one of openness, genuineness and directness, focusing on current events and interactions within the group, rather than a traditional, gnomic, psychoanalytic style. The patients benefited from the opportunity to discuss the difficulties of coming to terms with a chronic illness with a group of fellow sufferers. They therefore seemed to develop a culture of cohesiveness and support based upon shared experience. Sometimes they learned to recognise how their mood was affected by events in the outside world (more often immediate but occasionally remote). They also learned to explore how changes in their mood could impinge upon their environment and their social relationships.

The aim of these changes seems to have been to help sufferers accept that they were vulnerable to an illness, to come to terms with the implications of this and to recognise early manifestations of a potential relapse. This implies going further than an intellectual acceptance that they suffer from an illness and require medication, to a more fundamental grasp of what this means. As a result of these insights and the consequent changes, relapse should be reduced through better co-operation with the professionals involved in their treatment. This aspect of negotiating a therapeutic alliance is often called 'compliance'. As consumer groups have become increasingly sophisticated and expect to be involved in decision-making which affects their welfare, the concept of compliance seems to have become rather dated, in that it implies a paternalistic relationship with rather fixed roles. This shift from a more rigid professional–patient relationship to greater flexibility and co-operation, involving an adult negotiation between professional and patient, seems to have been a development in all the groups described. The conductors learned to discard the traditional and more distant therapist stance, and discovered that they were more effective when they became more open and focused on issues that made immediate sense to their patients. They displayed their skills through the interpreting process and revealed their knowledge by offering information. However, this was specifically not provided in the guise of expert advice. The learning experience described by the group therapists is also likely to have been educational for their patients, and to have had an impact on their outside relationships. All of these changes will have improved aspects of the individual patient's ability to socialise.

Anyone who suffers from a chronic fluctuating illness which can interfere seriously with their life, and which requires close co-operation between them and their care-givers, is likely to experience these concerns. Mood changes inevitably influence personality and behaviour and affect the way patients relate to others. Since they are also part of the human condition, people with manic depressive disorder additionally face an intense dilemma about how much of what they are experiencing is due to them as a person or to an illness.

The first difficulty to which patients must adjust is to accept that they have something wrong with them that requires treatment. Clearly, the emotional nature of this illness is likely to interfere with its progress, with the danger that a vicious spiral becomes established. The idealised picture of a patient who accepts that they have an illness, that they need to take medication regularly in order to prevent it, and that they must listen to friends and relatives who express concern about them during periods of relapse, is rarely met in clinical practice. People with manic depressive disorder are prone to excessive worrying or to denial, like everyone else. They also have the additional difficulty that their disorder is an extreme variation of normal human experience. This clearly raises the risk that an ordinary reaction becomes misread as relapse or, its alternative, that a relapse becomes discounted as an ordinary reaction. These are human problems and a group is clearly a good setting in which to address them.

In addition to coming to terms with the illness, people with manic depressive disorder are more vulnerable to loss and to complications in their interpersonal relationships. Both of these areas are specifically addressed by psychotherapy, and are therefore potentially very appropriate for treatment.

In manic depressive disorder the importance of medication cannot be overstated. Lithium therapy is essentially prophylactic, and therefore needs to be taken regularly, in therapeutic doses, to be effective. The decision to embark upon treatment with lithium should not be taken lightly. It has potentially serious side effects and once started, particularly when shown to be effective, is very difficult to stop. This is partly because of its biological action and the fact that withdrawing lithium runs a risk of relapse. It is also because of the dependence on it which develops in both the professional and the patient. If it works, the patient may feel no immediate benefit, and although they are likely to relapse if they discontinue, there may be a delay of a number of months, which makes it difficult to associate taking the medication to any sense of well-being. It is well known that many people do not take the medication prescribed by their doctors, not only when they are feeling well, but also when they feel ill. Although the considerable benefits of lithium prophylaxis have been amply demonstrated, and it is painful for patients to suffer damaging relapses in order to recognise this for themselves, it is easy to understand why they may not co-operate with their doctors' recommendations. Between one-fifth and one-half of patients prescribed lithium fail to take it, regardless of its therapeutic effect. This probably over-simplifies the situation, since individuals generally vary in their degree of co-operation throughout the course of their illness.

A number of factors increase the likelihood of people taking their medication (Goodwin and Jamison 1990). Not surprisingly, these include people with severe symptoms who consider treatment to be effective. The presence of obsessional personality traits also helps, presumably because this encourages habituation. Co-operation is further enhanced in those who have a stable social network. On the other hand, younger men who have had fewer episodes of illness and a previous history of non-co-operation are less likely to go along with treatment. These difficulties are particularly high during the first year of lithium treatment, especially in those people who experience a persistently elevated mood; it is not surprising that patients prefer to feel on the high side of normal and fear depression. Although the unwanted effects of medication are also important, clinicians and patients disagree about which ones matter. Weight gain and tremor, although less common than other effects, are particularly bothersome to patients, who also do not like feeling confused and having a poor memory. Psychiatrists, on the other hand, are particularly concerned about somatic symptoms, probably because they worry about the potential serious physical consequences (Jamison and Akiskal 1983).

Some people dislike using drugs to control their mood and see this as a sign of weakness. A number also fear losing their creativity, particularly if they experience more highs than lows. Not surprisingly, patients often reflect the attitudes of their psychiatrists, in that they are more likely to take medication if they believe that their clinician is motivated rather than ambivalent (Peet and Harvey, 1991).

Specific contributions from groups

A psychoanalytic model of the unconscious, which attributes meaning to behaviour and attempts to explore and understand defence mechanisms, can be applied to both individual and group therapy situations. However, there are specific group effects which may have a particular bearing on the management of people with severe and chronic psychological disorders. Among the curative factors in group therapy (Yalom 1985) a number appear to be particularly important for people with manic depressive illness, and seem to have emerged in the research described. These include the instillation of hope, the imparting of information, the development of socialising techniques, interpersonal learning and group cohesiveness. All these factors are likely to have been influenced, however, by the homogeneity of these groups. One of the central therapeutic elements of group analytic psychotherapy, a model of group therapy developed by Foulkes (1975), is that heterogeneity is beneficial. Foulkes's view was that a group represents the norm from which its members deviate, and that the wider the range of experience it contains, the greater the opportunity for new learning. Limiting groups to people with manic depressive illness, most of whom are men, who are receiving lithium, and who have had numerous hospital admissions, will obviously have an impact on this norm. The sense of cohesiveness that develops in such a situation is likely to arise out of the shared experiences of manic depression, which include a sense of stigma which has marginalised the group members from society, rather than out of universality, another of Yalom's curative factors. In a homogeneous group the instillation of hope and cohesiveness is likely to develop out of a sense of camaraderie, which is probably one of the therapeutic factors in self-help groups. Although this will develop to some extent in any psychoanalytic group, in a heterogeneous group the tendency to focus on a single issue will be subject to the modifying effects of a wider range of experiences and problems.

Yalom's warning of the disruption caused to a therapy group by someone with manic depressive disorder reflects a real concern recognised by many group therapists. However, there is plenty of clinical evidence that such people can benefit, although there is a risk that they may break down during treatment. There has not been any scientific investigation of the effects of group therapy on individual patients with manic depressive disorder, and it is difficult to imagine how this could be undertaken rigorously, given the problems of selection and observer bias. Nevertheless, the observation of a heterogeneous group which includes someone with this diagnosis offers an opportunity to observe those particular issues that might complicate or enhance the therapeutic experience.

The first of these is the universal nature of emotional reactions. Everyone has some experience of unhappiness or of joy. There is ample scope to empathise with these emotions in a group setting, particularly when their antecedents are understandable. Group situations provide an ideal opportunity to observe the meaningfulness of emotional responses, and to share those experiences where the grey areas of uncertainty merge into overt psychosis. The split between understandable emotional response and illness becomes apparent in a group setting. The conductor may experience this by feeling uneasy about his or her role, and by becoming torn between dealing with the issues that are being played out through the group process or becoming actively involved as a carer. This is potentially easier to address in a mature group, which has developed a sensitive and thoughtful culture. In such groups, which are likely to have been running for at least two years, members seem able to recognise intuitively the distress that an individual (and the group) can tolerate, and are also capable of confronting and sharing unusual and painful situations. In a new group, however, the overriding priority is to establish cohesiveness and trust, within clearly protected boundaries, and it is much more difficult to contain the needs of a disturbed individual, because they distract the group from its prime task, which is to survive. It can be very difficult for a patient to return to a group if they have required hospitalisation, because they often feel humiliated and ashamed, and their sense of trust can become shattered. The group can also experience intense guilt. The experience of someone becoming psychotic may leave the group extremely inhibited, and as a result it may take considerable time for it to recover its capacity to handle conflictual and painful issues. Under these circumstances the patient who has relapsed is likely to require additional individual support while re-entering the group.

Group therapy also provides an opportunity to observe and understand a number of psychological phenomena. These include phenomena 'borrowed' from individual psychoanalytic theory, such as projective identification and denial. When they manifest themselves in a group situation they may be more readily recognised and, because they frequently affect relationships between patients, they may be more accessible to them. However, there are also group-specific phenomena which offer additional mechanisms for understanding and treating patients. Classical examples of these include 'basic assumptions' (Bion 1959), the 'special patient' (Main 1957) and 'mirroring' (Foulkes 1964).

Bion described three basic assumptions, dependency, pairing, and fight and flight, when the group behaved as if the members were sharing a common belief, from which their mood emanated. He considered that when a group was in a basic assumption mode, which could be very variable in time, it would be distracted from its primary task, 'work', which was to understand its internal tensions. This perspective can illuminate the social perspective of behaviour because it emphasises the group as an organism and how an individual contributes to its overall culture. Main's special patient was generally a young woman from a professional background who was being treated in a psychiatric unit. She developed relationships with a number of staff in the unit which were characterised by each of them feeling that they were the only one who had a full understanding of her problem. Consequently the staff would become rivalrous for her attention and splits developed between them so that they stopped working as an effective team, particuarly in relation to the special patient. The value of this perspective is that it draws attention to group behaviour, the way in which staff inter-relate, and this illuminates the internal psychopathology of the patient. The final example, mirroring, occurs when two individuals seem to become enmeshed for no obvious reason. They may, for example, take an instant and exaggerated dislike to each other. It then becomes apparent that they may share certain experiences, such as a particular form of upbringing, of which neither has been aware.

These, and other, group phenomena may usefully illuminate the behaviour of people with manic depressive disorder. In addition, however, there are specific aspects of manic depressive behaviour which can resonate within a group setting, enhancing its recognition and understanding. An example of this is disinhibition, which occurs during the manic phase of the disorder, when the patient talks rapidly and freely about sensitive issues, and also becomes over-active and often distracted. Sometimes this may be more subtle, as when they introduce themselves and insist on shaking everyone's hand, however many people there are in the group. Occasionally the only manifestation is a psychological reaction in the group, which may be apparent even when the individual is absent and only being talked about. It is as if the manic mood is contagious and the group becomes slightly silly or flippant, with individual members cracking jokes or making puns. This can even be quite enjoyable, and if someone remarks on the absence of seriousness they are treated as a killjoy. If the prevailing mood in a manic phase is irritability, rather than extreme pleasure, the experience in the group will reflect this and become more upsetting or worrying.

An alternative reaction to a patient who is 'high' is to attempt to confront the extreme mood. Many people, particularly mental health professionals, find it much more comfortable to establish a relationship with someone when they are depressed than when they are manic, and when someone is high there seems to be a sense of satisfaction and achievement in talking them down, particularly when they then reveal the sadness and unhappiness which so frequently lies behind the manic shell. It is as if being depressed is a more real experience, and that mania is a state of denial. This has become incorporated into the concept of the manic defence, whereby splitting and grandiosity are perceived as protecting an individual from depression. This can manifest itself in a group in different ways. Humour, for example, is particularly useful as a method for dealing with an uncomfortable silence. Efforts to explore this in the group frequently result in the group allowing and encouraging the manic member to take over responsibility for communication. If someone, and it is often the conductor, tries to focus on this process, they are liable to be made a scapegoat. It can be very difficult to escape from this form of splitting, where all the capacity for thinking and for communication is felt to reside in the manic patient. If the group is unable to share these responsibilities, the conductor is likely to feel compelled to intervene in order to protect the manic patient, often without success. Although the particular session may be entertaining, the manic patient often disappears afterwards, and may never return.

Summary and conclusions

Despite the lack of empirical data, there is clinical evidence to support the assumption that group therapy is helpful for people with manic depressive disorder. Most of the research has focused on homogeneous groups, predominantly made up of men with long-standing, severe illness. The benefits are probably related to an improved co-operation with lithium therapy and an ability to recognise relapse early. The style of therapy which appears to be most helpful for these patients is more matter of fact and flexible, and involves a mixture of information-giving and understanding. These groups do, however, have a high drop-out rate, which suggests that considerable thought needs to be given to selection, and additional support given during times of stress.

The information regarding psychoanalytic group psychotherapy for individual patients is based on clinical experience. This suggests that therapy can be helpful for selected patients, since the introduction of a manic patient into a group can be damaging to all concerned. It needs to be clearly recognised that therapy will not cure the manic depressive disorder, although it can help with relapse prevention. The selection criteria should therefore focus on those issues, such as interpersonal conflict, which generally warrant psychotherapy, and the patients should show a capacity for reflection and an ability to cope with conflict. They should be prepared to co-operate with medication, and this needs to be consistently monitored by a psychiatrist outside the group. They should also have been stable for at least one year, and should be informed that there is a risk of relapse during treatment. These criteria will inevitably exclude from group therapy those patients who are most unwell. Finally, the therapist must evaluate thoughtfully the strengths and weaknesses of his or her group, since it needs to be sufficiently mature and secure to handle the complicated issues that are likely to arise.

References

American Psychiatric Association (1994) *Diagnostic and Statistical Manual of Mental Disorders (4th edition).* Washington, DC: American Psychiatric Association.

Bion, W.R. (1959) *Experiences in Groups and Other Papers.* London: Basic Books.

Brown, G. and Harris, T.O. (1986) *Social Origins of Depression.* London: Tavistock.

Foulkes, S.H. (1964) *Therapeutic Group Analysis.* London: Allen and Unwin.

Foulkes, S.H. (1975) *Group Analytic Psychotherapy.* London: Gordon and Breach.

Goodwin, F. and Jamison, K. (1990) 'Psychotherapy.' In F. Goodwin and K. Jamison (eds) *Manic-Depressive Illness.* Oxford: Oxford University Press.

Jamison, K. and Akiskal, H. (1983) 'Medication compliance in patients with bipolar disorder.' *Psychiatric Clinics of North America 6,* 175–192.

Kripke, D. and Robinson, D. (1985) 'Ten years with a lithium group.' *McLean Hospital Journal 10,* 1–11.

Leff, J.P. *et al.* (1985) 'A controlled trial of intervention in the families of schizophrenics: two year follow-up.' *British Journal of Psychiatry 146,* 594–600.

Main, T.F. (1957) 'The ailment.' *British Journal of Medical Psychology 30,* 129–145.

Peet, M. and Harvey, N. (1991) 'Lithium maintenance: one. A standard education programme for patients.' *British Journal of Psychiatry 158,* 197–200.

Scott, J. (1995) 'Psychotherapy for bipolar disorder.' *British Journal of Psychiatry 167,* 581–588.

Volkmar, F. *et al.* (1981) 'Group therapy in the management of manic-depressive illness.' *American Journal of Psychotherapy 35,* 226–234.

Winther, G. and Sorensen, T. (1989) 'Group therapy with manic depressives: dynamic and therapeutic aspects.' *Group Analysis 22,* 1, 19–30.

World Health Organisation (1992) *The ICD-10 Classification of Mental and Behavioural Disorders: Clinical Descriptions and Diagnostic Guidelines.* Geneva: WHO.

Wulsin, L., Bachop, N. and Hoffman, D. (1988) 'Group therapy in manic depressive illness.' *American Journal of Psychotherapy 42,* 263–271.

Yalom, I. D. (1985) *The Theory and Practice of Group Psychotherapy. (3rd edition).* New York: Basic Books.

CHAPTER 11

What Occupational Therapy Can Do To Help

Mandy J. Sainty

What is occupational therapy?

Occupational therapy developed as a health profession in psychiatry in the early 20th century in Britain. Occupational therapists are concerned with facilitating an individual to function at their maximum potential within their daily lives. As a holistic therapy, occupational therapy therefore considers all aspects of the individual's life, including personal and social activities, relationships, recreation and employment.

Occupational therapists may become involved in the assessment and treatment of a person whose function and independence has been affected by a mental health or physical problem or need. The key therapeutic medium is planned, structured activity, based on comprehensive assessment of the individual's specific circumstances.

The speciality of mental health is one field in which the occupational therapist may provide intervention, and therefore individuals suffering from manic depression may be referred for assessment and treatment by the consultant psychiatrist, or their general practitioner.

Where is occupational therapy provided?

Occupational therapists are key members of the multidisciplinary team within the field of mental health, and involvement with the individual suffering from manic depression may occur within a range of contexts. This reflects the cyclical nature of the illness and the adaptability of occupational therapy in responding to a variety of therapeutic environments.

Manic depression is characteristically cyclical, and potentially long term in its impact on the individual's life. This may necessitate the client to require assessment and treatment as an inpatient, within a day unit setting, or within the community. The occupational therapist may take a significant role in the care process within each context, although there will be variation in the focus of intervention. This focus will also be dependent on the presentation of the client for a particular episode of care, that is, whether the manic or depressive aspect of the illness is within the acute phase.

Inpatient facilities

The occupational therapist commonly has a role in providing a service to all patients within the ward environment as part of the overall management by the ward team. The ward may have a designated therapist, or the occupational therapist may be available for sessional periods only. Multidisciplinary team working is essential to ensure a consistent approach, and therefore the therapist must liaise and work closely with his or her colleagues. This is important particularly to gain the 24 hour perspective of the individual's needs from the primary nurse. Occupational therapy within the ward environment attempts to meet the needs of a variety of individuals with potentially varying problems and illnesses. A programme of both therapeutic group and individual interventions is usually co-ordinated by the occupational therapist, although these will obviously not all be appropriate for the client with manic depression. The therapist, together with the other team members and the client, will, however, identify those sessions which will facilitate ongoing assessment of need and will address individual treatment goals.

Day units

Day units offer multidisciplinary assessment and treatment for individuals who are usually in a less acute phase of their illness, and can provide invaluable support to prevent admission or to facilitate discharge from the inpatient environment. The occupational therapist working within the day unit may be involved with clients in two ways, one of which, as in the ward, concerns co-ordination and implementation of the therapeutic group programme with colleagues. The therapist may frequently, however, also have a keyworker role for specific clients. The keyworker role necessitates assessment of the individual's needs and strengths, co-ordinating the package of care and liaising with other team members regarding the client's progress in the therapeutic programme. The frequency of contact the therapist will have with their client (as a keyworker) will depend on the number of days attendance at the day unit and their client's mental health status and needs. This will change over time with the course of the individual's illness.

Community teams

Occupational therapists have a strong role within a community mental health team, and the chronic nature of manic depression means that the therapist may frequently have a keyworker role within the community setting. The role may be more extensive within this context as the therapist will essentially be working as an independent practitioner with the client, although liaison with other team members, and commonly other agencies, is vitally important. Intervention will take place usually on a one-to-one basis, either in the client's own home, the community team base or within other community settings. The occupational therapist within this context will implement specific occupational therapy activities, but there is also more role-blurring, in that he or she may become involved in issues related to medication, housing, benefits and the broader social context. The occupational therapist's role may therefore be considerably extended in relation to co-ordination of the care package; considering issues such as registration on the Care Programme Approach and long-term needs, support and interventions.

The occupational therapist can provide intervention within a variety of contexts, although the same therapeutic process is employed, that is, systematic care planning.

A systematic approach to care

The care planning process is essentially a logical problem-solving sequence which is used to help the health professional to identify the individual's needs and subsequent appropriate treatment. Assessment of needs and strengths enables goals to be established, which should be followed by the necessary therapeutic interventions. Evaluation and review is crucial to ensure goals are being met and to encourage revisions which reflect any changes in the individual's circumstances or mental health. This review process is essential given the cyclical nature of manic depression.

Assessment

Assessment is the cornerstone to any treatment, and a key philosophy of occupational therapy is to focus on the individual's strengths as well as their problems and needs. The process of assessment is a combination of informal observations, together with more formal collection of information using interview schedules and practical activities. The first contact with a client is only the beginning of the therapeutic relationship, and although the initial assessment may take anything up to three or four sessions, the process of assessment is continuous. The depth and nature of assessment will vary to some extent, depending on the involvement of other team members and the context within which the client is receiving the service. The client admitted to the ward or day unit may receive a comprehensive baseline assessment via the medical and nursing staff, and the emphasis therefore for the occupational therapist is the therapeutic group programme. In the community, however, the occupational therapist may be the main clinician involved, and this will therefore necessitate the therapist to implement an assessment which establishes a more detailed personal, medical and social history.

THE MODEL OF HUMAN OCCUPATION

A model or framework is important to facilitate the assessment process, and within occupational therapy, practice may be based on a range of frames of reference, including adaptive performance, psychodynamic, and developmental or occupational behaviour (Creek 1990). The author's preferred model for application within the mental health speciality is the Model of Human Occupation (Kielhofner 1985). This model is based on the occupational behaviour frame of reference, and provides an excellent consideration of the balance of work, play and self-care in the individual's life.

The model identifies humans as 'open systems' (p.12), and highlights the fact that we are always interacting with our environment, which facilitates either the *status quo* or change.

Three subsystems describe how occupational behaviour is 'motivated, organised and performed' (p.12). Assessment should identify how the individual is functioning in all three areas, which are volition, habituation and performance.

Volition reflects our beliefs, values and interests, and is at the top of the hierarchy of the three elements in that it influences our choices and decisions. This subsystem is frequently affected by the course of manic depression, and in many ways is the key to the intervention that follows. Any treatment will have minimal impact if the client can see no value in the goals or media used. Direct involvement in discussing beliefs and values is crucial to highlight areas which will enhance motivation and subsequent commitment to a treatment plan. This is extremely relevant to the choice of therapeutic activities within a programme.

Habituation involves the roles and habits within our day-to-day life. Illness can affect the balance of the roles the client may have, and alter their routine and management of time. Family, employment and social roles all need exploration, particularly as manic depression can have a destructive effect on the individual's roles and relationships. Identifying the roles which are important to the client, and ways of maintaining or re-establishing these, is an essential aspect of the care planning process.

The third subsystem concerns performance of skills and abilities to carry out activities of daily living. Dependent on the client's individual personal, social and mental health history (including institutional episodes), development of skills and independence in daily activities may be an essential feature of occupational therapy intervention.

All three subsystems need to work together to enable us to 'choose, routinise and produce occupational behaviour' (p.14). Assessment of these three areas enables the occupational therapist to identify goals for intervention. Specific assessment tools can be used, such as checklists for roles and interests, together with individual interviews and observation of participation in a range of activity-based groups. Use of a range of types of assessment is beneficial, as each has benefits and deficits, and together the combination of approaches establishes a more comprehensive interpretation of the individual's situation.

Goal-setting

Identification of needs and strengths leads to establishing goals or objectives of intervention.

Goals need to be negotiated between the therapist and client. Total prescription by the therapist is not viable, and the client must be as fully involved as possible to work together in addressing their quality of life. Goals need to be realistic and achievable, and should also be measurable to enhance demonstration of progress and outcomes. A short- and long-term focus may be required, and the nature of the goals will influence the treatment intervention that follows.

Treatment

Treatment by the occupational therapist will focus on achieving the goals identified in the care plan. Intervention may be a mixture of individual and group activities, but will consider some key principles:

- Time needs to be spent *with* the client, establishing a therapeutic relationship. This is essential in any context, but crucial in the keyworker role.

- Intervention during the features of mania aims at pacing the client within their activities, providing a structure and channelling energy constructively.

- Intervention during the depressive symptoms will focus on establishing the individual's self-esteem.

- An essential aspect of treatment concerns enabling the client to develop a balanced daily routine and lifestyle.

- It is important to identify whose problems are being addressed. Manic features are often perceived as more difficult for those around the client to deal with, rather than for the client personally. The reverse is often the situation for depressive symptoms. The perceptions of the client need to be acknowledged, as the impact of an acute episode on the individual can be significant.

○ Throughout intervention, ongoing assessment and observation of key features indicative of the client's mental health status occurs. This will include mood, activity, speech and concentration span. Medication side effects must also be considered.

Activity is the main medium for occupational therapy intervention, and both the process and end result can be therapeutic. The values of activity have been identified as including its ability to allow expression and exploration of feelings; the needs of esteem and purposefulness; stimulation; and play and social perspectives, together with the development of skills and competence (Finlay 1988, p.78). The range of activities used by the occupational therapist will reflect their value and the goals established for an individual. The occupational therapist's skill in activity analysis in relation to the demands of an activity (physical, sensory, perceptual, cognitive, emotional and social) is essential to ensure that the activity chosen does not put undue stress on the client. This also enables activities to be graded and so facilitate the process of change (Finlay 1988, p.89). The individual activity itself can be graded, as can the context in which it is carried out, that is, progressing from individual to group work.

Therapeutic activities used with the client suffering from manic depression may include relaxation techniques, support and counselling, personal and domestic activities of daily living (self-care, cooking, budgeting), and social and leisure pursuits (gardening, pottery, crafts, clubs, sports).

The range of potential activities is quite extensive, but it is important that choice reflects the individual's volitional and habituation needs and that the therapeutic goals are identified.

Evaluation

The evaluative phase of care planning is as important as assessment, and should again involve the client directly. Discussion of progress against the goals set, and in relation to any changes in the individual's mental health or circumstances, is crucial, particularly as occupational therapy contact may be potentially long term within the community setting.

Case studies

The systematic approach to care is best demonstrated by case examples which reflect the manic and depressive phases of the illness.

Case study 1: Janice

Janice, a 30-year-old lady, had been admitted to an inpatient unit following an exacerbation of manic symptoms, resulting in a shopping spree, persistent contact with a company requesting employment, and constant activity with subsequent exhaustion and dietary inadequacy. During her admission, the ward occupational therapist spent time with Janice, focusing on her activity levels. Intervention at this point was on an individual basis, as Janice was unable to cope with group activities, or her behaviour resulted in disruption detrimental to other clients (Table 11.1).

Table 11.1 Inpatient occupational therapy: Janice

Problem/need	Goal	Intervention
Constant activity	Janice to become more aware of her environment, in balance with her inner feelings	Short daily walks to comment on the environment, developing a new awareness
Unable to concentrate on any task for more than five minutes	Ability to sit for 30 minutes focused on an activity of Janice's choice	Therapist to engage Janice in individual interaction for increasing periods of time, gradually introducing the media chosen of drawings and reading
Restless pacing resulting in short-ness of breath and hyperventilation	Ability to carry out daily activities on the ward without becoming breathless	Relaxation sessions, grading from initial breathing exercises
Lack of attention to personal care and hygiene due to overactivity	Janice to spend at least ten minutes each day attending to her self-care	Individual time identified for Janice to attend to her appearance with supervision gradually reduced from the therapist

Janice's relapse had been partly the result of poor compliance with her medication, a situation which had been made worse by the death of her mother two months ago. Prior to this time, Janice's care had been managed at home by her general practitioner and the support of her mother, together with an outpatient visit to the consultant psychiatrist every three months. Janice responded well to a review of her medication, and began attending the day unit adjacent to the ward prior to her discharge home. The ward occupational therapist, who also was involved in the day unit programme, was able at this stage to carry out a comprehensive assessment using the Model of Human Occupation framework. This process identified Janice's values relating to a need to feel purposeful, and the change in roles she had experienced following the death of her mother (Table 11.2).

Table 11.2 Day Unit occupational therapy: Janice

Problems/need	Goal	Intervention
Lack of confidence in her cooking skills, as previously assisted by her mother	Cook meal independently	Cookery session in day unit kitchen once a week
Difficulty concentrating for more than 30 minutes Lack of purposeful work-related role and difficulty structuring time	Attend the day unit two half days each week and participate in two hourly sessions, involving activities of Janice's choice	Craft group Gardening group Initially individual activities but progressing to working alongside other clients and not the therapist
Janice has expressed anxieties to staff about living alone and dealing with situations which previously her mother had organised	Janice to feel able to discuss her anxieties about her change in life situation on an individual basis and identify problem-solving approaches to dealing with practical issues	Individual sessions of up to 45 minutes with the therapist at a pre-agreed time

Janice's strengths included a high level of motivation, a previously active interest in swimming and a small network of friends who remained supportive. She also had essentially a high level of performance in daily activities, but her breakdown had been partly due to the lack of a structured framework which had been facilitated in the past by her mother.

Janice attended the unit regularly while an inpatient, but she identified that she did not wish to continue attendance after her discharge from the ward. The multidisciplinary team therefore agreed with Janice that support on her return home could be provided by the community mental health occupational therapist. The community occupational therapist was identified as Janice's keyworker and, building on the work of her colleague at the hospital, identified with Janice those areas for future support and intervention (Table 11.3).

Table 11.3 Community occupational therapy intervention: Janice

Problems/need	Goal	Intervention
Lack of routine and balanced schedule of activities reflecting Janice's interests and values	Janice to have a weekly timetable of key activities, including one sports session a week at the local centre	Therapist assists Janice to initiate contact with local groups and clubs. Initially accompanies Janice to swimming pool
Janice would like an activity to fulfil her need for a role as a worker	Involvement one day a week (within six months) in a local scheme providing supported employment	Introduce Janice to the local aftercare scheme which provides support to seek employment/ voluntary work
Janice has gained confidence in her cooking skills, but remains apprehensive when dealing with budgeting	Ability to organise and deal with her finances independently	Work through actual budgeting requirement on a practical basis, liaising with the social worker as indicated
Janice needs to begin to take responsibility for monitoring her swings in energy to enable her to continue daily activities	Ability to recognise changes in her mood and energy and to implement strategies for balancing activity	Janice to keep a diary of activity, social contexts, sleep and eating habits, and feed back to the occupational therapist strategies adopted

Contact was initially twice a week following discharge from the ward, but this gradually reduced over a period of three months to fortnightly visits. Regular liaison with the consultant, and periodic advice from her social work colleague, was co-ordinated by the occupational therapist. Nine months after the admission, Janice was involved in two local clubs, was engaged one day in a sheltered workshop and was quite stable on her medication. At this stage she required only monthly contact from the occupational therapist for review which would facilitate early identification of any concerns Janice may have had, or any changes in her mental health and behaviour. This proactive approach, which enables Janice to feel supported, also encourages discussion with the consultant psychiatrist and other team members to ensure appropriate intervention to meet any change in needs.

Case study 2: Grace

Grace, a 65-year-old, lady was referred to the day unit by the consultant psychogeriatrician following a domiciliary visit to the residential home where she was living.

An inpatient over 12 months ago, Grace had subsequently been discharged to the residential home, although her sense of loss at leaving her own home of over 40 years was significant.

Assessment at the day unit by the occupational therapist found Grace to be withdrawn, self-isolating, her personal hygiene had been neglected, and the home staff reported her appetite to be poor. The home manager also informed the day unit that Grace's only son had been ill in recent months, and four weeks ago had been told he had lung cancer.

Table 11.4 Day unit occupational therapy: Grace

Problems/need	Goal	Intervention
Grace has become withdrawn and self-isolating, preoccupied with her son's illness	Grace has the opportunity to discuss her anxieties about her son's health within a supportive environment	Individual time is allocated at each attendance with an occupational therapist for supportive counselling, progressing to a support group
Grace has neglected her own personal hygiene, out of keeping with her normal habits	Grace regains interest in attending to her personal care, and home staff report a return to her usual routine	Self-care group Weekly liaison with home
Grace feels unable to gain any sense of achievement and has identified her loss of role since moving to residential care	Grace participates in therapeutic groups which reflect her interests and skills (progressing from working at a parallel level to integrally within the group)	Cookery group Social group
The home staff have limited mental health experience and understanding of Grace's needs	Residential home staff are able to report on Grace's progress effectively	Occupational therapist to visit the home to discuss Grace's needs

The occupational therapist's individual assessment of Grace, together with the team's observations on her assessment visit to the unit, identified a need for her to attend the day unit twice a week. The occupational therapist was allocated as keyworker, and she subsequently developed a care plan with Grace to focus on her anxieties about her son and the low self-esteem she had expressed in relation to her own role in life (Table 11.4).

Grace attended the unit for two weeks before she could be encouraged to leave a corner in the sitting room and join the groups agreed within her programme. She had, however, begun to respond to the individual sessions with the occupational therapist, and was starting to talk more about her thoughts and feelings.

Over the course of the next three months Grace began to take a more active role within the therapeutic groups, initially participating in the more practical activities (cookery, social groups), where her need to demonstrate group interaction skills was able to be graded in relation to her improvement. She was also able increasingly to function within the support group and share her feelings with her peers.

In parallel to this, Grace's personal hygiene had returned to her previous standards, and the home reported that her dietary intake and medication compliance was satisfactory.

A case review after six months established a continued need for attendance, now on a weekly basis, as a critical time had been reached in relation to stability of her mood and the potential for a change to increasing activity and excitability.

Discharge from the day unit was agreed after a nine month period, but with follow-up support from the community occupational therapist. The health of Grace's son continued to be an area of concern for her, and the need to explore the development of additional roles within the home for Grace was identified (Table 11.5).

The community occupational therapist was able to facilitate Grace to become involved in the local Women's Institute meetings with a volunteer befriender over a two month period. Grace had also become an active participant in social activities which had been introduced within the home with the recent employment of a sessional activities co-ordinator.

The occupational therapist was able to reduce her visits to monthly, although it was recognised that the intensity of intervention would need to be reviewed regularly to respond to any changes in Grace's mental health.

These case studies provide examples of the nature of intervention the occupational therapist can offer the individual with a manic depressive disorder. They demonstrate the potential for positive responses to treatment, but it is important to acknowledge that, given the individual nature of each client's needs, flexibility in approach is essential as well as an awareness that outcomes may not always reflect planned goals. A practical focus, a sense of humour and

Table 11.5 Community occupational therapy: Grace

Problems/need	Goal	Intervention
Grace's son remains unwell and his health causes her considerable stress	Grace has continued opportunity to discuss her anxieties and feelings	Occupational therapist visits fortnightly to offer individual supportive counselling
Grace has described a lack of activity and role within the home which reinforces her sense of loss of role and helplessness	Grace is able to identify and participate in activities which address some of her role and interest needs within the residential home environment	Occupational therapist discusses with Grace the roles she would like to develop within the home environment Contact to be made with local befriending service Advice to home regarding social activities
The home staff need to be aware of and sensitive to potential changes in Grace's mood and level of activity	Home staff are able to identify changes in Grace's mood which may indicate a need for formal review of intervention by the mental health team	Occupational therapist to discuss with the home staff coping strategies and possible action necessary in response to changes in Grace's mood

the ability to work *with* the client is an essential asset for the occupational therapist.

Summary

The occupational therapist has a significant role in helping the individual suffering from manic depression. Assessment based on the individual's unique volition, habituation and performance skills, enables the occupational therapist to facilitate the client's independence and quality of life. It is not possible for the occupational therapist to manage or treat the illness of manic depression, but he or she can assist the individual to 'manage his or her time and behaviour better within the context of their role' (Finlay 1988, p.120).

References

Creek, J. (ed) (1990) *Occupational Therapy and Mental Health*. Edinburgh: Churchill Livingstone.

Finlay, L. (1988) *Occupational Therapy Practice in Psychiatry*. London: Croom Helm Ltd.

Kielhofner, G. (ed) (1985) *A Model of Human Occupation. Theory and Application*. Baltimore: Williams and Williams.

CHAPTER 12

A Guide to Self-Management

David Guinness

In 1993 the Manic Depression Fellowship began a series of meetings on self-management. They employed a novel format. Members were asked in advance to send in posters containing descriptions of any techniques or ideas they found useful in managing their manic depression. These and other ideas were then discussed at length at the meetings. In 1995 the Fellowship published a booklet called 'Inside Out' which drew upon all this experience. It was funded by the Department of Health and was immediately successful. It contained workboxes for readers to fill in and also a detachable crisis card for use in emergencies. This chapter is from Inside Out.

What is self-management?

Self-management is a process of taking increasing responsibility for your health. It entails learning about the illness and developing the skills to recognise and control mood swings. It is about taking charge and finding out what you can do to help your condition. It is not an instant cure but can lead in time to increased self-reliance with less dependence on your GP or psychiatrist and greater trust in your own experience.

Why self-manage?

The indications are that people who self-manage have less frequent and less severe mood swings, more tolerance to stress, have stable relationships, more self-confidence, fewer hospital visits and are more able to hold down a job. The ability to do all this has a considerable impact on one's self-esteem. There are other reasons: for some people mood swings occur so rapidly that there just isn't time to seek specialist help. So, good self-management skills can give you the ability to cope when on holiday or abroad, miles away from your doctor. There is also the possible 'kindling' phenomenon of manic depression; the idea that the more highs you have had the easier it is to have another one. In these circumstances it makes sense to do all you can to improve your stability. Good self-management can greatly improve the quality of life of 'rapid cyclers' (people who have four or more highs in a year).

> *My main reason for wanting to self-manage is...*

How do I start?

Becoming a good self-manager takes time, determination and practice. The process will be unique to you, for everyone with a diagnosis of manic depression experiences the illness in a different way. The key to self-management is learning to recognise and understand the illness as it affects you personally. A good first step is to keep a journal. Make an agreement with yourself to enter at least one sentence a day in it; it could be just 'I felt depressed today'. A valuable addition would be to include a figure on a scale from say, -10 to +10 to describe your mood. Here 10 would be completely high, -10 totally depressed and 0 normal. A journal like this helps to develop awareness of moods. Another reason for keeping it is that if you do have a mood swing it is very important to be able to go back later and try and analyse what happened. At that stage a written record of the days preceding a mood swing can make very fruitful reading.

The next step is to try and find out as much about your illness as you can. Regular attendance at your local Manic Depression Fellowship (MDF) group will provide you with a wealth of information. Some of the books listed at the end of this chapter should be available through your local library. The MDF also produces leaflets and newsletters. You should then discuss with your doctor your wish to play a greater role in managing the illness. In particular, you should ask for full information about the drugs you are taking; at the very least the doctor ought to let you read literature such as the *Monthly Index of Medical Specialties* (MIMS), which lists the standard doses and side effects of most drugs. Just as important could be discussing your plans with a trusted friend or partner. While you are gaining practice in some of the skills mentioned here, someone you are close to and who cares about you could provide invaluable feedback and support with your beginnings in self-management.

Knowing your moods

The first skill of self-management of manic depression is *learning to recognise imminent mood swings*. This requires awareness of your current mood. Some of us may not find this so easy. If this applies to you, just get into the habit of asking yourself 'how am I feeling right now?' as you are walking down the street. Start with physical pains or discomforts and move on to your emotional state later. If you're feeling something you don't like, don't kick yourself for feeling that way; just try and accept it.

The other way is to ask a trusted friend or your partner. If they volunteer their concern without being asked, then you should definitely pay attention.

Right now I'm feeling...

Recognising mood swings

Very few people go high or low overnight. If a mood swing is developing you will usually have time to notice it. The signs of depression and mild mania are widely known. However, the important thing is to find what *your* clearest warning signals are. Think back on the last times you were depressed. You probably felt a number of these:

- tiredness

- poor concentration

- social withdrawal

- unclear thinking

- low mood

- hating yourself

- low self-image

- suicidal thoughts

- loss of libido

- waking early with anxiety

- loss of ability to enjoy things

- changes of appetite.

My signs of starting to feel depressed are...

Elation or hypomania (mild mania) is quite different. These are the common signs:

- unusually happy

- sleeping poorly and waking early

- grandiose ideas

- uninhibited sexual behaviour

- self-centredness

- hyperactive with many plans

- poor concentration

- rapid and pressured speech

- overspending

- excessive irritability.

If some of these are present you might well be getting 'high', but again you must establish what types of behaviour are the tell-tale symptoms for you.

> *My signs of beginning to get high are...*

Controlling mood swings

There are various ways of influencing mood swings. Whichever combination of methods you use, you must bear in mind two things. The first is that you *catch the mood swing early*. How quickly a depression becomes severe or an elation spirals into mania will depend not just on your own particular make-up but also on how quickly you act. Generally speaking, the *longer you leave it, the harder it will be to control.* For most people there is typically about a week in which to stop mild hypomania escalating into mania. If you don't catch it then, the choice is either hospitalisation or an untreated manic episode lasting several weeks with devastating consequences.

With depression, remember that many antidepressants take two to three weeks to work, so whether heading for a high or a low, it is definitely better to do something now before things start to slide. The attached crisis card (included with *Inside Out* (Manic Depressive Fellowship 1995), see Appendix) can provide you with a handy reminder of this. When you've completed it, it's a good idea to carry it with you.

The second is that, having noticed your early warning signs, *take them seriously.* If you're getting depressed you'll probably want to do something about it anyway. However, if you're beginning a high, particularly after months of depression, you may feel very inclined just to enjoy it. If so, remind yourself what your last episode was like, just how painful it felt afterwards, and what the damage was to relationships, work and personal finances. Then ask yourself whether it's worth having another.

> *Some of the features of my last high were...*

Self-medication

When you self-manage, the best way of using medication is to adjust the dose yourself according to your mood. You raise the dose when you experience symptoms and lower the dose to a maintenance level when they abate. This is called 'self-medication', and reaching this stage will involve some negotiation with your doctor. Your case will be strengthened if you can already show some knowledge of the drugs you are taking and journal entries indicating your ability to monitor your moods. If your doctor agrees, you will need – in addition to your normal dosages – a small supply of neuroleptics (anti-manic drugs).[1] Within limits agreed with your doctor, you can now take the appropriate medication as the occasion arises.

Self-medication is quite common in the USA. In this country an increasing number of GPs and consultants encourage it, but many do not. From the doctor's viewpoint this method involves an element of risk which they may consider unacceptable. The most common grounds for refusal are that they simply do not trust your ability to gauge your needs in this way. You may, for instance, have only just left hospital. Or it may be prejudice or a fear of prescribing in a way they have not done before. If they do refuse, you could ask how many patients in their practice are allowed to self-medicate. If questions such as these bear no fruit your local advocate might help – or you could move to another practice.

If the negotiations with your doctor are successful, then having in your pocket the means to affect your moods should make you feel better already. Agreeing to try you on self-medication will have been an act of trust on your physician's behalf and obviously you abuse it at your own risk. The better you self-manage, the happier he/she will be.

Self-medication is/isn't right for me because...

Controlling moods by other means

If your doctor is not happy to let you self-medicate, there is still a range of techniques you can use to control your moods, and these have other advantages. If you run out of tablets on holiday, for instance, you are less likely to be at the mercy of a mood swing. And several psychotropic drugs, especially if taken over a long time, carry a risk of tardive dyskinesia, a currently untreatable condition causing uncontrollable muscular movements and facial contortions. It is therefore better to avoid extra medication – if you can. Apart from practical

---

1 Under supervision, lithium can be used as an anti-manic drug as well. See Schou (1993).

reasons most people find a deep sense of satisfaction in being able to have some personal influence over their condition. It narrows the gap between the normal and the abnormal and raises self-esteem.

A word of caution must be added. Most of the following techniques are easily learnt and apply anywhere at any time. However, a wide variety of methods is listed and not all will work for everybody. One of your tasks will be finding out *which ones work best for you*. To begin with, most people should regard these methods as a tentative supplement to medication, seeing the medication as a safety net if the technique fails. As you find which ones are best for you, you may want to use the techniques more and medicate less. In addition, the earlier advice about acting early and taking your mood swing very seriously must be re-emphasised. And if the techniques do not seem to be working and you are just getting worse, then you should definitely get help from your doctor as soon as you can.

COPING WITH DEPRESSION

You can find many books telling you how to get out of a depression. However, many of these were not intended for people with manic depression. So just as antidepressant pills can send you high, you need to be on your guard in case a self-help technique does the same. One of these could be 'positive affirmations' – for example, if you are feeling totally worthless, repeating 'I'm an important person' many times a day (see p.174 for more information on affirmations). If that starts to happen, remember that you're in charge; just stop using that method and try another. The principal strategies are:

1. Do something physical. It could be something that needs to be done, like cleaning or ironing, or just going for a walk. Whichever one you do, it should help to change your thinking and help you to discover a way forward.

2. Find someone to talk to, preferably about your depressed feelings. A burden shared is a burden halved and a sympathetic listener can be of great help.

3. Use cognitive therapy. This is a method of changing your feelings by changing your thinking. When depressed we have lots of negative thoughts and we believe them – despite strong evidence to the contrary. Part of cognitive therapy is to subject the thoughts to experimental test, for example by looking at the objective evidence. This process can challenge the negative thoughts, in turn lifting the mood. Research has shown that a course of cognitive therapy is as effective as a course of antidepressants and has long-term effects as well. The proper way to learn cognitive therapy is either from a qualified teacher or a book, such as Burns (1990). In the absence of

these, a good start is to write down your negative thoughts and for each one, write the evidence to the contrary. For instance, if the thought was 'I'm a failure' some of the evidence to the contrary might be, for example, 'my partner appreciates me' or 'I passed my driving test last month'. This should affect your thinking and, in turn, your mood.

4.   Try and turn your depression into anger. Many therapists regard depression as *anger turned inwards*. Techniques such as co-counselling, gestalt therapy, transactional analysis, and many types of psycho- and group therapy all encourage outward expressions of anger. This can be a very quick way both of relieving your depression and also finding what it was about. You can do this on your own using the following process: Find somewhere you can sit upright and make some noise; failing this put something over your mouth to deaden the sound. Now repeatedly shout 'No' and punch your fists in front of you as hard as you can. If words come into your mind while you are doing it, for example, 'I won't', 'I can't take your lies anymore', shout them out instead of the 'No'. After only three or four minutes of this you should be feeling much better.

5.   People who suffer from manic depression generally have their worst depressions after a high. Not only have you the depression to grapple with, but also a horrible return to reality and the gradual realisation of the impact of recent actions. Add to this the possible withdrawal – or desertion – of a close friend or partner and the combined effect can be cripplingly painful. The way out of this is *action*. Do anything you can to begin to repair the damage, however small the initial step, and congratulate yourself on whatever you manage to do. Then tackle the larger matters: unnecessary purchases, an overdrawn credit card, or making it up with a hurt or angry friend... It is remarkable how understanding people can be if approached in the right way. Managing to sort out some of the 'hangover' can do wonders to restore your self-confidence.

Next time I'm depressed I will try...

STOPPING A HIGH

There is very little published material about stopping a high. So, much of the following comes from the shared experiences of people who have tried these techniques. You probably have a week in which to act – after that, self-management could be vastly more difficult. So the warnings above about catching it early and taking it seriously apply now again – even more so.

Currently these are the main techniques:

1. *Cutting out stimulants and stimulation.* If you are on the verge of going high, you will have plenty of energy. *There is absolutely no point in hyping yourself up further.* You will know what your stimulants are: alcohol, tobacco, tea, coffee and caffeine-based products are probably the strongest. Whatever they are, the more you can cut them out, the more you will improve your chances of quickly returning to normal. Antidepressants can induce mania so if you're still taking them, discuss stopping them with your doctor. Stimulating or stressful situations can be just as bad. Meetings, parties going on until late – however enticing, these are not the best places to be at the moment.

2. Coupled with this is *planning for a good night's sleep.* Studies have shown that one of the quickest ways to send a person with manic depression high is to deprive them of sleep. A few really good nights' rest will be of great benefit. So, together with cutting out stimulants:

   a) Take plenty of relaxing exercise during the day, particularly those types which help you sleep. Swimming is good if you can; a walk before bed helps most people.

   b) Eat well. Digesting a good meal will lower your mental energy.

   c) If your doctor prescribes you sleeping pills this is a good time to take them. Otherwise, herbal remedies such as 'Quiet Life' can be just as effective.

   d) You may well find yourself waking in the early morning full of ideas. Although it may be very hard to do, by far your best policy is just to stay in bed. And if you are on a maintenance drug such as lithium or carbamazepine, this is an ideal time to take it. Should you lie awake till dawn comes, fine. You can use the time for planning the day or, better still, considering what further steps you can take to bring yourself down.

3. The third main strategy is to *protect yourself against yourself.* The next few days are a time when you may easily do things you could later seriously regret. So:

   a) Put off any major decisions – such as leaving your job or moving your home.

   b) Cancel any critical meetings or engagements over the next few days.

c) Put a ceiling on your financial spending capacity. This might mean giving your cheque book or credit cards to a friend.

d) Try to structure your day. Although the temptation is to do a lot, do the minimum. In a near-high state it is very easy to get diverted and miss appointments, forget to go shopping, and so on. Write down a plan for your day, allocating time for each event (including meals) and stick to it.

e) Limit or cut out driving, especially if taking haloperidol or largactil. These can further impair your driving skills.

4. A good overall strategy is to *actively do those things which calm you down.* Many authorities regard mania as a way of denying or escaping from depression. So if you think you're going high, it makes sense to try to reconnect with this underlying depression. Move slowly, talk slowly, think slowly. If you have some unpaid bills and boring chores to do, now is just the time to do them. Adopting an attitude 'if I'm going to go high, then I'll do so with the flat clean/my desk clear/the kitchen cupboards sorted/etc.' *and carrying these out* can be very grounding. Or if you have a friend who is depressed, arrange to pay a visit. Some of your enthusiasm may rub off on them and some of their deliberation may be transferred to you.

Try and alter your thinking as well. Rather than enthusing about your latest schemes and ideas at the end of the day, persuade yourself to do something quite different: focus on the parts of the day that have not gone so well, occasions where you did things you might really regret either now or later. Perhaps you're starting to have a grandiose fantasy, seeing yourself as Jesus, the Virgin Mary, Batman, Superman, whatever. Counter this false self with negative affirmations such as, 'I'm just an ordinary person', 'it's my manic depression talking' or make up another which affects you more strongly.[2] These calming techniques can be done anywhere at any time – the chief difficulty in an elated state is remembering to do them. Don't just tie a knot in your handkerchief, write a reminder on your hand and words such as 'I'm at risk at the moment' on conspicuous pieces of paper in your room.

---

2   Affirmations are phrases which you repeat over and over to yourself, with as much meaning as you can, preferably out loud. They can be positive (for example, 'I'm a totally wonderful person') or negative. If you want a really powerful negative affirmation, recall your most common recurrent thought when depressed (for example, 'I'm worthless/I'm no good/I'm a failure, and so on) and say that to yourself slowly several times over. At the very least it should make you feel sleepy.

> *Next time I think I'm going high my strategy will be... (and write it on your crisis card)*

COMING BACK TO NORMAL

With mood swings such as these it may be difficult deciding when you are back to normal – at least enough to cease these rather demanding activities. Normality means things such as:

- ○ reasonable powers of concentration
- ○ sleeping well
- ○ being able to plan and manage your day.

Some people regard the onset of anxiety as a sign that you've stopped a high; whatever it is, it is worth thinking about what 'normal' means for you.

> *I'm normal when...*

Long-term self-management

Many of the features about a good long-term self-management programme also get pushed at people who have never had the illness at all: take plenty of exercise, watch your diet, enjoy your relationships, work well, find a hobby, and explore and attend to your spiritual needs. Here are some additional suggestions oriented towards manic depression:

Know your trigger(s)

Very often it will be clear that your last high started around a particular situation, and a previous high might have begun with something very similar. This could be your 'trigger'. It might be moving house, a success, having a baby, a long-distance flight or a personal loss, with quite different triggers applying to different people. You need to find – maybe with the help of your journal – what form your trigger takes. It indicates the type of situation to which you are most vulnerable.

What to do about it? There are two strategies. One is consciously to avoid anything that looks like your trigger situation, so that you never meet up with those circumstances again. This is a bit like a 'never cross the road' strategy, leading to a half-life dominated by the fear of a recurrence. A more positive approach is to reckon that you will meet trigger-type situations again, and plan around them. You may actually see one coming; if so, warn your doctor and friends that you may have a difficult patch, make sure you have medication, and get yourself into physical shape by taking exercise. After all this you may find that the trigger does not produce a mood swing at all. If the unconscious can't catch us by surprise, it often won't bother.

Looking back suggests my triggers might be...

'Cultivate your garden'

For most of us, however far we have got with our manic depression, there is always the chance of another episode. Times of relative normality are a good opportunity to build up reserves against this possibility. Building up fitness, increasing your job security, cultivating friends and carers, joining an evening class; these can be of great value if things get difficult again. Although it involves caffeine withdrawal symptoms, some people might find it helpful to cut out tea and coffee completely. If you do get depressed you can always go back on; you'll probably find a cup of tea/coffee is much more potent then, too.

Another is keeping promises with yourself. Some of the self-management techniques require effort and discipline. You can build up self-discipline quite easily with a simple technique. Each day make a simple, private promise to yourself. But make it with one proviso, you only promise what you can *absolutely definitely* carry out. It might be 'I won't have another cigarette for the next five minutes' or 'I'll clean the bath today'. Keep this promise and next time try something a little more adventurous. If you break the promise (and you shouldn't need to), forgive yourself and try again. Repeating this builds up a sense of self-trust which will develop into a strong self-discipline. Try it.

With things that *have* to be done (or avoided) a different technique can work well. It consists of: (a) exploring your feelings; (b) stating them to yourself; and (c) adding '*and* I'm (not) going to do...' For example, for getting up in the morning, it might go like this: 'I'm feeling tired, depressed, loth to move, *and* I'm getting up'. Much more powerful than it sounds.

General activities found to help are: keeping a pet, hobbies, music and, of course, joining a local MDF group.

I'm going to try these long-term strategies...

Knowing yourself

Whether planning for the future, improving your relationships or getting into more satisfying work, increasing your self-knowledge will be a big help. Activities designed to increase self-knowledge tend to increase self-esteem

(Hendricks (1987) describes a powerful technique for increasing self-esteem) which in turn leads to more energy and better self-direction. This sort of work may also help unearth some of the background causes of your manic depression. Those people who have got through their manic depression and have now been off drugs for years – and there are such people – mostly claim to have done it by means of this 'inner work'.

However, this is an area littered with pitfalls and cul-de-sacs. And many bits of self-knowledge don't come from personal growth classes but come out of an unanticipated situation – or perhaps quietly ruminating while working with your hands.

Your best way forward is to find what has worked for other people with manic depression – maybe members of your local group – and discuss it with them. Meditation is a safe starting point which is widely taught; doing it twice a day for 20 minutes can work wonders for your relaxation and ability to manage your day. Yoga and Tai Chi have also been found to be helpful. Should you be just too stressed up for activities like this, then try the age-old technique of taking a few really long, slow deep breaths. Sounds silly? It's the standard technique used by mountaineers with vertigo and actors with stage fright.

Next come the one-to-one therapies, including psychotherapy, focusing, psychoanalysis and counselling. For some people, psychotherapy and counsel-ling have provided a solution to their manic depression. Others never found the right therapist (Dorothy Rowe (1991) writes that a good therapist 'should be rather like a good friend') or it was just too expensive. If you can get into it (you need to do a 'fundamentals' course first), co-counselling is much cheaper than any of those and more flexible. It takes place between equals so power issues are less of a factor. However, since you will have to act in a listener role part of the time it is not suitable if you are overly elated or depressed. Ordinary counselling is available on the NHS, but waiting lists vary.

What results can I expect?

Self-management has some of the characteristics of going solo – in driving a car, for instance. The notion that you are much more in charge is exhilarating and gives you a feeling of achievement. And then if you do get into trouble you know much more about what really helps you. How much you gain from self-management depends very much on what you put into it. One sign of progress is when you can continue working through your highs and lows and are no longer incapacitated by them. Another is when you start to do things which, before you developed the illness, were beyond you. All this implies a growth in wisdom and understanding. Anyone who applies themselves should certainly see tangible results within a year. And given time you might even manage yourself right out of the condition altogether.

Self-management: a summary

Self-management is a process of taking increasing responsibility for your health.

Practising it should lead to:

- fewer hospitalisations
- better relationships
- increasing ability to hold down a job

First steps

- Keep a journal – minimum one sentence each day.
- Find out as much about the illness and your medication as you can.
- Ask your doctor if you can adjust your medication according to your moods – called 'self-medication'.
- Get better at recognising your moods and warnings of a mood swing.

Then

You can either control your mood swings by self-medication or/also use other ways of controlling mood. There are many techniques; you must find those which work best for *you*.

1. For depression:

   - do something physical, even going for a walk
   - find someone to talk to, if possible about your depression
   - cognitive therapy (changing your mood by changing your thoughts)
   - express it as anger (in private).

2. For stopping a high:

   - cut out tea, coffee and other caffeine-based stimulants
   - sleep is vital: alter your day to ensure you sleep well
   - protect yourself against yourself ; no major decisions and take steps to avoid overspending
   - actively try to calm yourself. Act as if you were depressed; counter grandiose notions with negative affirmations.

In the long term

Realise that there's plenty you can do. For a start:

- Get to know yourself better.
- Stay physically healthy.
- Nurture supportive relationships.

References

Burns, D. (1990) *The Feeling Good Handbook*. New York: Plume Books.

Hendricks, G. (1987) *Learning to Love Yourself*. New York: Prentice Hall.

Rowe, D. (1991) *Breaking the Bonds*. London: Fontana.

Schou, M. (1993) *Lithium Treatment of Manic Depressive Illness: A Practical Guide*. Basle: Karger Press.

Further reading

Burns, D. (1980) *Feeling Good: The New Mood Therapy*. New York: Penguin Books. An early book on cognitive therapy.

Copeland, M. (1992) *The Depression Workbook: A Guide for Living with Depression and Manic Depression*. Oakland, CA: New Harbinger Press (USA). The first real workbook on self-management. Highly recommended.

Copeland, M. (1994) *Living Without Depression and Manic Depression. A Workbook for Maintaining Mood Stability*. Oakland, CA: New Harbinger Press (USA). Quite as good as her previous book, with more recent techniques.

Goodwin, F.K.. and Jamison, K.R. (1990) *Manic Depressive Illness*. New York: Oxford University Press. The standard work on manic depression, designed to be read by professionals and laymen alike. Regarded as one of the classics of psychiatry.

Lacey, R. (1993) *The Complete Guide to Psychiatric Drugs*. London: MIND. A comprehensive primer on over 100 drugs and their side effects.

Lindenfield, G. (1993) *Managing Anger*. London: Thorsons. Clear, practical advice on how to manage your own and other people's anger.

McKeon, P. (1986) *Coping with Depression and Elation*. London: Sheldon Press. A thorough description of the illness and also some advice on self-management.

MDF (1994) *Drug Treatment of Manic-Depression*. The Manic Depression Fellowship, 8–10 High Street, Kingston-Upon-Thames, Surrey, KT1 1EY. Good value for your money.

MDF (1995) *Inside Out*. The Manic Depression Fellowship, 8–10 High Street, Kingston-Upon-Thames, Surrey KT1 1EY.

Rogers, C. (1992) *On Becoming a Person*. London: Constable. If you only read the first chapter, that's enough.

Rowe, D. (1988) *Depression: The Way out of your Prison*. London: Routledge. A classic. Describes how we make ourselves depressed and what we can do to get out of it. Mind Book of the Year 1983.

Wilson, P. (1995) *Instant Calm – Over 100 Techniques for Dealing with Stress*. New York: Plume-Penguin books. An excellent variety of self-help techniques.

Appendix
Reproduction of Crisis Card (included with *Inside Out*)

Front

WHEN DEPRESSED

- Medication
- Do something physical
- Talk about it
- Cognitive Therapy
- Try and get angry

My techniques are:

....

....

....

MD FELLOWSHIP

Reverse

WHEN GOING HIGH

- Medication
- Cut out stimulants
- Target on sleep
- Avoid major decisions
- Actively calm yourself

My techniques are:

....

....

....

MD FELLOWSHIP

The Contributors

Eia K. Asen is Consultant Psychiatrist at the Maudsley Hospital and at Marlborough Family Consultation Centre, London.

Khaver Bashir is Research Fellow in the Department of Psychiatry, Royal Free Hospital School of Medicine, University of London.

Dennis Friedman is Honorary Lecturer in Psychiatry at St. Bartholemew's Hospital, London.

Myra Fulford is Director of The Manic Depression Fellowship, UK.

Paul Gilbert, Professor of Clinical Psychology, University of Derby and Southern Derbyshire Mental Health Care Trust, Kingsway Hospital.

Maurice Greenberg is Head of the Student Counselling Service at University College, London, and is a Consultant Psychiatrist and Psychotherapist at Camden and Islington NHS Community Health Services Trust and at the Group-Analytic Practice, London.

David Guinness is Chair of the Manic Depression Fellowship, UK.

Cosmo Hallström is Consultant Psychiatrist, The Charter Clinic, London.

Alison Jenaway is a Clinical Research Associate in the Department of Psychiatry, Addenbrook's Hospital, University of Cambridge.

David Kingdon is Medical Director of the Nottingham Healthcare Trust.

Charles Lund is Consultant Psychiatrist in Psychiatry at the Regional Department of Psychotherapy, Royal Victoria Infirmary, Newcastle-upon-Tyne.

Paul Needham is Senior Lecturer in Health Sciences at Thames Valley University.

Jean Nursten is Visiting Professor of Social Work, Department of Community Studies, University of Reading.

Denis O'Leary is Clinical Lecturer in the Department of Psychiatry, Addenbrook's Hospital, University of Cambridge.

Anne Palmer is Clinical Psychologist in the Department of Clinical Psychology, Hellesdon Hospital, Norwich.

Jill G.C. Rasmussen is a Clinical Psychopharmacologist in Dorking, Surrey.

Mandy J. Sainty is an Occupational Therapist, currently employed as Quality Development Facilitator for Mid Essex Community and Mental Health NHS Trust, Witham, Essex.

Malcolm Weller is a Consultant Psychiatrist at St Ann's Hospital, and Honorary Senior Lecturer at the Royal Free Hospital School of Medicine, University of London.

Ved P. Varma was formerly Educational Psychologist with the Institute of Education, University of London, the Tavistock Clinic and the London Boroughs of Richmond and Brent. He has edited or co-edited more than 30 books in education, psychology, psychiatry, psychotherapy and social work.

Subject Index

Author Index